D1083387

EUROPEAN WOMEN
in BUSINESS and
MANAGEMENT

EUROPEAN WOMEN
in BUSINESS and
MANAGEMENT

Edited by
Marilyn J. Davidson and Cary L. Cooper

Manchester School of Management,
University of Manchester Institute
of Science and Technology, UK

P·C·P

Paul Chapman
Publishing Ltd

331.481
E89

Copyright © 1993 Paul Chapman Publishing Ltd

All rights reserved

Paul Chapman Publishing Ltd
144 Liverpool Road
London
N1 1LA

Apart from any fair dealing for the purposes of research or
private study, or criticism or review, as permitted under the
Copyright, Designs and Patents Act, 1988, this publication may be
reproduced, stored or transmitted, in any form or by any means,
only with the prior permission in writing of the publishers, or
in the case of reprographic reproduction in accordance with the
terms of licences issued by the Copyright Licensing Agency.
Inquiries concerning reproduction outside those terms should be
sent to the publishers at the abovementioned address.

British Library Cataloguing-in-Publication Data.
European Women in Business and Management
  I. Davidson, Marilyn J.
  II. Cooper, Cary L.
  658.0082

  ISBN 1−85396−138−8

Typeset by Setrite Typesetters Ltd., Hong Kong
Printed by The Cromwell Press, Melksham, Wiltshire SN12 8PH

A B C D E F G H   9 8 7 6 5 4 3

CONTENTS

University Libraries
Carnegie Mellon University
Pittsburgh PA 15213-3890

CONTRIBUTORS

Marilyn J. Davidson *Editor*; Manchester School of Management, University of Manchester Institute of Science and Technology, UK

Cary L. Cooper *Editor*; Manchester School of Management, University of Manchester Institute of Science and Technology, UK

Janne Albertsen; Director, In—Company and International Programmes, Management Education, The Danish Employers' Confederation, 52 Oester Alle, DK-8400 Ebeltoft, Denmark

Beverly Alimo-Metcalfe; Senior Lecturer in Occupational Psychology, The Nuffield Institute, University of Leeds, Fairbairn House, 71—75 Clarendon Road, Leeds LS2 9PL, UK

Ariane Berthoin Antal; Director, International Institute for Organizational Change — Ashridge, International Business Park, French-Geneva Campus, F-74166 Archamps, France

Bolette Christensen; Management Development Consultant, Management Education, The Danish Employers' Confederation, 52 Oester Alle, DK-8400 Ebeltoft, Denmark

Rita Campos e Cunha; Lecturer, Human Resources Management, Faculdade de Economia/MBA, Universidade Nova de Lisboa, R. Marques de Fronteira 20, 1000 Lisboa, Portugal

Camilla Krebsbach-Gnath; Managing Director, KG & D Management und Unternehmensberatung, Kronberg und Berlin, Wissenschaftzentrum Berlin für Sozialforschung, Reichpietschufer 50, 1000 Berlin 30, Germany

Jacqueline Laufer; Professor, Département Management et Ressources Humaines, Groupe HEC, 78351 Jouy-en-Josas Cedex, France

Poly Miliori; Journalist, 35 Filadelfeos Street, 14562 Kifissia, Athens, Greece

Yvonne Murphy; Barrister-at-Law, 19 Palmerston Park, Dublin 6, Ireland

Federica Olivares; Managing Director, *Edizioni Olivares*, Publishing Society in Milano, Via S. Pietro all'Orto 9, Milano 20121, Italy

Kea Tijdens; Organizational Psychologist, Senior Lecturer, Women in the Labour Market, University of Amsterdam, Department of Economics and Econometrics, Roetersstraat 11, 1018 WB Amsterdam, The Netherlands

Matilde Vázquez Fernández; General Deputy, Women's Institute of Spain, Subdirectora Gral. de Estudiois y Documentacion, Instituto de la Mujer, C/Almagro, 36–1, 28010 Madrid, Spain

Colleen Wedderburn-Tate; Associate Lecturer in Management Development, The Nuffield Institute, University of Leeds, Fairbairn House, 71–75 Clarendon Road, Leeds LS2 9PL, UK

Alison Woodward; Associate Professor, European Studies and Women's Programmes, Vesalius College, Vrije Universiteit Brussel, Pleinlaan 2, B-1050 Brussel, Belgium

1.

AN OVERVIEW

Marilyn J. Davidson and Cary L. Cooper

INTRODUCTION – WORKING WOMEN IN THE EUROPEAN COMMUNITY

Throughout the European Community (EC) women's advance into what have been traditionally men's jobs, particularly into the higher-status professions in business and management, has been very slow (Davidson and Cooper, 1992). Nevertheless, over the past decade there has been an increasing change in legislation, including the EC's Social Protocol, to enforce issues related to equal opportunity such as equal pay and sex discrimination (Hammond and Holton, 1991).

Certainly, within the EC, the proportion of women in the workforce has increased and between 1979 and 1988 women's economic activity grew in every single state. Between 1985 and 1988, 58% of the 4.8 million jobs created in the EC were occupied by women (Commission of the European Communities, 1990a). Figure 1 illustrates that Denmark and the UK have the highest female work activity rates, i.e. 60.5% and 50.8% respectively. Furthermore, these rates are predicted to continue increasing, particularly among younger women. In the UK, for example, about three-quarters of women are expected to be working by the year 2001 (Commission of the European Communities, 1990a).

Figure 2 shows the increasing employment rate in the member states of married women aged between 25 and 49 years. Once again, Denmark has the highest percentage of married working women at over 80%, followed by the UK at around 65%, and Portugal and France, both around 60%.

Hammond and Holton (1991) point out that the increasing numbers of part-time jobs and changing social attitudes are just two factors in the change process (see Figure 3). Moreover, while the percentage of women returning to work has increased, with the highest percentages in the Netherlands, the UK, Ireland and Portugal, evidence suggests

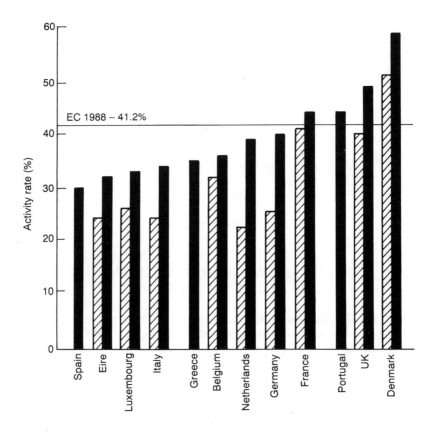

Source: Commission of the European Communities (1990) *Employment in Europe 1990a*

Figure 1 Activity rates of women in the member states of the EC, 1979 (▨) and 1988 (■).

that an increasing number accept part-time employment out of necessity rather than choice. Hammond and Holton (1991) also emphasize a number of disadvantages associated with part-time employment:

> The growth of part-time work may also have played a part in the number of women with second jobs, which more than doubled between 1983 and 1988 in the European Community; this suggests that women want − or need − to work more hours.
> The popularity of part-time work has an impact on the average number of hours worked by men and women during a week. Typically, men in the UK average 43.5 hours, against 29.8 for women. It also has a bearing on the training women receive. Women working full-time are twice as likely to receive training as their part-time equivalents (EOC, 1991).

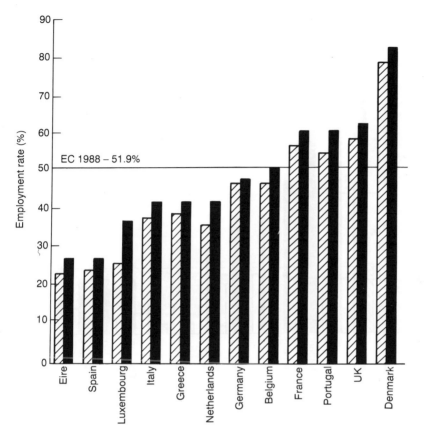

Source: Commission of the European Communities (1990) *Employment in Europe 1990a*

Figure 2 Employment rates of married women aged 25–49 in the member states of the EC, 1985 (▨) and 1988 (■).

Fewer hours bring lesser rewards. Though the underlying trend is for women's rates of pay increasingly to match those of men, when hourly rates are compared, women in the UK average 78% of the men's rate (Spence, 1991).

This remains the case throughout the European Community. Despite the beneficial intentions and impact of equal pay legislation, the gap between men's and women's pay remains significant. Men in manufacturing employed on manual jobs, for example, earn an average 25% more per hour than women. In Denmark and Italy the gap appears to be closing with greater rapidity than elsewhere. In those countries women are paid 85% of the men's rate. In France and Greece, similar progress is being made with women receiving 80% (Commission of the European Communities, 1990b, p. 8).

(Hammond and Holton, 1991)

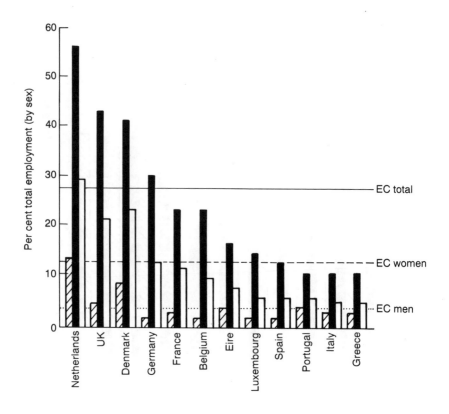

Source: Commission of the European Communities (1990) *Employment in Europe 1990a*

Figure 3   Part-time employment as a share of total employment in the member states of the EC, 1988. ⌓⊠= men; ■ = women; □ = total.

Nevertheless, women throughout Europe remain significantly less well paid than men. Table 1 outlines the history of the equal pay policy in the EC countries. Furthermore, a recent analysis by Marvani (1992) concludes that despite the existence of increasingly egalitarian legislation and growth in women's economic activity, in some countries, such as Portugal, Denmark and Italy, the pay differential between men and women's salaries has actually widened!

Women have also been hit very hard by high unemployment levels, and throughout Europe women constitute over 40% of Europe's unemployed. This means that there are more women out of work than men in proportion to their share of the total workforce. Not only are women more frequently unemployed than men, but they receive less compensation and are unemployed longer. Marvani views the signific-

Table 1 Equal pay policy in the member countries of the European
Community

Country	Year	Designation	Sanctioning bodies
Belgium	1975	National Employment Council's collective agreement on labour no. 25, enforced by royal decree	Parties to the collective bargaining process
Denmark	1973	Collective agreement at national level on wage parity	
France	1972	Law no. 72/1143 on gender wage parity	Ministry of Labour; Commission for Women's Affairs
Germany	1980	Code of civil law (para. 612)	Ministry of Labour and Social Affairs; industrial tribunals
Greece	1984	Law no. 1414/84 on the application of gender parity in employment	Ministry of Labour
Eire	1974	Anti-Wage-Discrimination Act (amended by the Equal Opportunities Act)	Employment Equality Agency; industrial tribunals
Italy	1960	Agreement on wage parity in industry	Parties to the collective bargaining process
	1964	Agreement on wage parity in industry	Ministry of Agriculture
Netherlands	1975	Equal Pay Act	Civil courts
	1984	(Revised) Equal Treatment Act (integrating the Equal Pay Act of 1975 and the Equal Treatment Act of 1980)	Civil courts
Portugal	1979	Equal opportunities legislation (work and employment)	Commission for Equality; Labour Inspectorate
Spain	1980	Worker's status	Industrial tribunals; Labour Inspectorate
UK	1970	Equal Pay Act	
	1975	(in force)	Industrial tribunals
	1984	(amended)	

Source: OECD, *Employment Prospects 1988*, pp. 181–2.

ance of this as both massive and complex: 'It is the manifestation of the difficulties that women have finding work, but it is also a sign that women are remaining on the labour market rather than opting for inactivity' (Marvani, 1992, p. 34).

In 1992, at Maastricht, 11 member states of the EC, excluding the UK, signed the Social Protocol, which enabled them to act by qualified majority voting on 'equality between men and women with regard to labour market opportunities and treatment at work'. The Directive would impose a maximum 48-hour week, extend rights on redundancy, sick pay, holidays and training to part-time workers on a pro rata basis, and entitle working women to 14 weeks' maternity leave without any qualifying conditions. As with all employment conditions and

benefits, there is a wide variety of maternity leave and childcare
facilities in the different member state (see Figure 4).

In the UK, for example, the average maternity leave pay is about half
of salary and fewer than 50% of children aged between 3 and 5 years
have access to childcare provisions. Conversely, Portugal and the
Netherlands offer full maternity leave pay and over 90% of French
children aged between 3 and 5 enjoy childcare facilities (Hammond
and Holton, 1991) (Table 2).

Indeed, Marvani (1992) proposes that this is an interesting issue in
which there is the greatest diversity between European countries. She
concludes that the strategies for coping with family obligations have a

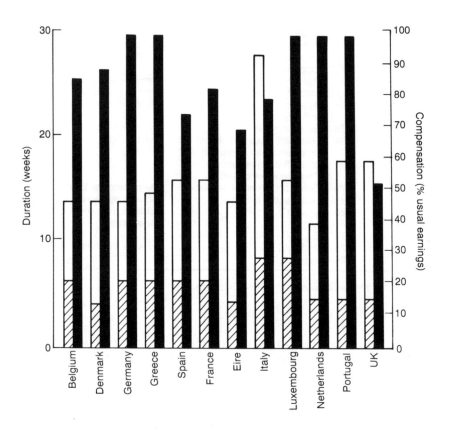

Source: Commission of the European Communities (1990) *Employment in
Europe 1990a*

Figure 4   Duration of maternity leave and average weekly compensations as
percentage of usual pay in the member states of the EC, 1988. ▨ =
antenatal leave; □ = postnatal leave; ■ = compensation.

Table 2 Places in publicly funded childcare services, as percentage of all children in the age group, in the member countries of the European Community

Country	Date to which data refer	For children under 3 years (%)*	For children from 3 to compulsory school age (%)	Age when compulsory schooling begins (years)	Length of school day (including midday break) (hours)	Outside school hours care for primary school children (%)
Germany	1987	3	65–70	6–7	4–5 (a)	4
France	1988	20	95+	6	8	?
Italy	1986	5	85+	6	4	?
Netherlands	1989	2	50–55	5	6–7	1
Belgium	1988	20	95+	6	7	?
Luxembourg	1989	2	55–60	5	4–8 (a)	1
UK	1988	2	35–40	5	6½	(–)
Eire	1988	2	55	6	4½–6½ (b)	(–)
Denmark	1989	48	85†	7	3–5½ (a,b)	29
Greece	1988	4	65–70	5½	4–5 (b)	(–)
Portugal	1988	6	35	6	6½	6
Spain	1988	?	65–70	6	8	(–)

Key: ? = no information; (–) = less than 0.5%; (a) = school hours vary from day to day; (b) = school hours increase as children get older.
* This percentage should be expressed as a percentage of the children whose ages exceed the end of the maternity leave rather than percentage of 0- to 3-year-olds, in which case it would be 55% for Denmark instead of 48%.
† Does not include preschool classes.

Source: Women of Europe Supplement, no. 31, August 1990.

greater influence on female employment activity rates than either the availability of childcare or the number of children. This would help explain why a country such as the UK has one of the lowest levels of childcare facilities and yet one of the highest female employment rates. Conversely, Danish women have the highest activity rate and have a fertility rate very close to that of Dutch women, whose activity rates are among the lowest. Marvani (1992) also emphasizes the importance of higher levels of education and training achieved by women through-out the EC on sources of female economic activity throughout the past decade.

Throughout all the EC countries there is still job segregation based on gender, and over half of women are employed in the service sector which includes trade, education, retail, healthcare and clerical duties. About a quarter of women workers are employed in the textile and food industries, and a larger number in the chemical and electronic sectors. In comparison, men are employed in a wider range of occu-pations and a wider range of industries (Marvani, 1992). In the UK, for example, just under half of all men and two-thirds of all women in employment are in non-manual occupations (Social Trends, 1992). Moreover, Marvani (1992) points out that increased female activity rates throughout the 1980s have further perpetuated this gender segrega-tion, as they have been in the traditional sectors of female employ-ment, where new jobs have been created. In the words of Marvani (1992, p. 12) 'Female economic activity has not risen only because women's behaviour has changed. It is also because the supply was met by a demand' (see Tables 3 and 4).

AIMS OF THIS BOOK

On a more optimistic note, with more women working there has also been an increase in the number of women entering business, including entrepreneurs, and management throughout all the EC countries. This book seeks to explore the past, present and future position of women managers in each of the respective EC countries. The only country not included is Luxembourg. This is due to the very small size of its population (400,000), the diversity of its employers, and the unavail-ability of statistics on workforce participation at managerial level. In addition, many of the employees in Luxembourg are not Luxembourg nationals − 26% of the population are citizens of other countries and 63% of the employees in the service sectors are non-national (Snyder, 1992).

The contributors to each chapter not only detail more fully the most recent available employment statistics, but also help to unravel some of the reasons for similarities and differences between member states. Here, discrepancies based on such issues as differing traditions, his-torical events, education, training, legislation, attitudes and behaviours,

Table 3 Women's share in employment in 1989

Employment area	Germany GFR (%)	Germany GDR (%)	Belgium (%)	Denmark (%)	Spain (%)	France (%)	UK (%)	Greece (%)	Ireland (%)	Italy (%)	Luxembourg (%)	Netherlands (%)	Portugal (%)
Agriculture	44.8	37.4	26.7	23.3	26.7	34.9	19.4	44.6	9.5	34.3	33.3	24.5	49.1
Energy and water*	10.7	40.8	13.0	0.0	6.9	19.3	15.2	12.5	0.0	9.3	0.0	12.5	11.6
Extraction of minerals; chemical industry†	23.8	35.9	14.1	32.7	13.4	24.6	24.3	17.0	17.1	19.5	7.1	13.9	24.0
Metal manufacture; mechanical, electrical and instrument engineering	22.4		14.6	22.2	10.3	21.9	22.2	10.3	30.1	17.6	16.7	11.9	15.3
Other manufacturing industries	39.4	56.5	34.8	40.8	32.5	40.9	38.5	41.4	32.8	45.0	18.2	25.6	51.2
Building and civil engineering	10.5		5.0	10.2	2.4	8.2	8.7	0.0	3.9	5.2	7.7	7.8	3.1
Industry: total	24.2	72.2	19.0	26.1	16.3	24.3	23.3	23.4	22.0	24.7	10.9	15.6	30.6
Distributive trades, hotels and catering	52.3		45.4	45.2	37.8	45.6	53.0	34.3	41.0	36.4	48.4	42.7	38.4
Transport and communication	25.1	35.4	13.6	26.7	11.5	26.0	23.6	11.2	20.0	14.0	20.0	19.5	19.4
Banking, finance and insurance	45.9		38.9	46.1	29.1	48.7	48.9	39.1	43.8	37.9	47.4	35.8	33.1
Public administration	34.2		37.0	50.5	30.4	46.2	40.7	30.9	27.9	29.4	30.8	28.8	34.6
Other services‡	64.9	72.4	63.3	73.2	65.4	67.8	69.7	53.9	62.2	53.4	60.0	63.4	75.4
Services: total	49.3		45.9	55.1	41.4	51.9	53.9	36.1	44.7	39.1	46.6	46.3	47.0
Total (where a sector is declared)	39.0		36.8	45.4	31.3	42.3	43.1	35.0	32.8	34.1	35.5	37.1	41.7

* Industry in the GDR.
† Small-scale private manufacturing industry in the GDR.
‡ Other non-manufacturing sectors in the GDR.

Sources: EUROSTAT, *Labour Force Survey*, Table T43, 1983–9 and German Report for the GDR, Spanish Report for the 1983 data. Calculations DULBEA.

Table 4 Breakdown of 1983–9 employment growth rates by country, sector and gender

	Germany (GFR) (%)	Belgium (%)	Denmark (%)	France (%)	UK (%)	Greece (%)	Ireland (%)	Italy (%)	Netherlands (%)
Men: 1983–9 growth rates									
Agriculture	-21.8	8.6	-14.2	-14.4	2.6	-13.4	-9.5	-21.0	-1.8
Energy and water	-6.8	-32.2	57.1	-1.7	-24.6	13.5	-13.3	3.2	-3.4
Extraction of minerals; chemical industry	2.6	-12.2	25.0	-17.9	-5.6	-14.1	-12.1	1.2	17.4
Metal manufacture; electrical and instrument engineering	9.5	8.7	-8.1	-11.2	-2.8	-1.9	8.5	-14.2	8.2
Other manufacturing industries	0.1	-3.3	1.3	-2.9	6.2	4.3	-12.4	-8.3	12.4
Building and civil engineering	-6.5	5.1	18.4	-3.0	20.1	-12.2	-22.3	-17.4	10.9
Industry: total	2.2	-1.8	6.0	-7.4	2.5	-4.1	-12.2	-11.6	10.6
Distributive trades, hotels and catering	4.1	-2.0	16.2	-1.7	19.0	13.8	0.8	3.0	17.2
Transport and communication	4.7	-5.1	4.4	0.5	6.5	-4.5	2.1	-0.7	9.7
Banking, finance and insurance	21.1	21.4	60.5	17.8	48.2	30.4	8.7	22.1	49.6
Public administration	0.9	-0.4	10.8	13.6	3.0	28.8	-6.4	8.8	3.3
Other services	34.0	7.3	3.8	11.6	12.9	15.6	7.4	30.6	20.2
Services: total	10.8	2.5	15.5	6.6	17.5	13.3	2.4	10.6	19.7
Total (where a sector is declared)	4.9	0.9	8.8	-1.2	9.9	1.0	-5.4	-2.0	14.9
Women: 1983–9 growth rates									
Agriculture	-36.4	-3.0	-16.7	-19.1	-4.2	-9.0	-38.5	-25.1	29.6
Energy and water	-5.3	50.0	-100.0	3.8	-14.6	20.0		11.1	33.3
Extraction of minerals; chemical industry	7.6	13.0	13.3	-5.1	2.6	0.0	20.0	11.2	38.9
Metal manufacture; electrical and instrument engineering	19.3	0.0	2.4	-11.9	8.9	0.0	29.4	-15.0	33.3
Other manufacturing industries	-4.3	-4.6	17.4	-8.6	6.2	16.0	2.7	-6.0	18.1
Building and civil engineering	3.6	10.0	35.7	-2.2	40.5	-100.0	-25.0	13.8	43.5
Industry: total	5.6	0.0	12.7	-8.3	7.8	11.6	9.5	-5.2	26.1
Distributive trades, hotels and catering	1.7	5.1	0.5	3.1	13.4	28.1	9.1	15.2	38.8
Transport and communication	25.7	0.0	20.9	6.6	37.9	8.0	-7.7	29.6	51.1
Banking, finance and insurance	23.5	33.3	68.6	18.2	55.9	53.5	11.4	61.2	60.8
Public administration	-4.0	42.4	44.6	11.4	12.0	58.3	-15.0	0.6	43.0
Other services	22.5	15.8	1.8	16.3	24.2	26.0	12.1	25.2	33.6
Services: total	12.0	16.2	11.1	12.0	23.9	31.4	7.9	20.6	38.9
Total (where a sector is declared)	6.8	12.7	10.2	5.6	20.4	11.9	4.7	7.7	37.0

Source: EUROSTAT, *Labour Force Survey*, Table T43, 1983–9. Calculations DULBEA.

employment conditions, rights and benefits, childcare provisions, equal opportunity policies, and positive action programmes are discussed. In particular, the authors isolate specific problems and barriers being experienced by women in business and management in their countries. In addition, they examine the effects on these women and organizations, and suggest ways of reducing these problems so that the opportunities to enter business and management, and climb up the corporate ladder, are as accessible to women as they are to men.

Throughout this book it will be evident that of the issues raised by the authors in each of the chapters some are specific to their own country and a number are common across many EC countries. Let us explore, therefore, what are some of the commonalities between countries with regard to the plight of women in management and business and the ways in which particular countries are dealing with it.

Common experiences and trends throughout the European Community

Childcare

In many of the EC countries there is great concern about the provision of childcare facilities, which are felt to be prerequisite to encouraging women to enter either the world of business or corporate life. In a number of countries, particularly the UK, Eire and the Netherlands, there is emphasis on the need for a widespread and professional service, as well as the infrastructure to enable women financially to avail themselves of the facilities. This could be done by the state or through the state by substantial income tax relief, which could stimulate the private sector. By whatever method, the reality of maintaining both a job and a family requires the provision of affordable, convenient and professional childcare arrangements either in the workplace, or in the local community or by the local or state authority. Without this, the desire of many women to enter management or start their own businesses will be severely undermined.

Positive or affirmative action

Another issue that seems to emerge is the mechanism by which women obtain management jobs in the first place. In a number of EC countries the issue of either voluntary or legislated positive action is now on the agenda. After many years of women being confronted by barriers at the 'gates of entry' to management jobs or to more senior levels within corporate structures, there is a growing interest in exploring the alternative of affirmative action. For example, in Greece it has been suggested by the Co-ordinating Committee for Quotas that an obligatory quota of 35% be introduced as a minimum target for women in senior jobs in both the public and private sectors. These issues are also being discussed actively in Belgium, Italy and Germany. It is obvious that exposure to the US experience in this field has led many in EC countries to consider this approach, given the continuing problems that women confront not only in obtaining a job in the first instance, but also in breaking through the proverbial 'glass ceiling' into senior or top management positions.

Selection of women into management

Also noted in the various chapters is the concern about gender bias in selection of prospective managers. It has been suggested for example, that in Spain, one of the reasons why women succeed in obtaining management jobs in the public sector, but not in the private sector, is that the selection techniques and criteria are more gender free, less subjective and ultimately less biased. The call in most countries is for ensuring more equal opportunities for selection procedures for women in the first place, and ultimately in the assessment of women for future promotion. The use of assessment centres and testing, in terms of minimizing gender bias, might be more useful than originally thought.

Mentoring

Linked to some extent to the promotion of women to more senior roles is the notion of mentoring. In the chapters on Denmark, Belgium, Greece and Ireland, it is felt that mentoring is extremely important in providing women in management with the self-confidence and modelling skills to pursue career advancement and promotion. For many years, women who have achieved success in their careers have been forced to rely on male mentors, without the benefit of female role models. However, with the increase, albeit small, of women in senior positions, there is now an opportunity for more systematic help and support, which should be considered by organizations concerned about developing and retaining women in management.

Training of women managers and businesswomen

In many of the EC countries there is a concern that the training provision for women is inadequate, because women have access to less appropriate training than that available to men. In addition, there is a feeling that the needs of women in business and management are different, whether it is a need for assertiveness training in Eire or for the basic business or financial skills required in Italy, Spain or Denmark. Specific training provision for women in the workplace, or even all-female training groups, might seem an anathema to male senior executives, but the reality of life in corporate environments is such that these training needs are real and potentially useful to women in their career progression. In addition, as has been suggested by the Danish experience, training for women managers and business leaders will be different at different levels and stages of their careers. It is important for training to be considered throughout the career process, and not just at landmark temporal points, for example trainee period, entry to middle management.

Parental leave

Although most European countries provide maternity leave, the explosion of the dual-career or two-earner families means that increasingly if women are to achieve any degree of success in their careers, they will need the back-up and total commitment of their partners to share the domestic workload. If working women are to pursue both careers and families, it will become increasingly important for organizations and governments to help with provisions for parental leave. A number of chapters in this book highlight this requirement, suggesting, as in the Dutch case, the need not only to have a corporate and/or statutory commitment, but also the need to change attitudes amongst men about familial responsibility and role sharing. In some cases, the former is easier than the latter, as we have seen in recent years in Sweden where the provision for parental leave is available but men just do not take it up in any great numbers.

Corporate women versus businesswomen

It can be seen in Table 5 that women in corporate environments tend to be at the bottom of the managerial hierarchy, even after a decade or more in management jobs, with fewer than 5% in senior management roles. Many of the difficulties women experience in corporate environments have been highlighted in this and in many other books in the field, such as Davidson and Cooper (1992), and although some progress is being made to develop strategies to help women managers, these barriers have also encouraged many to consider setting up their own businesses. As can be seen in Table 5, between 15% and 30% of entrepreneurs or business owners are women. This trend seems to be increasing, and although many of these businesses are small they are

Table 5 Women in management and business in the European Community

Country*	Working females as a percentage of all:			
	Managers	Middle managers	Senior managers	Entrepreneurs/ self-employed
UK	26	—	2	25
Eire	17.4	—	—	31.5
Denmark	11	10	5	—
Netherlands	13	18	—	24
Germany	6	—	—	17
France	25	44	4.6	16[†]
Belgium	—	12.5	5	—
Greece	14	—	8	14
Italy	—	—	3	25
Portugal	—	—	—	—
Spain	10	5	5	37

* Category definitions vary between countries.
† Head of firms with 10+ persons.

growing in number and size. Perhaps the flexibility and control that owning your own business provide are a greater attraction to working women, particularly those with children, than any hierarchy-driven corporate culture.

Corporate culture

Corporate culture is another issue of importance, since many women in the EC countries feel that organizational life is too imbued with the 'male values' of competition, aggression, dominance, and 'transmitting' rather than 'receiving' communications. As the chapters on France and Denmark highlight, European corporate cultures need to change to encourage negotiation, support, problem resolution, listening skills, co-operation and participation. Such change in the workplace will benefit men as well as women. Increasingly, the evidence is mounting that competition, confrontation and the 'macho' management style are producing more workplace stress and less productivity (Cooper and Payne, 1988). Organizations are demanding long hours and total commitment, at a time when both partners are working. Corporate cultures and management styles which support and reward people, and that take into account their personal circumstances, are the ones that will survive the 1990s and beyond.

CONCLUSION

Ultimately the European work environment should be the habitat of both men and women in roughly equal numbers. The Europe of the future will no longer be dominated by men, nor will men's career paths be the blueprint. We must accept this reality, and design work organizations and the wider business community to help promote both men and women. As the EC document *The Position of Women on the Labour Market* suggested in 1992,

> The increase in the economic activity of women is now an irreversible, lasting, widespread reality. Throughout Europe women are continuing to enter the labour market by the millions, despite the labour crisis. This is a basic trend that is redrawing the contours of the labour market. The 'feminization' of the working population, especially in white-collar jobs, is one of the most important social developments of the late twentieth century and one that will leave its imprint on the ongoing construction of Europe.
>
> This does not mean that women have won occupational equality. Also throughout Europe, women are gearing up under the sign of discrimination. Discrimination and segregation continue to reign. The feminization of the working world has not led to a real equal distribution of jobs between the sexes any more than it has reversed the tranquil current of occupational inequality of all sorts. Finally, whilst the employment crisis has not chased women off the labour market, it has not protected them from the unemployment and precarious positions, either.

Women are now working more in the EC, but they are also unemployed
more: more today than yesterday, more than men, and longer than men.

(Maruani, 1992, p. 2)

REFERENCES

Commission of the European Communities (1990a) *Employment in Europe 1990*, Luxembourg.

Commission of the European Communities (1990b) Wages and labour costs, *Employment in Europe 1990*, Luxembourg.

Cooper, C. L. and Payne, R. (1988) *Causes, Coping and Consequences of Stress at Work*, John Wiley, Chichester.

Davidson, M. J. and Cooper, C. L. (1992) *Shattering the Glass Ceiling – The Woman Manager*, Paul Chapman, London.

Equal Opportunities Commission (1991) Training for those at work, in *Women and Men in Britain 1991*, EOC, London.

Hammond, V. and Holton, V. (1991) *A Balanced Workforce – Achieving Cultural Change for Women: A Comparative Study*, Ashridge Management College, Ashridge.

Maruani, M. (1992) *The Position of Women on the Labour Market*, Commission of the European Communities, Brussels.

Snyder, P. (1992) *The European Women's Almanac*, Scarlet Press, London.

Social Trends 1992 (1992) HMSO, London.

Spence, A. (1991) Pay in Great Britain, *Employment Gazette*, November, p. 6.

2.

THE UNITED KINGDOM

Beverly Alimo-Metcalfe (formerly Alban Metcalfe) and
Colleen Wedderburn-Tate

INTRODUCTION

In 1990 the Hansard Society, whose aims are 'to promote wider knowledge and understanding of parliamentary government so as to strengthen the full and informed participation of all citizens in our democratic system', published a report on the findings of its own commission, entitled *Women At the Top* (Hansard Society, 1990). The commission's mandate was to 'identify barriers to the appointment of women to senior occupational positions, and to other positions of power and influence, and to make recommendations as to how these barriers could be overcome' (p. xiii).

Its findings make sobering reading for those who may have thought that the UK had made steady progress towards producing a society in which discrimination on the basis of gender was a historical phenomenon, and that equality of opportunity for women and men was at least approaching realization. It concluded that in the UK the barriers to equality for women are general and pervasive and include: outmoded attitudes about the role of women; direct and indirect discrimination; the absence of proper childcare provision; and inflexible structures for work and careers.

If ever there was a powerful opportunity for change in the employment of women, the 1990s should be providing it.

THE CHANGING PATTERN OF WOMEN IN
THE LABOUR FORCE IN THE UK

The most conspicuous change in the labour force in the UK in the last few years, and expected to continue in the next decade, is the greater participation of women. Whilst the economic activities of men aged 16 and over showed a slight fall over the period spring 1984 to spring 1989 (from 75.9% to 75.6%), the female activity rate has shown a steady rise over the same period from 49.3% to 53.0% (Labour Force Survey, 1989). Married women made up two-thirds of the growth in the labour force between 1983 and 1987, most of them working part time or in unskilled or semi-skilled work. Projections into 2001 note that women are expected to make up nearly 90% of the increase in the labour force, by which time they are expected to comprise over 50% of the paid workforce (compare with 22% of women in France). In comparison with other European countries the relatively slower increase in participation of women in the labour force, plus the fact that the UK contains an extremely high proportion of part-time working women, can be interpreted as reflecting the lack of serious initiatives in the UK to assist the entry of women into employment (Hirsh and Jackson, 1990).

Women are desperately needed to fill the 'black hole' created by the shortfall of 1 million workers in the 16–24-year-old bracket. Large organizations, including major high street banks and building societies, are taking urgent steps to recruit more women, and to develop the largely untapped reservoir of potential amongst their female employees. But that women's significant contribution to the UK workforce will be in areas other than those in which they currently dominate, namely low-status, low-paid, part-time, low-interest jobs, seems unlikely.

The Henley Centre for Forecasting (Stewart, 1989) suggests several reasons for women's greater participation which include: the increased importance women are placing on their careers; the larger numbers of women who are delaying having children and who return to work before their children reach school age; and the larger proportion of single-parent families of which the female is the lone parent.

THE POSITION OF WOMEN IN MANAGEMENT

In terms of the managerial population, it is difficult to establish accurate figures for the proportions of women in management in the UK since definitions of management used by different studies may vary. However, from the sources listed in Table 1, there may be some evidence that the proportion of women in management is increasing.

However, figures given for women in senior management remain negligible. One to two per cent is the most commonly stated figure (e.g. Hirsh and Jackson, 1990). A survey of 100 top Confederation of British Industry (CBI) employers conducted for the Hansard Society (1990) report revealed that 6.7% of senior managers were women, and that only 3% of the companies sampled had women on their main boards as executive directors. A further 16% were non-executive directors. Five per cent of the members of the Institute of Directors are women (Marketing Business, 1990); 22% of publishing directors;

Table 1   Proportion of women in management

Year	Proportion of women in management (%)	Source
1975	10	Marshall (1984)
1977	19 OPCS (1980)	Labour Force Survey 1977
1979	20 OPCS (1982)	Labour Force Survey 1979
1985	22 OPCS (1987)	Labour Force Survey 1985
1989	26	Labour Force Survey 1989

10% of heads of BBC regions; 7% of senior managers in industry; 5% of under-secretaries in the civil service; 3% of professors; and 2% of university vice-chancellors and principals are women (Hirsh and Jackson, 1990).

Management as an occupation is clearly gender segregated. In 1985 a labour force survey estimated that probably more than 50% of the female managers were in office work, retail and catering (Labour Force Survey, 1985). In general the structure of UK employment has changed as manufacturing has declined and employment in the service sector has increased. A survey of 1,470 male and 412 female members of the British Institute of Management (BIM), the largest professional group for managers in Britain (Alban Metcalfe and Nicholson, 1984) found that far more women than men were in service as opposed to manufacturing organizations and that significantly more women were in education and training, government, and professional services. There were also contrasts by job function. The largest proportion of female members in the sample were in personnel/training, management services, and office administration, in that order, whereas the largest proportion of men were in management services, finance/accounting, and general management. The BIM study also found that the female managers were more likely to be functional specialists than general managers. Clearly the chances of rising to senior management are greater when joining the general management career track.

The BIM sample cannot be taken as representative of the UK management population, for example it may underrepresent women in fields such as education and other professions. However, the researchers also noted that whilst most members were in full-time employment, twice as many women were in less secure positions, namely they were self-employed or on fixed-term contracts. A more recent survey of women in the BIM (Rycroft, 1989) shows that 27% were employed in education and the public sector. One-fifth of this sample worked in very small organizations, i.e. employing fewer than 20 people.

Women in local government

With a disproportionate number of women employed in government organizations one might have expected a more hopeful picture of their employment at senior management levels. The civil service, which comprises 50% female staff, mainly at lower clerical grades, has only 8% of principal grades, 4% of higher grades and 2% of civil service permanent secretary posts filled by women. An investigation by Corby (1982) into the possible reasons for such a dearth of female senior managers within the civil service identified several contributing factors including poor quality appraisal interviews, slower promotion rates than those enjoyed by men, placement in less visible posts which meant that they were not readily identified for general management, and promotion within specialities rather than into general management.

A recent study of more than 1,000 women managers in local government in England and Wales (Young and Spencer, 1990) found that whilst there were no common patterns amongst them with respect to their backgrounds, experiences, responsibilities, working context and job content, the one feature that they did share in common was 'their minority status at the management level'. The researchers remark on the 'near absence of women from top management positions in local government' and moreover that there would appear to be little evidence of the status quo changing since there was an 'overwhelming preponderance of men at middle and lower levels' (Young and Spencer, 1990, p. 6).

One might expect that as women tend to be employed in greater numbers in public sector organizations, and in particular occupations such as education, or 'caring' professions, one would find them well represented here in senior management. Alas, this appears not to be the case. In primary education 40% of headteachers are female. The figures for higher educations are worse: in the universities, although the proportion of women undergraduates increased from 35% to 42% between 1975 and 1988, only 3% of professors and 2% of university vice-chancellors and principals are women.

Nursing is a highly popular occupation for women who comprise 90% of qualified nurses (Hutt, 1985), yet only 55% of chief nursing officers are female. One-third of all NHS nurses are women who work part time (Beardshaw, 1990). The British National Health Service is the third largest employing organization in the world; 78% of its total workforce are women, yet only 4% are general managers.

BIOGRAPHICAL DATA ON WOMEN MANAGERS

Two large-scale studies in particular have provided detailed biographical information on women managers. The first, by Davidson and Cooper (1984), sampled female and male managers in a wide cross-section of industries. The second, by Alban Metcalfe and Nicholson (1984), has already been referred to.

Study by Davidson and Cooper (1984)

The sample comprised 696 females and 185 males at supervisory, junior, middle, and senior management levels in a wide cross-section of different industries. The following biographical differences between women and men were found.

Women were more likely to be slightly older, and less likely to be married than were men (56.5% and 74.6% respectively); women were more likely to be childless, and if they had children they had fewer in number; twice as many women as men were divorced or separated – 15.12% versus 8.1%.

Whilst women had lower educational qualifications overall, there was little difference between the numbers of women and men with first degrees and postgraduate qualifications. Women were also more likely to have professional qualifications. With respect to their work profile the women were more likely to be concentrated in lower levels of management, to supervise fewer people, and receive on average lower annual salaries. The researchers also found that the average female manager is more likely to be the first of her sex to hold the particular job title compared to her male counterpart.

Study by Alban Metcalfe and Nicholson (1984)

The second study concentrated on middle and senior managers in the British Institute of Management. The sample comprised 371 female and 993 male middle managers, and 41 female and 477 male senior managers. Overall in the BIM study, the women were generally younger, less likely to be married (60.9% versus 93.3%), almost four times more likely to be divorced (11.9% versus 2.7%), and more likely to be childless (controlling for age effects). Half of the married women had no children; those who did have children tended to have fewer than their male counterparts (again controlling for age effects).

When comparisons were made between occupation of manager's partner, dramatic differences emerged. Of the female managers 90% had partners in full-time employment, whereas only 25% of men in the sample were in a similar position. The women obtained a lower proportion of school and further educational qualifications than men, and a roughly equal proportion of first degrees, but almost twice the proportion of postgraduate diplomas and higher degrees. Interestingly this is the opposite to the findings of Davidson and Cooper. An earlier study conducted by Ashridge Management College (1980) suggested that women tended to follow different career routes from men. Women were more likely to enter management careers following degree qualifications, whereas men typically chose the professional qualifications route.

Alban Metcalfe and Nicholson summarize the biographical data obtained in their study as follows:

The results show that women managers are found more in service organizations/occupations and in specialist functions. They also tended to be younger and more highly qualified than males. Women in management are much more likely to be in dual-career marriages than men. All in all these results suggest that women managers have to surmount greater obstacles than men to reach equivalent positions; they require higher educational attainments and have to overcome or forego competing domestic demands.

(Alban Metcalfe and Nicholson, 1984, p. 15)

The interim report of the study of women managers in local government does not allow for a detailed comparison with the other two studies; however, all three studies feature important common elements relating to the female manager's experience of work and of balancing work with home life. All three studies identified the problem the women managers had with respect to attempting to combine a satisfying career with domestic responsibilities. All three clearly portray the unequal burden still placed on women to provide by far the major proportion of childcare.

THE EXPERIENCES OF WORKING AS A WOMAN MANAGER

Most female managers have male bosses and are more likely to have female than male staff. Whilst it is also true that they are working in traditionally 'female' functions as already noted, given the preponderance of men in the most influential and controlling positions, women managers often remark on the male dominance of the organization and on the sense of discomfort or tension, which may be experienced as a major stressor.

The subject of stress amongst women managers in the UK has been an issue of particular interest in the last few years. Davidson and Cooper's (1984) investigation represents the most detailed study. The authors remark that whilst management as an occupation is regarded as stressful, 'women managers at all levels of the managerial hierarchy were experiencing higher stresses both at work and at home compared to their male counterparts. In terms of stress manifestations, female managers reported more often experiencing a far greater number of psychosomatic symptoms compared to men'. (Davidson, 1989, p. 32).

The work-related pressures included prejudice and discrimination. 'Compared to married male managers, married female managers were much more likely to experience higher pressures in respect of career and spouse/partner conflicts, career/home conflicts, and career and marriage/childbearing conflicts' (Davidson, 1989, p. 32).

Single women managers were likely to experience pressure from colleagues who perceived them as 'odd' and who might exclude them from social and business events, but they also experienced the stress of making decisions relating to the form of a relationship with a partner – to marry or to live together or not to live together, and the quandary, sometimes exacerbated by pressures from others, of whether to have children, and when.

Davidson corrects the myth that it is senior managers who experience the most stress. In fact it was the junior- and middle-level female managers in the sample studied who experienced the greatest number of combined high stressors. Prejudice and sexual discrimination were particularly strongly experienced by junior management women.

There were many parallels to be found in the BIM study, which comprised mainly middle-level female managers. In addition to the problems identified in Davidson and Cooper's study, there were examples of female managers experiencing pressures from teenagers who resented their mother's 'career'. The guilt felt by women experiencing role conflict often led to remarkable personal sacrifices on the women's part. Several women managers stated that their career emerged almost by chance, developing from success and enthusiasm for what was initially a temporary or part-time job, but the strong sense of self-esteem and satisfaction of using one's potential overrode the cost of the personal sacrifices they felt were necessary. (For examples of comments made by female managers see Davidson and Cooper (1984) and Alban Metcalfe (1984).)

Additional sources of stress and frustration mentioned included not being taken seriously; being excluded from decision-making situations which in some way involved them; not being sought for advice despite their 'expert' knowledge; being told that they were receiving preferential treatment by virtue of being a female; lack of development opportunities that were offered to male colleagues; and an overriding sense of isolation and alienation. Several women felt that they had experienced clear discrimination with respect to pay and promotion and a few mentioned that they had considered taking their case to the industrial tribunal which legislates on equal pay matters, but that the price of being labelled 'a troublemaker' would damage their future opportunities.

One of the objectives of the BIM study was to investigate how male and female managers perceived themselves at work and outside work. A self-concept semantic-differential scale was used. Of the 15 dimensions only three significant differences emerged between the males and females in the sample (controlling for age effects) (Alban Metcalfe, 1987). These were: that the females perceived themselves as more intellectual than the males perceived themselves (perhaps not surprisingly given their higher educational qualifications); females were less likely to keep feelings to themselves; and the females perceived themselves as more tense than the males perceived themselves. Women frequently made reference to the fact that they felt themselves to be under the close scrutiny of male colleagues and bosses, and were constantly aware of a suspicious audience looking for opportunities to exploit any *faux pas*.

Alban Metcalfe (1987) expresses concern, not only with the higher levels of perceived tension, but with the fact that the female and male self-concepts were so similar. For example, the females perceived themselves as equally creative, forceful, confident, ambitious and controlling. On the face of it these data may be taken as offering weight to the argument that women are no different from men. However, placed alongside some of the remarks made by some of the females, they may be seen as more sinister. These comments include: '[Through completing the questionnaire] I noticed that my "work personality" is far less attractive. It certainly reflects my dislike of feeling it necessary to change my personality at work to reflect what my male management want to see' (Alban Metcalfe, 1984, p. 15).

For many women the sense of alienation arising from working in a masculine' environment where there was an overriding emphasis on competition and aggression, and where they were strongly sanctioned if they did not comply, meant that in order to succeed they had to behave in an entirely 'unnatural' way. These data may resemble those from US studies of women in non-traditional roles (managers) who, when compared with women in traditional roles, resembled more closely the self-characteristics of male colleagues. Moore and Rickel (1980) ominously note that the higher up the organizational hierarchy the female was, the more she rejected 'even the few positively-valued feminine traits they earlier endorsed' (p. 32), replacing them with the male model of managerial success. Such might be the potency of organizational socialization for women (Alban Metcalfe, 1985).

Organizational socialization places pressures on individuals to perform according to the norms and values of the dominant powerful group, which for women may be at variance with their preferred style. Marshall's (1984) in-depth study of women managers entitled *Women Managers: Travellers in a Male World* provides a rich source of commentary on women's experiences in male-dominant organizations.

WOMEN AND MANAGEMENT STYLE

There has been substantial research in the USA conducted into management or leadership style and investigating the possibility of gender differences which has concluded that there is no greater difference between women and men than between women and women. However, two British studies may have obtained interesting and potentially important findings, if the relatively small sample on which they were based were found to be true of the wider population. The first, by Vinnicombe (1987), compared scores obtained by male managers responding to a scale devised by the US Center for Creative Leadership which was based on a combination of the Myers Briggs Type Indicator (Myers Briggs, 1976) and Mintzberg's managerial roles (1975). A comparison of scores obtained from a small sample of 87 female managers with a large sample of 849 (almost exclusively male) managers showed far smaller proportions of 'traditionalist' managers amongst the women, and significantly more 'visionaries' or 'catalysts'. Vinnicombe comments that 'visionaries' are supposed to be the 'natural' strategic managers. Referring to the description of 'catalyst', she quotes Bates and Kiersey (1984):

> Catalysts are excellent in public relations and shine as organizational spokespersons since they work well with all types of people. They can sell the organization to its customers and can make employees feel good about themselves and the organization. They are excellent in the top position if given free rein to manage, but they may rebel and become disloyal if they perceive themselves as having too many constraints.
>
> (Bates and Kiersey, 1984)

A recent study by Ferrario (1990) of 124 female managers and 95 male managers compared the scores for the two groups on a wide range of management style and sex role measures. Despite the widely held assumption that women are more people oriented and men more task oriented she found that the women obtained significantly higher self-report scores on both dimensions of 'consideration' and 'initiating structure' than did the men. She adds, 'when the two sexes were compared, more women managers had a team management, which emphasizes not only a high regard for people, but also a high regard for task. In contrast, a higher proportion of men managers were identified as *laissez-faire*'. Whilst adding the caveat that these two studies were based on relatively small samples (although there have of course been examples of major psychological theories constructed from similar sized populations, e.g. Herzberg's theory of motivation based on data from a mere 200 employees) one cannot be expected to ignore the data.

Viewed in the context of the changing shape and culture of organizations (e.g. Barham, Fraser and Heath, 1988; Harrison, 1987), where values of co-operation and caring, and visionary leadership are expected to be at least as important as task orientation, one might well presume that women have qualities and styles best suited to leading them.

WOMEN MANAGERS: WHAT DO THEY WANT FROM A JOB?

Amongst the many myths extolled by male senior managers in the UK as reasons for women's conspicuous absence at senior levels, is the one relating to their different patterns of motivation. Clearly if women are less concerned with advancement, challenge, autonomy and development, then when it comes to a selection or promotion decision into middle or senior management, or on to a fast career track development programme, women are less of a good investment. Schein's classical studies of male and female manager's perceptions of characteristics of effective managers have provided substantial evidence of the classic stereotypes, held almost equally strongly by females and males. Since her initial studies in the USA in 1973 (Schein, 1973, 1975) Schein has repeated her survey in 1989 (Schein, 1989) and in 1990 (Schein and Mueller, 1990), extending her sampling frame beyond female and male middle managers, to include young business students in the USA, Germany and the UK. Sadly there has been little or no modification in attitudes as to characteristics of effective managers or, as Schein puts it, 'Think Manager equals Think Male'.

Whilst Schein asked managers what they perceived as characteristics of female and male managers and effective middle managers, in other words they may well be basing judgements on sterotypes, an extension of the BIM study already cited, which finally included 1,497 male and 805 female managers, obtained results which were very different with respect to what managers *themselves* believed to be important in a job (Alban Metcalfe, 1989). When age was controlled, since clearly it affects work preferences, the top five out of 17 items were identical for women and men and, in fact, contrary to commonly held assumptions, the women rated nearly all the items either equally important or even significantly *more* important than did the men. Amongst the 10 items which the women rated significantly more highly than did the men were: a challenging job, opportunity for development, quality of feedback, working with friendly people, and autonomy. Men on the other hand were significantly more concerned with extrinsic factors to the job, such as high earnings, fringe benefits and job security. Some readers might understandably conclude from these data that women represent a better organizational investment than do male managerial employees.

Comparisons were also made by gender and sector of employment, that is public versus private sector (see Table 2). Public sector managers, irrespective of gender, were significantly more concerned with security and having a job which made a contribution to society, but less concerned with the quality of senior management, whilst both men and women in the private sector regarded high earnings and fringe benefits as more important than did those working in the public sector. Alban Metcalfe concluded that 'the patterns of work preferences appear more similar with respect to an individual's gender than to the sector of employment in which they work' (p. 103). Table 3 shows the actual rating of importance that the female and male managers in the different sectors gave.

WOMEN ENTREPRENEURS

Given the problems that women experience working in organizations — most of which are male dominated — it is perhaps not surprising that the number of women entering self-employment between 1981 and 1987 has shown a dramatic increase of 70%. The corresponding increase

Table 2 Mean scores and analysis of variance (ANOVA) for attitudes to work scores of females and males working in private and public sector organizations by sector with age as covariate

	Females				Males			
	Private $\bar{x}$ (n = 447)	Public $\bar{x}$ (n = 326)	Age Sig. of F.	Sector Sig. of F.	Private $\bar{x}$ (n = 1,045)	Public $\bar{x}$ (n = 412)	Age Sig. of F.	Sector Sig. of F.
Advancement	4.11	3.82	<0.0001	<0.003	3.90	3.75	<0.001	ns
Friendly people	4.03	4.06	ns	ns	3.78	3.87	<0.001	ns
Challenge	4.68	4.63	ns	ns	4.52	4.48	ns	ns
Being appreciated	4.28	4.25	ns	ns	4.11	3.97	<0.02	<0.005
Highly regarded organization	3.66	3.46	<0.001	<0.001	3.66	3.62	<0.001	ns
Opportunity to develop	4.34	4.35	ns	ns	3.92	3.93	<0.001	ns
Autonomy	4.15	4.18	<0.01	ns	4.15	4.01	ns	<0.01
Fringe benefits	2.78	2.20	<0.001	<0.001	3.04	2.39	ns	<0.001
Non-work fit	3.22	3.24	ns	ns	2.90	2.88	ns	ns
Security	3.45	3.67	<0.01	<0.02	3.66	3.85	ns	<0.01
High earnings	3.66	3.20	<0.001	<0.001	3.79	3.28	<0.001	<0.001
Location	3.40	3.52	<0.01	ns	3.25	3.21	<0.001	ns
Contribution to society	3.12	3.79	<0.001	<0.001	2.91	3.57	<0.001	<0.001
Influence	3.59	3.71	<0.001	ns	3.82	3.76	ns	ns
Task specificity	2.78	2.91	<0.001	ns	2.92	2.96	<0.001	ns
Feedback	3.66	3.61	ns	ns	3.42	3.32	<0.01	ns
Senior management	4.30	4.19	<0.001	<0.02	4.30	4.09	<0.01	<0.001

ns = not significant.

Source: Alban Metcalfe, B. (1989) What motivates managers: an investigation by gender and sector of employment, *Public Administration*, Vol. 67, no. 1, pp. 95–108.

Table 3 Ranking of importance of aspects of a job by females in private and public sector organizations and males in private and public sector organizations

Ranking	Females		Males	
	Private sector	Public sector	Private sector	Public sector
Important to very important	Challenge Opportunity to develop Quality of senior management Being appreciated Autonomy Advancement Friendly people	Challenge Opportunity to develop Being appreciated Quality of senior management Autonomy Friendly people	Challenge Quality of senior management Autonomy Being appreciated	Challenge Quality of senior management Autonomy
Moderately important to important	Highly regarded organization High earnings Feedback Influence Security Location Non-work fit Contribution to society	Advancement Contribution to society Influence Security Feedback Location Highly regarded organization High earnings	Opportunity to develop Advancement Influence High earnings Friendly people Highly regarded organization Security Feedback Location Fringe benefits	Being appreciated Opportunity to develop Friendly people Security Influence Advancement Highly regarded organization Contribution to society Feedback High earnings Location
Of little importance	Task specificity Fringe benefits	Task specificity Fringe benefits	Task specificity Contribution to society Non-work fit	Task specificity Non-work fit Fringe benefits

Source: Alban Metcalfe, B. (1989) What motivates managers: an investigation by gender and sector of employment, *Public Administration*, Vol. 67, no. 1, pp. 95–108.

for men was 30% (*Employment Gazette*, 1988). Women now comprise at least 25% of the self-employed population of UK-based organizations.

The profile of the female British entrepreneur compared with her male counterpart is an interesting one. Davidson and Cooper (1987) in their review of the literature cite research which found that females tended to be younger when they started their businesses, with an average age of 39 years compared with 42 years for men (Devine and Clutterbuck, 1985); they were more likely to have entered a business venture of which they had no prior experience when compared with the men (more than 50% versus 5%, Davidson, 1985); compared with women managers who were not self-employed they were far more likely to be married and have children (80% and 73% respectively, quoted in Knight, 1985); and in comparison with American female entrepreneurs, they were far less likely to have degrees (14% versus 86%, Devine and Clutterbuck, 1985).

However, Simpson (1991) in a more recent review warns that research results are often contradictory, citing several British studies including, for example, two in which women were found to be as well qualified as men (Johnson and Storey, 1989; Watkins and Watkins, 1986), and one in which women entrepreneurs were found to have higher educational qualifications than men (Carter and Cannon, 1988). With respect to age some studies have found that women entrepreneurs are younger than their male counterparts (Birley, Moss and Saunders, 1986; Welsh and Young, 1982, cited in Simpson, 1991, p. 114) whilst others have found that they are older (Hisrich, 1986; Johnson and Storey, 1989).

The single common factor that has been identified, and which is equally true for females and males, is that previous employment/work experience predominantly drives the choice of new business formation (Brotherton, Leather and Simpson, 1987).

Simpson (1991) cites some of the reasons why women may choose to start their own business. These include the frequent experience of suffering downward mobility after a period of childrearing, or the inflexibility of organizations in accommodating domestic responsibilities (Brotherton, Leather and Simpson, 1987), unrewarding experience in employment (Brotherton, Leather and Simpson, 1986; Goffee and Scase, 1985), and the considerable frustration with the inequality of career prospects.

If the move into self-employment is stimulated by the need to free oneself from gender discrimination in organizational life, Simpson warns that there is no guarantee that women will be free of such forces once they set themselves on the road to self-employment. She states that entrepreneurship is essentially viewed as a male phenomenon and most research on the subject, like the vast bulk of management research, has until recently concentrated on all-male samples: 'The rhetoric indicates "opportunity for all", although even a superficial analysis reveals messages reflecting a predominantly male image of enterprise' (Simpson, 1991, p. 114).

Whilst the British government has invested millions of pounds of public money in promoting enterprise initiatives such as the Enterprise Allowance Scheme (EAS) or the Business Enterprise Programme, Simpson states that the demand for various schedules are underestimated as women are frequently ineligible due to either lost National Insurance contributions or not being in receipt of benefit (1991, p. 114). 'Of the successful EAS applicants between April and October 1987, 28.7% were women compared to 71.3% men (EOC, 1988). Statistics on the number of failed applications (by gender) were not available. All in all, women are largely ignored' (Simpson, 1991, p. 114).

The founder director of one of the newest and most successful computer programming organizations – F International – with a turnover of over £15 million, is a woman. Her initial attempts at establishing the new business almost floundered. How did she succeed? She changed her name from Stephanie to Steve, and the customers rolled in. All its employees were women working from home.

The kinds of problems women have to cope with when embarking on the self-employment road include negative attitudes from agencies and other commercial sources of advice, almost exclusively staffed with male advisers; and not being taken seriously. Another common experience of women is the lack of morale and practical support from partners for domestic responsibilities or help in the business itself, particularly in its start-up phase. Typically men in a similar position receive substantial and unpaid support from a partner who is more likely to ensure that domestic responsibilities do not interfere with the entrepreneur's effort (Scase and Goffee, 1980, 1982). Women experience the same pressures and stresses as male entrepreneurs, but apparently more powerfully. These include worry about finance, or the lack of it, business failure and lack of business skills. For example, women are less likely to have access to the collateral required to raise capital and often lack the 'track record', interpreted according to certain male-stereotyped criteria as experience in business, particularly in the manufacturing sector (Halpern, 1989). Given the considerable additional problems they face, it is not surprising that women's need for independence and challenge (Nicholson and West, 1988; Simpson, 1991) needs to be combined with a remarkable level of resilience in combating the many potential attacks on their self-confidence. Whilst clearly no defence for the situation, perhaps women's experience of organizational life in some way prepares them better.

WOMEN AND CAREER PROMOTION

Mobility of job changes appears to have increased over the last 15 years in Britain. In 1976 a survey of BIM members (figures by sex are not provided and therefore presumed to be almost all male) found that managers changed employers, on average, 3.0 times in their careers.

Davidson and Cooper (1983), in a sample of female and male managers, obtained an average of 3.7 for both women and men. Alban Metcalfe and Nicholson found in 1984 that women had changed employers more frequently than men (3.6 times and 3.4 times respectively).

Many working women have discovered the 'glass ceiling' in organizations: the invisible, intangible, but ambition-proof barrier to their progress. Assuming that women sampled in British management surveys give a clear indication of their solid educational qualifications and ambition apparently equal to that of men, one can only hypothesize as to why they do not achieve equal rates or levels of promotion, as appears to be the case. A longitudinal study of a sample of 4,000 UK graduates who graduated in 1982 has reported that women were in lower status jobs, had limited promotion prospects, and earned significantly less than men (Chapman, 1986, 1989a, 1989b). Studies of women in the civil service (OMCS, 1988) and of nurse managers in the NHS (Hutt, 1985), and graduate entrants to the NHS fast-track management training scheme (Dixon and Shaw, 1986) have shown similar patterns. Whilst taking a career break is an obvious and oft-quoted explanation, we should recall that significant proportions of women in managerial careers are single and childless (Davidson and Cooper, 1987; Alban Metcalfe and Nicholson, 1984). Moreover, referring to the longitudinal graduate study, Hirsh and Jackson (1990) state that it was 'certainly too early for it to be blamed on having children' (p. 27). Other reasons posited are that the early career choices or job selection women make may be 'deviant' from the male model of management progression, which was vividly referred to in a study of NHS career progression as the uninterrupted 'yellow brick road' to senior positions (Davies and Rosser, 1986).

There is evidence of gender discrimination in recruitment techniques and selection interviews in which women applying for out-of-role jobs, that is, managerial ones, are regarded as less suitable candidates (Ashridge Management Centre, 1980; Iles and Robertson, 1988). More specific and challenging data have been collected by the civil service which monitors the data of candidates applying for and being selected to join their 'fast-track' programme. Hirsh and Jackson (1990) report that whilst equal numbers of females and males applied for the scheme only 29% of the 'successful' candidates were women. They suggest that the scoring method may provide a major barrier to women. As assessment techniques become more 'sophisticated' and complex, concerns have been expressed elsewhere about the increasing difficulty of 'challenging' potential sources of discrimination (Alimo-Metcalfe, 1992).

Reference has already been made to the substantial data which suggest that women are more likely to be found in specialist or support roles in organizations, and moreover to be promoted within them rather than moving out into the more general management senior-track career path (e.g. Rycroft, 1989; Ashridge Management Centre, 1980; Corby, 1982; Alban Metcalfe and Nicholson, 1984). The reason is frequently given that women choose this path; however, it may also be true, or even more true that they have little say in the matter of job placement or the type of promotion they are offered. A longitudinal study of the original BIM members sampled by Alban Metcalfe and Nicholson (1984) conducted a year or so later showed that women were more likely than men to make 'outspiralling' moves, changing employers and functions and experiencing a promotion (Nicholson and West, 1988). This might provide evidence for the point made that women have to move out of the organization to be recognized as having the potential for promotion. In the last few years research has been published on women's career opportunities, or lack of them, in the banking sector in the UK. Collinson (1987), through the use of case study material, provides evidence of major career barriers for women by way of types of job allocation, closed promotion systems in which jobs are not advertised internally, and false or inaccurate assumptions made by personnel and line managers about women's career intentions and mobility. A survey by Ashburner (1989) of the building society sector in Britain provides a powerful indictment of antediluvian and clearly chauvinistic attitudes amongst a substantial proportion of its managers.

EQUAL OPPORTUNITIES LEGISLATION

In the late 19th and early 20th centuries there was an endless debate between employers, feminists, trades unions and other interested groups about how best to protect women from the hazards of the workplace. This so-called protective legislation focused on women as actual or potential mothers and aimed to regulate the hours worked. Maternity leave was first introduced in the UK in 1891 and the 1970s saw the start of today's equal pay and sex discrimination legislation (Lewis and Davies, 1991).

As Lewis and Davies point out, equal pay for equal work was an attempt by male employers to maintain the sexual division of labour. All-female occupations were covered by any legislation on women in the workplace (Lewis and Davies, 1991).

The arguments about protective legislation have continued to the present day but do not necessarily focus on women's concerns about working in organizations. One area where specific legislation is needed is sexual harassment. This is regarded as direct discrimination under the Sex Discrimination Act 1975. In a study of organizational attitudes to sexual harassment, Davidson and Earnshaw (1990) found that, while personnel directors favour preventive measures, few have policy state- ments. Sexual harassment contravenes the EC equal treatment Directive but there is an urgent need to clarify just what constitutes sexual harassment. What seems 'harmless fun' at the office party may, for the woman concerned, be offensive and upsetting. The lack of direct legislation on sexual harassment leaves the woman in the position of having to prove her case. Employers are also disserved because policy is not guided by any national consistency.

However, in areas where there is legislation concerning working women, benefits are not what they seem nor do they accrue to all.

POSITIVE DISCRIMINATION

Most job advertisements in the UK include a statement to the effect that the organization is 'working toward equal opportunities' or 'is an equal opportunity employer'. Other 'welcome applications from women and members of the ethnic minorities who are currently underrepresented at this level'. While the absence of such statements should be no reflection of the organization's lack of intention to 'equalize' its workforce, the reality is very different. The equal opportunities legislation of 1975 requires that no applicant for a job is denied equal opportunity to compete because of 'sex, religious orientation, disability, colour or race'. This has not prevented organizations from treating men and women differently at job interviews. Women are still asked questions about plans for a family or childcare arrangements, and are turned down for jobs because they are too bright, too articulate, too attractive, overqualified or, in at least one case, are wearing the wrong perfume! (Iles and Robertson, 1988).

The arguments against positive discrimination are fought on the grounds that women should not be made 'special cases' but allowed to compete on the same terms as men. Proponents of such discrimination insist that, given the skewed nature of organizations, women need to be assisted to obtain positions which have traditionally been the preserve of men. Most of these arguments ignore the fact that many women who have the choice have been quietly voting with their feet and setting up their own businesses, albeit against tremendous odds, working in co-operatives, or simply quitting the workplace. There is something offensive in the current rush to discriminate positively in favour of women when organizations are short of skills and people. Ironically, when women arrive in the workplace, they find that support systems, in terms of maternity leave, childcare provision and pensions, leave much to be desired.

MATERNITY LEAVE

Maternity leave legislation is fraught with complexity and exclusion clauses. For example, the right to paid time off work for antenatal care is not afforded to all women. Some 50% of working women in the UK receive no maternity leave, and those who are entitled to this benefit may not always know; neither may their employers. Only a minority of women (10%) benefit from extended maternity leave arrangements. In general, women in public sector organizations are better provided for than those in the private sector. However, in the light of the EC Directive on the treatment of pregnant women at work, and before formal implementation, some private sector firms, for example Shell UK, are offering women employees much enhanced maternity benefits, including up to 6 months' leave on full pay.

The UK, of all EC countries, gives the most maternity leave (40 weeks). This apparent generosity is in lieu of any other provision for childcare leave, and the combined requirement of number of hours worked and length of service with the employer results in many women not qualifying for this benefit. The concern over this patchy legislation is heightened by increasing reports of women being dismissed from their jobs because of pregnancy (Robson-Scott, 1990). In such cases the burden of proof is on the woman and not the employer.

The proposed EC Directive on pregnant women at work grants all women access to a range of maternity leave benefits with no eligibility conditions (EC Directive, 1989). In 1991 a government minister responded to this proposed Directive by stressing the disadvantage to employers because of high cost, warning that women's employment opportunities would be particularly at risk (Robson-Scott, 1990). The experience of other countries which have legislation forbidding the dismissal of women employees because of pregnancy, for example Sweden, disproves this theory.

If legislation on maternity leave has the look of a giant honeycomb with many honey-denuded areas, childcare provision has even greater deficiencies.

CHILDCARE PROVISIONS AND FACILITIES

As part of a relocation package, British Petroleum (BP) recently became the first UK employer to offer workers an independent childcare information service. The Body Shop has financed and built the UK's only dedicated childcare development centre. At the other extreme there are unregistered childminders and a constant juggle to meet job and family needs. The issue of childcare is emotive: many working women experience guilt, anxiety and shame at 'farming out' their children to other women (and a few men) while they hold down much needed employment. The apparent ambivalence towards the need for a comprehensive policy on and provision of childcare in the UK is related to the widely held view that a child needs its mother if it is to grow up a whole, non-delinquent person. This view collides with the reality, which is that, contrary to popular opinion, women work from financial necessity rather than for pin money, and the nuclear family is now largely a myth. The debate is now usefully shifting to consideration not of where childcare is provided but the quality of that provision (Phillips,

1990). Some organizations make provision through private nursery places or by directing resources to out-of-school care. The latter is the preferred choice of one of the private sector leaders in childcare provision, the Midland Bank.

Most women pay for childcare, for which there is no tax relief. Of those women who can pay, 14% use workplace crèche facilities and 23% employ childminders. A very small proportion have live-in nannies, trained or untrained. This minority offers evidence of women's generally lower earnings and reliance on relatives, for whom they may also care. One organization has endeavoured to provide self-help for working mothers: the Working Mothers Association (WMA) formed in late 1985 offers support and advice to working parents through self-help groups, relying primarily on voluntary contributions from members, and runs, for example, BP's childcare information service mentioned above.

There is no national policy for funding of childcare facilities. Where workplace nurseries exist (at the time of writing there are 120, 20 of which are run by private companies), they are concentrated in the affluent south east. Only 300 out-of-school care schemes exist, while Kids Club Network estimate a need for 25,000 (EOC, 1990b). As with maternity leave, the public sector is generally better provided than the private sector, perhaps because these organizations employ proportionately more women. One major exception is the UK's and Europe's largest employer, the National Health Service (NHS): although 78% of their workforce are women, only 50% of NHS health authorities provide childcare facilities.

The contradiction underlying the lack of childcare provision and employers' expressed need to recruit and retain women workers is revealed in the report of a survey of over 2,000 organizations employing between them more than 10% of the female workforce in Britain. Whereas only 25% have facilities to attract women returners, 71% experienced labour shortages. Clearly, the present government's hope that market forces would stimulate initiatives in childcare provision has not been realized.

The deficiencies in childcare facilities are likely to be exacerbated by the current recession. Midland Bank recently announced that it would halve the planned number of nurseries, and other employers are scrapping plans to provide childcare, because of financial pressures. Nevertheless, the government continues to reject calls for a national strategy on childcare (Lowe, 1991). The government has attempted to modify a key area of concern to many workers' pensions. And again the driving force has been the rulings from the European Court of Justice.

PENSIONS

Papadakis and Taylor-Gooby (1987) chart the history and context of recent debates about pensions especially the continuing support for state pensions among employees and most employers. Despite the present government's attempts to shift the emphasis from state to private provision of pensions, most people seem to view pensions as an intangible asset, unlike shares in, say, British Telecom.

For many working women, access to company pension schemes is ruled by many of the same eligibility criteria as maternity leave. The majority of part-timers, mainly women who work fewer than 30 hours each week, are excluded from company schemes. Even where trades unions are successful in winning pension provision for women a minimum of 16 hours per week is specified for eligibility (Maier, 1991). In an international comparison of labour law and social security, Maier (1991) reports that permanent part-time work actually reduces the final value of a pension because schemes are based on at least 30–40 years of full-time working. Pension schemes in the public sector have generally been fairer, but with the increase in the contracting out of some services, usually catering and domestic, to the private sector, women have lost many of their pension rights because it is mainly in these areas of public sector organizations that they are employed. Private contractors keep overheads low and therefore can make competitive bids because they do not provide pension schemes for employees and tend, in any event, to employ mainly part-time staff. Indeed, the public sector has failed to protect the pension rights of many of its employees because, in bidding to contract for its own services, it has often increased part-time and less than part-time working to remain competitive with private bidders. Ward argues that, for women, the state earnings-related pension scheme (SERPS) is 'considerably better' than most private schemes. However, even here there are drawbacks as SERPS pays out on what is put in; in other words, the lowest paid get smaller pensions (Ward, 1984). The 1986 Social Security Act has been modified so that SERPS is now based on lifetime earnings and not, as previously, on the best 20 years. Further, women who have breaks in employment will have their rights protected. This modification is in contrast to the 1985 Green Paper which proposed the abolition of SERPS.

The late acknowledgement of women's right to company pensions has undoubtedly been the result of several rulings of the European Court of Justice on UK pension violations of Article 119 of the Treaty of Rome. As more women enter the workforce, the pace of, and the arguments for, change in this area will become more focused on ensuring not only that UK company pension schemes fall into line with the rest of Europe, but that employers see that not making company pensions available to all employees is simply poor company practice.

It is also poor practice not to provide comprehensive training and development for women workers. It is in this area that most of the progress has been made for British working women.

TRAINING AND DEVELOPMENT

The UK record on training and development is probably the worst in Europe. However, good practice does exist, both because of the need to attract women into the workforce in response to demographic changes and because wise employees see training and development as sound investment. In both the public and private sectors, women workers now have many more opportunities than they did even 10 years ago. Much more remains to be done but at least there are good examples of what can be achieved with concentrated thinking.

The report of the Hansard Society (1990) entitled *Women at the Top* gives several examples of organizations, in both the public and private sectors, which have developed a variety of programmes to overcome barriers that prevent women reaching the top. The report also lists some of the barriers and the change strategies used to overcome these.

Sections 47, 48 and 49 of the 1975 Sex Discrimination Act permit employers to take 'positive action' in favour of women, without breaching the principle of non-discrimination.

The University of Manchester Institute for Science and Technology (UMIST) has developed a single-sex management development programme, the objective of which is to increase the number of women in middle and senior management positions (Smith *et al.*, 1984). The programme has four broad foci – women's issues, career planning, personal and interactive skills and management knowledge. The preferred method of single-sex training enables women on the programme to acquire knowledge and skills in a psychologically secure setting and avoids the tendency to follow traditional patterns of interaction that can occur in mixed training. Men do have a role in the programme, as tutors and voluntary participants in workshops, after the initial stages of the programme.

In a more recent collaboration, the *Guardian* newspaper and the Manchester Business School have launched the *Guardian* Women in Management Scholarship, the first six of which were awarded in April 1991. In an earlier and similar scheme, the Prudential Insurance company funded two women to undertake the 10-week intensive management development programme at the London Business School. This scheme has been discontinued.

For women returners there are many organizations with innovative and long-term training and development schemes. An institute of Manpower Studies report (Rajan and van Eupen, 1990) on women returners highlighted the growing recognition that women are vital resources in their own right, not just stopgaps in times of demographic change and falling birthrates. Many employers are also becoming more aware that, in a labour market where 80% of the labour force will be returners, the majority of them women, they will be disadvantaged if they do not provide training and other facilities. Notwithstanding the slow pace of these developments, a recent survey finds that, for women returners, the UK is better than most countries in Europe (Falconer, 1991). Consideration of such findings should take into account the fact that the UK is starting at a lower base than other countries surveyed.

It is fair to say that the private sector has set the pace with training and development for women workers, especially returners. The largest employer in Europe, the NHS, has no national policy on women returners, opportunities for women in management or specific training for women managers. The level of training and development for women in the UK is part of the overall malaise about training in the UK. All the initiatives in this area have come from organizations with their own problems to solve or from professional associations. For example, the scheme for women engineers returning to employment, The Fellowship Scheme for Women Returners to Science and Engineering, has enabled this group of women actively to contribute to their field, even after several years away from professional practice. Some women on the scheme commented particularly on the support received from male colleagues (Jackson, 1991). The returners' schemes offered by the private sector, for example Boots plc, Lloyds Bank, Barclays, and the public sector, for example Leicester City Council, The British Council, The Electricity Council, have a similar focus and similar results (NEDO/ RIPA, 1990).

For all this activity, Coward (1991) reports on a rising trend among some middle-class women who are returning, but returning home rather than to work: they are giving up careers and well-paid jobs to look after their children. Many see raising a family as a timely break from the frustrations of work. At the risk of increasing the idealization of childrearing, and therefore leaving the male structure of organizations intact, these women may well encourage more women who may have hesitated to take this step. These women do not want to give up active employment, but want a less fragmented and organization-dominated life: a choice that some men wish they could exercise?

CONCLUSION

The future for working women in the UK is mixed. On the one hand, the moves by private and public sector organizations to recognize the value of women in the workforce provide a blueprint for further initiatives. On the other hand, the apparent lack of political will to have national strategies on childcare provision is the single biggest obstacle to women participating fully in the economy. The lack of a national training strategy is also a minus. Women themselves seem markedly reluctant to fuss about such things as pension benefits, until personal experience necessitates action.

Britain's membership of the EC has been an unexpected boom for working women in the UK, and if EC Directives on maternity leave, pension rights and equal treatment are fully adopted, then the future is indeed of a rosy hue.

However, EC Directives cannot change the persistent belief that women work just to 'fill in' time between babies. Whatever measures are taken to ensure women's full integration into the workforce, this underlying belief will have to form part of the debate for change.

Organizations of the future will have to review their emphasis on full-time work as the norm. Handy (1989) argues that organizations as we know them will cease to exist and people will work from home. If this is to be a positive change, and not increase the invisibility of women in the workforce, government, employers and women will need to state clearly that women's contribution to work is needed and valued.

Maternity leave, childcare facilities, unemployment pay, pensions, cannot for much longer only apply to those women working in enlightened organizations. If the UK is to remain competitive and make the best use of increasingly scarce skills, then women, soon to comprise more than half the workforce, must have a more visible role in the economy, and reap the benefits of that involvement. It should not be forgotten that there is evidence that as modern orgnizations are changing dramatically in structure and in the leadership styles to be adopted, women may provide a particularly crucial resource.

If significant change is to take place, then it will require pressure on those in influential positions, and in particular the law makers. The Hansard Society (1990) reported that Britain was 'at the bottom of the league table of modern democracies' (p. 4). With almost all senior judges being male, and only 42 out of a total of 650 members of parliament in 1990 being female, it is clearly going to require not only sustained effort on the part of women, but an honest and serious recognition on the part of men to enable full equality of opportunity to be realized.

REFERENCES

Alban Metcalfe, B. (1984) Current career concerns of female and male managers and professionals: An analysis of free-response comments to a national survey, *Equal Opportunities International*, Vol. 3, no. 1, pp. 11–18.

Alban Metcalfe, B. (1985) The effects of socialization on women's-management careers, *Management Bibliographies and Reviews*, Vol. 11, no. 3.

Alban Metcalfe, B. (1987) Male and female managers: an analysis of biographical and self-concept data, *Work and Stress*, Vol. 1, no. 3, pp. 207–219.

Alban Metcalfe, B. (1989) What motivates managers: an investigation by gender and sector of employment, *Public Administration*, Vol. 67, no. 1, pp. 95–108.

Alban Metcalfe, B. and Nicholson, N. (1984) *The Career Development of British Managers*, British Institute of Management Foundation, London.

Alimo-Metcalfe, B. (1992) Different gender − different rules?: assessment of women in management, in P. Barrer and C. L. Cooper (eds.) *Managing organizations in 1992: Strategic Response*, Routledge, London.

Ashburner, L. (1989) Man managers and women workers: women employees as an under used resource. Paper given at the Third Annual Conference of the British Academy of Management, Manchester Business School, 10−12 September.

Ashridge Management College (1980) *Employee Potential: Issues in the Development of Women*, IPM and Ashridge Management College, London.

Barham, K., Fraser, J. and Heath, L. (1988) *Management for the Future*, Ashridge Management Research Group and the Foundation for Management Education, London.

Bates, M. and Kiersey, D. W. (1984) *Please Understand Me*, Prometheus Neamesis Book Company, California.

Beardshaw, V. (1990) Battle to stem the shortage tide, *Health Service Journal*, 25 October, pp. 25−6.

Birley, S., Moss, C. and Saunders, P. (1986) The difference between small firms started by male and female entrepreneurs who attended small business courses, in R. Roustadt, J. A. Hornaday, R. Peterson and K. H. Vesper (eds.) *Frontiers of Entreprenurial Research 1986*, Proceedings of the Sixth Annual Babson College Entreprenurship Research Conference, Babson College, Wellesley, Mass.

Brotherton, C., Leather, P. and Simpson, S. M. (1986) Social psychological dimensions in job creation. Paper given at the Occupational Psychology Conference of the British Psychological Society, University of Nottingham, January.

Brotherton, C., Leather, P. and Simpson, S. M. (1987) Job creation: new work for women? *Work and Stress*, Vol. 1, no. 3, pp. 249−59.

Carter, S. and Cannon, T. (1988) *Female Entrepreneurs: A Study of Female Business Owners; Their Motivations, Experiences and Strategies for Success.* Development of Employment Research Paper No. 65, Department of Employment, London.

Chapman, T. (1989) Women graduates in management and the professions, *Women in Management Review and Abstracts*, Vol. 4, pp. 10−14.

Collinson, D. L. (1987) Banking on women: selection practices in the finance sector, *Personnel Review*, Vol. 16, pp. 12−20.

Corby, S. (1982) *Equal Opportunities for Women in the Civil Service*, HMSO, London.

Coward, R. (1991) When home is where the work is, *The Guardian*, 25 April, p. 36.

Davidson, M. J. (1985) *Reach for the Top − A Woman's Guide to Success in Business and Management*, Piatkus, London.

Davidson, M. J. (1989) Women managers and stress: profiles of vulnerable individuals, *Clinical Psychology Forum*, Vol. 22, pp. 32−4.

Davidson, M. J. and Cooper, C. L. (1983) *Stress and the Woman Manager*, Martin Robertson, London.

Davidson, M. J. and Cooper, C. L. (1984) Occupational stress in female managers: a comparative study, *Journal of Management Studies*, Vol. 21, no. 2, pp. 185−205.

Davidson, M. J. and Cooper, C. L. (1987) Female managers in Britain − a comparative perspective, *Human Resource Management*, Vol. 26, no. 2, pp. 217−42.

Davidson, M. J. and Earnshaw, J. (1990) Policies, practices and attitudes towards sexual harrassment in UK organizations, *Personnel Review*, Vol. 19, no. 3, pp. 23–7.

Davies, C. and Rosser, J. (1986) *Processes of Discrimination: A Study of Women Working in the NHS*, Dept. of Health and Social Security, London.

Devine, M. and Clutterbuck, D. (1985) The rise of the entrepreneuse, *Management Today*, January, pp. 63–107.

Dixon, M. and Shaw, C. (1986) *Maximizing Investment in the NHS*, King Edward's Hospital Fund for London, London.

EC Directive (1989) HMSO, London.

Equal Opportunities Commission (1988) *Women and Men in Britain: A Research Profile*, HMSO, London.

Equal Opportunities Commission (1990a) *Pregnant Women at Work: A Response to the EC's Proposed Directive*, EOC, Manchester.

Equal Opportunities Commission (1990b) *The Key to Real Choice: An Action Plan for Child Care*, EOC, Manchester.

Falconer, H. (1991) Crèche bandwagon runs out of steam, *Personnel Today*, 19 March–1 April, p. 1.

Ferrario, M. (1990) Leadership Styles of British Men and Women Managers, unpublished MSc dissertation, University of Manchester, Faculty of Management Sciences, Manchester.

Goffee, R. and Scase, R. (1985) *Women in Charge*, Allen & Unwin, London.

The Guardian (1991) Six of the best in business, 30 April, p. 17.

Halpern, M. (1989) Business creation by women, and financing. Paper given at the Women and Enterprise/University of Bradford Women Entrepreneurs Conference, University of Bradford, April.

Handy, C. (1989) *The Age of Unreason*, Penguin Business Books, London.

Hansard Society (1990) *Women At the Top*, The Hansard Society for Parliamentary Government, London.

Harrison, R. (1987) *Organization Culture and Quality of Service: A Strategy for Releasing Love in the Workplace*, Association for Management Education and Development, London.

Hirsh, W. and Jackson, C. (1990) *Women into Management: Issues Influencing the Entry of Women into Managerial Jobs*, IMS Report No. 158, Institute of Manpower Studies, University of Sussex.

Hisrich, R. D. (1986) The woman entrepreneur: Characteristics, skills, problems and prescriptions for success, in D. L. Sexton and R. W. Smilor (eds.) *The Art and Science of Entrepreneurship*, Ballinger, Cambridge, Mass.

Hutt, R. (1985) *Chief Officer Profiles: Regional and District Nursing Officers*, IMS Report No. 111, Institute of Manpower Studies, University of Sussex.

Iles, P. A. and Robertson, I. T. (1988) Getting in, getting on, and looking good: physical attractiveness, gender and selection decisions, *Guidance and Assessment Review*, Vol. 4, no. 3, pp. 6–8.

Jackson, D. F. (1991) Problems facing women returners, in J. Firth-Cozens and M. A. West (eds.) *Women at Work*, Open University Press, Buckingham.

Johnson, S. and Storey, D. (1989) Male and female entrepreneurs and their business: a comparative study. Paper given at the Woman in Enterprise, University of Bradford Women Entrepreneurs Conference, April.

Knight, J. (1985) Self-employed satisfaction, *Sunday Times*.

Labour Force Survey (1977) no. 1, HMSO, London.

Labour Force Survey (1979) no. 2, HMSO, London.

Labour Force Survey (1985) no. 5, HMSO, London.

Labour Force Survey (1989) Preliminary results (1990) *Employment Gazette*, April, pp. 199–212.

Lewis, J. and Davies, C. (1991) Protective legislation in Britain 1870–1990: equality, difference and their implications for women, *Policy and Politics*, Vol. 19, no. 1, pp. 13–23.

Lowe, K. (1991) Slump devastates nursery hopes, *Personnel Today*, April, p. 4.

Maier, F. (1991) Part-time work, social security protections and labour law; an international comparison, *Policy and Politics*, Vol. 19, no. 1, pp. 1–11.

Marketing Business (1990) An end to lip service, February, pp. 16–17.

Marshall, J. (1984) *Women Managers: Travellers in a Male World*, Wiley, Chichester.

Mintzberg, H. (1975) *The Nature of Managerial Work*, Harper & Row, New York.

Moore, L. M. and Rickel, A. U. (1980) Characteristics of women in traditional and non-traditional managerial roles, *Personnel Psychology*, Vol. 33, pp. 317–33.

Myers Briggs, I. (1976) *Introduction to Type*, Centre for Applications of Psychological Type, Florida.

National Economic Development Office/Royal Institute of Public Administration (1990) *Women Managers the Untapped Resource*, Kogan Page, London.

Nicholson, N. and West, M. A. (1988) *Managerial Job Change: Men and Women in Transition*, Cambridge University Press.

Office for the Minister for the Civil Service (1988) *Equal Opportunities for Women in the Civil Service. Progress Report 1984–87*, Cabinet Office, Office for the Minister for the Civil Service, London.

Papadakis, E. and Taylor-Gooby, P. (1987) *The Private Provision of Public Welfare: State, Market and Community*, Wheatsheaf Books, Sussex.

Phillips, A. (1990) At the end of the day, *The Guardian*, 2 October, p. 38.

Rajan, A. and van Eupen, P. (1990) *Good Practices in the Employment of Women Returners*, Report No. 183, Institute of Manpower Studies. University of Sussex.

Robson-Scott, M. (1990) Labour pains, *The Guardian*, 23 October, p. 19.

Rycroft, T. (1989) *Survey of Women Managers – Interim Report*, British Institute of Management, London.

Scase, R. and Goffee, R. (1980) *The Real World of the Small Business Owner*, Croom Helm, London.

Scase, R. and Goffee, R. (1982) *The Entrepreneurial Middle Class*, Croom Helm, London.

Schein, V. E. (1973) The relationship between sex-role stereotypes and requisite management characteristics, *Journal of Applied Psychology*, Vol. 57, no. 2, pp. 95–100.

Schein, V. E. (1975) Relationships between sex-role stereotypes and requisite management characteristics among female managers. *Journal of Applied Psychology*, Vol. 60, no. 3, pp. 340–4.

Schein, V. E. (1989) Sex-role stereotypes and requisite management characteristics past, present and future. Paper given at the Current

Research in Women in Management Conference, 24–26 September, 1990, Queen's University, Ontario, Canada.

Schein, V. E. and Mueller, R. (1990) Sex-role stereotyping and requisite management characteristics: a cross-cultural look. Paper presented at the 22nd International Congress of Applied Psychology, 22–27 July, Kyoto, Japan.

Simpson, S. M. (1991) Women entrepreneurs, in J. Firth-Cozens and M.A. West (eds.) *Women at Work*, Open University Press, Buckingham.

Smith, J. M., Wood, J. R., Langrish, S. V., Davidson, M. L., Mogridge, C. and Smith, M. K. (1984) A Development Programme for Women in Management. Gower, Aldershot.

Stewart, F. (ed.) (1989) *Family Futures*, Report of the Henley Management Centre for Forecasting, Henley.

Vinnicombe, S. (1987) What exactly are the differences in male and female working styles? *Women in Management Review*, Vol. 3, no. 1, pp. 13–21.

Ward, S. (1984) Pensions for women, in *Social Security: The Real Agenda: The Fabian Society's Response to the Government's Review of Social Security*, Fabian Society, London.

Watkins, J. and Watkins, D. (1986) The female entrepreneur: her background and determinants of business choice – some British data, in J. Curran, J. Stanworth and D. Watkins (eds.) *The Survival of the Small Firm, Vol. 1: The Economics of Survival and Entrepreneurship*, Gower, Aldershot.

Young, K. and Spencer, E. (1990) *Women Managers in Local Government: Removing the Barriers*, INLOGOV, Birmingham.

3.

IRELAND

Yvonne Murphy

INTRODUCTION

Between 1981 and 1986 the population of Ireland increased from 3.44 million to 3.54 million. Although the 1971/1981 period had an exceptionally high rate of increase of 1.5% a year, this average went down to 0.6% a year in the 1981/1986 period. The proportion of women in the total population is 50% and the proportion of persons of working age (15 to 64) who are women is 49.5%. As can be seen in Table 1 women comprise 30.5% of the labour force and 32.1% of those in employment. Blackwell (1984) points out that the proportion of the labour force which consists of women has increased from 29.1% in 1981 to 29.4% in 1984 and to 30.9% in 1987. He also notes that the proportion of the female labour force which consists of married women has increased from 30.2% in 1981 to 41.3% in 1988.

Ireland, like most other European countries, has been experiencing a decline in its birthrate although this decline started about 10 years later than in the rest of Europe. While there is increased participation of women in the labour force, the level of participation by women in management and in self-employment and business is relatively small (see Table 2). O'Connor (1987), in her study *Women in Enterprise 1987*, points out that a number of factors have influenced women's involvement in business over the years. These include education, legislation and attitudes of women themselves. An analysis of where self-employed people work can be seen in Table 3. It will be noted that the majority are in the commerce, insurance, finance and business services.

WOMEN IN MANAGEMENT

Table 4 shows where women actually work and again it can be seen

Table 1 Overview of the labour force*, 1987, 1988 (000)

	1987	1988
Population aged 15−64		
Total	2,142.3	2,149.1
Women	1,061.4	1,064.4
% of women to total	49.5	49.5
Labour force (LF)		
Total	1,319.2	1,309.8
Women	407.7	399.5
% of women to total	30.9	30.5
Married women in LF[†]		
Total	161.6	164.8
% of female LF	39.6	41.3
Employment		
Total	1,087.6	1,091.2
Women	352.5	350.5
% of women to total	32.4	32.1
Unemployed		
Total	231.6	218.5
Women	55.2	49.0
% of women to total	23.8	22.4

* The labour force consists of those who are employed together with the unemployed. The unemployed include those who are looking for a first regular job.
† Includes separated and divorced.

Source: Labour Force Survey, 1988.

Table 2 Persons at work classified by employment status and by sex, 1988

	Women (000)	Men (000)
Employers	7.3	50.4
Self-employed	18.2	57.7
Assisting relatives	8.3	15.2
Employees	316.7	506.9
Total	350.5	1,091.2

Source: Labour Force Survey, 1988.

that a large proportion of working women are clerical workers, shop assistants and service workers.

Traditionally in Ireland, public service and the teaching profession have provided employment opportunities for women. Until the early 1970s women had to resign their jobs in the public service on marriage, and Table 5, which analyses the percentage distribution of women in the public sector, illustrates that it is only in recent years that there has been an increase in women filling some of the management jobs.

Table 3 The non-agricultural self-employed by industrial broad sector and by sex, 1987

	Females (000)	Males (000)
Industry		
Building and construction	0.1	10.9
Other production industries	0.9	8.1
Commerce, insurance,		
finance and business services	5.7	21.0
Transport, communication		
and storage	0.2	5.4
Professional services	2.1	5.9
Public administration and		
defence	—	0.1
Others	2.9	4.0
Total	11.8	55.4

Source: Labour Force Survey, 1987.

Table 4 Persons at work by occupational group and sex, 1987

Occupation	Females (000)	Males (000)	Ratio of women to all persons (%)
Farmers	5.1	114.9	4.3
Other agricultural workers, forestry			
workers and fishery workers	6.6	39.9	14.2
Electrical and electronic workers	7.2	30.8	18.9
Engineering and related trades workers	3.6	45.2	7.4
Woodworkers	0.3	17.7	1.7
Leather, leather substitute,			
textile and clothing workers	15.0	8.5	63.8
Food, beverage and tobacco workers	4.2	14.8	22.0
Paper and printing workers	1.6	6.2	20.5
Workers in other products			
(incl. mining, quarrying and turf)	4.2	15.4	21.5
Building and construction workers	0.3	31.7	0.9
Forepeople and supervisors			
of manual workers	1.3	9.6	11.8
Labourers and unskilled workers	0.4	33.6	1.2
Transport and communication workers	4.3	47.6	8.3
Warehouse staff, storekeepers,			
packers and bottlers	4.8	13.7	25.9
Clerical workers	96.2	33.6	74.1
Proprietors and managers	10.5	39.2	21.1
Shop assistants and bar staff	31.8	27.1	54.0
Other commercial workers	2.6	24.2	9.7
Professional and technical workers	89.7	88.6	50.3
Service workers	54.0	45.6	54.2
Administrative, executive and			
managerial workers	7.1	33.6	17.4
Others (incl. not stated)	1.4	13.8	9.2
	352.5	735.1	32.4

Source: Labour Force Survey, 1987.

Table 5 Gender composition of general service grades 1987–90

	Year							
	1987		1988		1989		1990	
Grade	F (%)	M (%)	F (%)	M (%)	F (%)	M (%)	F (%)	M (%)
Secretary	Nil	100	Nil	100	Nil	100	Nil	100
Deputy secretary	Nil	100	Nil	100	Nil	100	Nil	100
Assistant secretary	1	99	1	99	3	97	3	97
Principal	5	95	7	93	8	92	9	91
Assistant principal	23	77	20	80	21	79	22	78
Administrative officer	26	74	21	79	19	81	20	80
Higher executive officer	34	66	30	70	28	72	29	71
Executive officer	44	56	42	58	43	57	46	54
Staff officer	67	33	64	36	60	40	61	39
Clerical officer	68	32	68	32	68	32	71	29
Clerical assistant	83	17	83	17	84	16	65	15
Paperkeeper	4	96	5	95	5	95	5	95
Messenger	2	98	2	98	2	98	2	98
Service attendant	2	98	1	99	1	99	1	99
Cleaner	96	4	96	4	96	4	93	7

F = female; M = male.

Source: Department of Finance, 1991.

In the teaching profession, where women did not have to resign on marriage, they comprise fewer than 50% of school principals in the primary sector despite the fact that they occupy over 75% of the teaching posts in that sector (see Table 6).

DECISION-MAKERS

The Council for the Status of Women (CSW, 1990), which is an umbrella body of more than 90 women's organizations, has surveyed a number of state boards and ascertained that women comprise just 15% of the members of state boards, an increase of only 3% since 1985. In fact, the CSW survey reveals that the participation rate by women on all state boards had increased only 5% between 1981 when there were 10% and 1990 when there were 15%.

Since that survey was completed, an interim report from the Second Commission on the Status of Women recommended that at least 40% of all state and semi-state boards should comprise women. Some government ministers have responded to this with one minister appointing women to just over 50% of the vice-chairs of the Employment Appeals Tribunal in early 1992. Another government minister appointed women to seven semi-state boards, many of these boards being in the major industrial areas.

Private companies have also been influenced by the call from the Council for the Status of Women to increase the numbers of women on boards. Many banking, insurance and financial institutions have appointed women to their boards. The pattern, therefore, is changing rapidly and it is likely that any comprehensive survey done within the next year or two will reveal a different picture than that presented in the survey by the Council for the Status of Women.

GOVERNMENT LEGISLATION

As already noted, the activity rate among women in Ireland is lower than in most other European Community (EC) countries. Employment rates of mothers are closely related to the number of children they

Table 6 Membership of Irish National Teacher Organizations* 1991/92

	Women	Men	Total
General	14,916	4,568	19,584
Principals	1,840	1,969	3,809

* The trade union body for primary teachers.

Source: INTO.

have. For women aged 20 to 24 years, the percentage drop in employment rate is 60% for those with one child under 15 and 62% and 26% for those with two and three children respectively. In the age group 25 to 34 years, which includes twice as many women, the decline is 50%, 52% and 44% for women with one, two and three or more children respectively. It is in this context that the provisions relating to maternity leave and childcare must be considered.

MATERNITY LEAVE

Maternity leave lasts for 14 weeks with 4 weeks to be taken before the birth and a further 10 weeks to be taken before or after so that postnatal leave can be between 4 and 10 weeks; a further 4 weeks postnatal leave can be taken on request. These last 4 weeks are unpaid, but during the remainder of the period women receive benefit equivalent to 70% of earnings subject to a minimum of 70% of the average industrial earnings for women which are currently £76 per week. There is also a maximum amount which will be paid and this is £154 per week. The payment is tax free so that, in some cases, women will receive the equivalent of their full net earnings. Women in the public sector and in some of the large private companies receive full pay as a result of collective agreements. There is no official paternity leave. Mothers, whether or not they are working, receive a small monthly child allowance on a scale amounting to just over £15 for one child or £47 for three children.

MEMBERSHIP OF THE EUROPEAN COMMUNITY 1973

In 1973 Ireland's entry into the EC saw the introduction of the Anti-Discrimination (Pay) Act of 1974 to establish the right to equal pay of men and women employed on like work by the same or by an associated employer. The Act became law on 31 December 1975 and provides for remedies and penal sanctions if there is a breach. The Equal Treatment Directive was adopted into Irish Law through the Employment Equality Act which was passed in 1977. This Act prevents discrimination on the grounds of sex or marital status in recruitment for employment, in training, in conditions of employment or in the provision of opportunities for promotion. The Act also provided for the setting up of the Employment Equality Agency with aims of working towards the elimination of discrimination in relation to employment and promoting equality of opportunity between men and women in relation to employment. While in general most employees are covered under this legislation, the members of the defence forces, the police, those employed in the prison sector, and those employed in private residences or by a close relative are excluded from the Employment Equality Act.

CHILDCARE SERVICES IN IRELAND

McKenna (1988), in her *Childcare and Equal Opportunities — Policies and Services for Children in Ireland*, has produced a table showing the type of provision for children under the age of 6, the numbers attending this service in each year and the percentage of all under-6s cared for by that service (see Table 7).

It can be seen that the greatest number of under-6s being provided for in a service outside their own home is 26% in formal education. Whereas the statutory age for beginning school is 6 years, in fact 54.6% of 4-year-olds and 99.7% of 5-year-olds are already attending primary school in infant classes at national school on a voluntary basis.

Playgroups

As can be seen from the table, the next largest group of children in care outside their own home area is the playgroup sector with 5%. There is also an Irish language playgroup which caters for approximately 2,500 children. McKenna also includes figures relating to the provision of services, mostly state funded, for disadvantaged and handicapped children.

Workplace nurseries

A final interesting figure to emerge from McKenna's study was that relating to workplace nurseries, but, as can be seen, few children are catered for in such nurseries. At the time McKenna (1988) wrote her report, only four public sector or semi-public sector nurseries existed in the country and she could find no data on any nurseries in private firms in Ireland. Since the completion of that study, the Bank of Ireland Group has established a childcare centre for its staff, and a study on childcare in the EC 1985 to 1990 (Commission of the European Communities, 1990) thought that the number of public sector employers providing day nursery facilities was slightly higher at around five or six but they claimed that, as private services do not as yet have to be approved and registered, there were no statistics for private nurseries and mixed-age centres, family daycare and own home care. Private family daycare, however, they concluded, was widespread. Overall, one can say that there has been increased public interest in childcare and there has been a political response in that the Minister for Labour has set up a working group to look into private and public sector initiatives that could be adopted to provide childcare services for employed parents. The Second Commission on the Status of Women will also be looking at this area.

Table 7 Provision for the under 6s

	0–1	1–2	2–3	3–4	4–5	5–6	Total	(%)
No. in cohort	64,800	64,800	64,800	64,800	64,800	67,940	392,018	26
Early primary education					35,430	67,700	103,130	5
Playgroups				10,000	10,000		20,000	2
Social services centres							6,681	0.6
Naíonrí*				1,250	1,250		2,500	0.5
EHB van Leer**	1,000	1,000					2,000	
Travellers'					175	175	350	
Day fostering	60	60		50	51		120	
'Rutland Street'							101	
Mentally handicapped		175	175	175	175	400	1,100	0.3
Physically handicapped			35	57	101	42	235	
Workplace nursery	15	17	14	14	7	4	70	
Third-level nursery	32	26	30	40	38	2	168	
Private (45+30)	450	450	450	450	450	10	2,260	0.5
Total	1,557	1,712	669	12,154	47,576	68,116	138,430	
% of cohort	2	3	1	19	73	100		

* Irish-speaking play groups
** Easter Health Board Foundation

PENSIONS AND RETIREMENT PLANS

Any person who has been paying earnings-related social insurance contributions will qualify for a retirement pension at the age of 65. 'Retired' means not having a full-time job. To qualify for the retirement pension a person would need to have paid social insurance before the age of 55, have paid at least 156 contributions and have a yearly average of 24 contributions paid or credited from 1953 or the year in which contributions insurance was first paid, whichever is later, until the April before reaching 65. The current retirement pension is approximately £64 per week. Women in management are likely to be contributing to the earnings-related social insurance scheme but self-employed women are generally not entitled to a retirement pension unless they have made private arrangements. They are required to contribute to the social insurance scheme but many of them will not be eligible for an old-age pension until 1998 as the scheme was only introduced in 1988. There is no provision for the spouses of self-employed people who are involved in the business, even though an EC Directive exists in relation to the treatment of the self-employed.

Pensions Act

A new Pensions Act was passed in mid-1990 and came into effect in January 1991. The aim of the Act was to regulate occupational pension schemes and provide for equal treatment for men and women in occupational pension schemes. The Pensions Board was established to supervise these schemes. It is estimated that in the private sector about two-thirds of employees are also members of occupational pension schemes in addition to being covered by the social welfare retirement pension scheme. In the public sector most employees would not be eligible for a retirement pension but they would have an occupational pension scheme and, while some are non-contributory, all would be considered to provide adequate coverage. Before the advent of the new legislation, one problem with employees' pension schemes was the fact that employees lost their pension rights if they changed jobs. The new Pensions Act provides that anyone leaving their job before reaching the normal retirement age is entitled to retain the rights acquired after the Pension Act came into effect.

Self-employed people

In addition to their contributions to the social welfare retirement fund, self-employed people are required to make their own arrangements in relation to pension schemes.

PUBLIC SERVICE POLICIES AND INITIATIVES TOWARDS WOMEN

Women in Business Enterprise Campaign

One of the most interesting initiatives taken to encourage women to set up their own enterprises was the Women in Business Enterprise Campaign which was initiated by the Office of the Minister of State for Women's Affairs in 1985. The project was discontinued following a change of government but while it existed it provided a freephone information service backed up by a countrywide free business consultancy provided by women. There was also a series of seminars held to inform and encourage women to set up their own enterprises. When the government changed, the Office of the Minister of State for Women's Affairs was abolished but in recent months it has been re-established.

Foras Aiseann Saothair (FAS)

The training and employment authority, FAS, has been conscious of the need to improve the activity rate of women on its courses. Although there has been an excellent record of women attending the FAS enterprise courses, with in some cases women comprising 58% of the participants, FAS is aware of the fact that it has been difficult to entice women on to its apprenticeship courses, with the result that often many potential avenues of promotion are not available to them. In the 1990s FAS has initiated a positive action programme (FAS, 1990) which seeks to begin to redress the imbalances not only, as its Director General says, 'for reasons of equity, but also to ensure that the human resource potential of the Irish labour market is fully tapped'. The authority is aware that women still continue to cluster in a narrow range of traditional occupations and that the types of jobs they are in offer limited promotional prospects. It recognizes that there are few women in management and fewer still in senior managerial posts. Among the initiatives and targets they have set themselves is a significant increase in the rate of female participation in apprenticeship, and among the ideas employed to try and achieve this are the promotion of apprenticeships at regional level, a bursary scheme, a national apprenticeship target and an induction programme into apprenticeship.

Return to work courses

One range of courses with which FAS has achieved positive results has been the return to work courses. These are specifically aimed at women and are often offered on a part-time basis as part of its positive action programme. The authority intends to increase the throughput on the courses.

Development agencies

The development agencies such as the Shannon Development Company
and The Industrial Development Authority have also provided encouragement to women by designing and implementing special women in
industry promotions and encouraging women to apply for a range of
services which they offer for all potential entrepreneurs including their
very attractive feasibility study grants.

While these developments are useful, it is the view of O'Connor
(1987) that they provide only a starting point and that 'a co-ordinated
programme to encourage women entrepreneurs needs to be developed
and channelled through the main agencies .

Department of Education grants

The Department of Education provides up to 20 grants for women
aged 25 years and over who are unwaged or on a low income, to
enable them to pursue an approved undergraduate degree, diploma or
certificate. The grants amount of £1,000 per year and are given to those
who have completed at least 1 year of their course.

Other agencies

Ireland has always sought to encourage enterprise of all kinds because
of its high level of unemployment and to this end there are a range of
agencies committed to assisting the growth and development of all
kinds of enterprises. While the services are not specifically related to
women in business they are, nevertheless, available to all those engaging
in enterprise.

PRIVATE SECTOR INITIATIVES

The private sector has been to the fore in encouraging women to climb
the corporate ladder. Ten years ago there was only one female bank
manager in Ireland, but now one-third of the managerial positions in
the two main banks are held by women. One of the main banking
groups, The Bank of Ireland, found that women were getting less
encouragement and often there was a perception that they were not
interested in promotion. To address some of these problems it undertook
a personal development programme for women from senior clerical
level upwards. In the 4 to 5 years that the programme has been going
over 700 women have attended and in that time the female representation in management grades increased from 18% to 30%. The aim of
the course was to raise women's confidence levels and encourage them
to think in terms of banking as a career. The *Sunday Tribune* newspaper
produced in 1991 a table illustrating the progress made by women

during the last number of years in some of the banking and insurance areas (Table 8).

Veuve Clicquot Award

An award that has played an important role in recognizing women entrepreneurs is the Veuve Clicquot Businesswoman of the Year Award sponsored by that company and Gilbeys. The award itself attracts a great deal of publicity and past recipients of it have found themselves sought after for appointments to boards and other bodies.

Networking

Network is a group which encourages women to help each other to advance in their respective jobs and brings together self-employed and employed women. It has provided a support group for many women and, particularly for those wishing to go into business, it has been a source of information and advice.

Women's Talent Bank

The Council for the Status of Women has produced a booklet which contains a list of women who are available for appointment to the boards of companies and state and semi-state boards, together with a description of their qualifications and interests. Women are invited to send in their names and qualifications if they wish to be considered for inclusion in the Talent Bank.

Table 8 Women in banking and insurance

Organization	Total employees	Women employees	Women managers
Bank of Ireland	7,500	4,350	30% of managers are women (both branch and group managers); 1 woman executive director; 2 women on the board of directors
Allied Irish Bank	8,800	5,149	33% of managers are women (both branch and group managers); 1 woman executive director; 1 woman on the board of directors
Trustee Savings Bank	490	294	1 female manager; no female branch managers
ICS Building Society	139	78	6 female managers; no female branch managers
Irish Permanent	792	455	77 female managers (both branch and group)

Source: Sunday Tribune (1991)

Federation of Irish Employers

The Federation of Irish Employers has produced guidelines on equal opportunities and has encouraged companies affiliated to its organization to implement an equal opportunities policy. It provides guidelines on the drawing up of such a policy and helps with its implementation.

INITIATIVES IN THE SEMI-STATE SECTOR

Many of the semi-state bodies have positive action programmes, foremost among them the Electricity Supply Board, the National Radio and Television station and the Airport authorities. Interestingly, when the national radio and television station arranged training courses to improve the position of women they found that women were reluctant to join them because the courses were sneered at by men and undervalued precisely because they were for women only. This was in direct contrast to the Bank of Ireland's experience.

RESEARCH ON WOMEN IN BUSINESS AND MANAGEMENT

O'Connor's study (1987) *Women in Enterprise 1987* was the first detailed examination of women in enterprise in the manufacturing area and many of the issues raised in the research apply to all entrepreneurs. Her study found that the typical woman entrepreneur:

- was aged between 31 and 40 years;
- was middle class;
- had a spouse employed in a professional or technical occupation;
- had an average of two children, the eldest usually being 11 years or younger;
- regarded home and family commitments as of crucial importance;
- had a history of family involvement in business;
- had third-level education in the arts, social sciences or crafts and design area, or undertook jobs in secretarial areas;
- was involved in business in the traditional female areas of crafts, textiles and food;
- was involved in one-product companies, typically its sole promoter;
- had a low level of business training, business skills or work experience immediately relevant to manufacturing industry;
- was similar to the male entrepreneur in personality profile (differences emerged in the areas of achievement, self-fulfilment and control of their lives).

Interestingly, one of the many problems which O'Connor found in her study was that many women entrepreneurs were unaware of the existence and functions of certain agencies, had little or no knowledge of the detailed incentives and advice available, and were uncertain as to how to use the resources available to them.

Growing Concerns is the title of a pilot study conducted by O'Connor and Ruddle (1988) of growth-oriented women entrepreneurs. It was also undertaken as a contribution to the debate about women in enterprise. Forty female-led businesses from different manufacturing sectors were identified on the basis of the length of time in operation and their employment level, and from this group 10 businesses were inspected using a simple random sample. The object of the study was to complement the *Women in Enterprise 1987* study and also to help create awareness of possibilities for women in business.

The Joint Oireachtas Committee on Women's Rights has commissioned a number of major studies on the changing attitudes to the role of women in Ireland and issues relating to equal employment and opportunity and has recently completed in 1991 a study entitled *Motherhood – Women and Equal Opportunities* which looks at women in the civil service.

One of the disappointing conclusions to emerge from some of these studies was that there was no difference in the level of perceived discrimination between 1975 (when the anti-discrimination legislation became operative) and 1986 in the areas of training or in the kind of work or quality of work experience which women had. From a promotional point of view, single women reported slightly less discrimination over this period but married women reported a good deal more discrimination.

McCarthy, in her study entitled *Transitions to Equal Opportunity at Work in Ireland – Problems and Possibilities* (1986), looked at the question of promotion criteria applied to women in particular in the context of promotion policies in general and the changes in promotion policies over the period 1972–83. She has produced an interesting table on the reasons given as to why women's promotional prospects are less favourable than those of their male counterparts (Table 9). She recommends in her conclusions the need to focus specifically on male managers to enable them to understand their own role in reinforcing barriers to equal opportunity and also the need actively to encourage them to develop and promote more of their women subordinates.

CONCLUSIONS

The barriers to women succeeding in business and management are well defined and much has been studied and written about these barriers over the past 10 years. There is an urgent need to tackle the problems which have been identified and progress has been slow in that area. Priority must be given to establishing training courses which are likely to lead women into management or into establishing their own businesses. This training should include assertiveness training

Table 9 Reasons given as to why women's promotional prospects are less favourable than those of their male counterparts

Reason	Percentage agreeing
1. Women are less committed than men to their jobs	17.7
2. Women are less professionally competent than men	17.7
3. Women are less geographically mobile than men	39.2
4. Women are not assertive enough in their jobs	46.4
5. Women display less leadership ability than men do	29.6
6. Women have a lower level of further training than men have	31.0
7. Women's work experience is less varied and more limited than men's	53.5
8. Women are less ambitious in their jobs than men are	60.7
9. Women stay for shorter periods in an organization than men do	36.8
10. Other	4.8
11. No data	9.75

Source: McCarthy (1986)

designed at giving women confidence to advance to the top. Men also need to be educated about the potential that women offer in the workplace and in business and this education needs to start in early schooling. Finally, the issue of childcare will have to be tackled both by industry and by the state who must consider granting income tax relief in respect of childcare expenses both to working parents and to employers providing workplace nurseries.

REFERENCES

Blackwell, J. (1989) *Women in the Labour Force*, Employment Equality Agency, Dublin.

Commission of the European Communities (1990) *Childcare in the European Communities 1985 to 1990*, Commission of the European Communities, Brussels.

Council for the Status of Women (1990) *Who Makes the Decisions*, Council for the Status of Women, Dublin.

FAS — Training and Development Authority (1990) *Positive Action Programme in Favour of Women*, FAS, Dublin.

Joint Oireachtas Committee on Women's Rights (1991) *Motherhood — Women and Equal Opportunities*, Joint Oireachtas Committee, Dublin.

McCarthy, E. (1986) *Transitions to Equal Opportunity at Work in Ireland — Problems and Possibilities*, Dublin.

McKenna, A. (1988) *Childcare and Equal Opportunities — Policies and Services for Children in Ireland*, Employment Equality Agency, Dublin.

O'Connor, J. (1987) *Women in Enterprise 1987*, Industrial Development Authority, Dublin.

O'Connor, J. and Ruddle, H. (1988) *Growing Concerns*, Industrial Development Authority, Dublin.

4.

DENMARK

Janne Albertsen and Bolette Christensen

INTRODUCTION

Figures for the total Danish workforce in 1990 show that 54% are men and 46% are women (Statistic Information, 1991), and it is predicted that by the year 2000 the division will be 50% and 50%. However, men and women are by no means equally distributed throughout the workforce, as is shown in Figure 1. It is evident that there are still certain jobs filled predominantly by men and others filled predominantly by women.

Women are much more likely than men to be working part time: in 1989 36% of women and 9% of men worked part time. Of the other European countries, only Norway has a higher percentage of part-time women workers (see Figure 2). In Denmark a large number of women working part time do so within the private sector.

A closer look at the 48% of women who are in the Danish workforce reveals few in middle or senior management positions. Approximately 10% of women in both the public and private sectors are in middle management positions (Tables 1 and 2).

In the private sector there has been a 100% increase between 1982 and 1989 in women's percentage share of middle management jobs but the proportion is still undeniably small. Table 3 shows that in local government women occupy 65.2% and 12.8% of middle management positions in Group 1 and Group 2 respectively. The apparent contradiction in these figures is explained by the fact that the traditionally female-dominated occupations are concentrated in Group 1.

The figures for female representation in senior management for 1987 and 1989 range from 2.3% to 4.5% for local government and the private sector respectively (see Tables 4, 5 and 6). There has been an increase of between 30% and 300% in women's percentage share of senior management jobs but in 1987 and 1989 more than 95% of

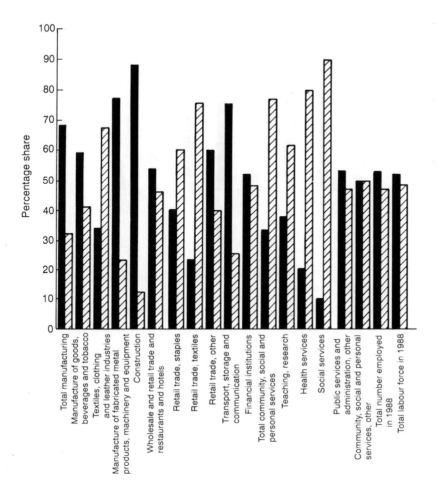

Source: The Danish Employers' Confederation (1991), *Equal Opportunities –
Introduction to a debate*

Figure 1 Percentages of men (■) and women (▨) employed in certain
occupations, 1988.

Denmark's top managers were still men. A survey of 3,700 of Denmark's
largest companies shows that out of the 755 directorship appointments
made in 1991 only 31 (approximately 4%) of the posts were filled by
women (Børsens Nyhedsmagasin, 1991).

EQUAL OPPORTUNITIES AND DANISH LEGISLATION

There have been five Danish acts of parliament dealing with equal

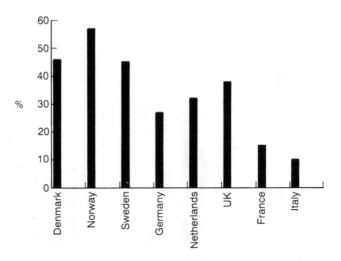

Source: The Danish Employers' Confederation (1991), *Equal Opportunities —
Introduction to a debate*

Figure 2 Percentage of women working part time in certain countries in
Europe.

Table 1 Middle managers in the public sector by total numbers and women's
share of total, 1983–7*

Year	Total	Total women	Women's share of total (%)
1983	1,635	153	9.4
1984	1,617	162	10.0
1985	1,627	171	10.5
1986	1,692	182	10.8
1987	2,136	216	10.1

* This group includes the following positions: head
of department, ambassador, principal (and vice-
principal), head of office, chief engineer, head of
school, forest supervisor, inspector of customs
department (and deputy inspector of customs).

Source: Statistic Information (1985:16, 1986:20,
1988:18, 1989:3, 1989:20) *Labour Market*.

opportunities. Two of these stipulate that both a man and a woman
must be nominated when members of public councils, boards and
committees are appointed. The others include the Equal Opportunities
Act, the Equal Treatment Act and the Equal Pay Act.

Table 2 Middle managers* in the private sector, by men's and women's shares, 1982–9

Year	Men		Women		Men + women (number)
	Number	%	Number	%	
1982	13,667	95.1	707	4.9	14,374
1983	15,580	94.2	957	5.8	16,537
1984	16,539	93.1	1,126	6.9	17,665
1985	17,518	92.3	1,457	7.7	18,975
1986	19,033	91.9	1,673	8.1	20,706
1987	19,486	90.9	1,942	9.1	21,428
1988	20,733	90.6	2,059	9.4	22,892
1989	23,588	89.4	2,797	10.6	26,385

* The group of middle managers is defined as position categories incorporating the words 'Head of...'.

Source: Danmark Statistics (1983–90) *Salary and Income Statistics*.

Table 3 Middle managers within local government by total numbers and women's share of total, 1983–7*

Year	Total	Total women	Women's share of total (%)
Group 1			
1983	4,818	3,138	65.1
1984	4,938	1,245	65.7
1985	4,117	2,670	64.9
1986	4,182	2,714	64.9
1987	4,117	2,685	65.2
Group 2			
1983	3,220	391	12.1
1984	3,237	410	12.7
1985	3,454	439	12.7
1986	3,544	469	13.2
1987	4,267	546	12.8

* Since by far the greatest number of female middle managers are employed in the positions of principal, vice-principal and head of an institution (Group 1), these women are separated from the rest.
Group 2 consists of administration manager, fire brigade officer, harbour master, head of clinic, department manager (and assistant department manager), chief physician, chief dentist, chief of city and municipal gardening, chief of city and municipal engineering, principal of junior school.

Source: Statistic Information (1985:16, 1986:20, 1988:18, 1989:3, 1989:20) *Labour Market*.

Table 4 Senior managers in the public sector by total numbers and women's share of total, 1983—7*

Year	Total	Total women	Women's share of total (%)
1983	338	9	2.7
1984	334	9	2.7
1985	324	9	2.8
1986	313	11	3.5
1987	304	10	3.3

* This group includes the following positions: permanent secretary of state, director.

Source: Statistic Information (1985:16, 1986:20, 1988:18, 1989:3, 1989:20) *Labour Market*.

Table 5 Senior managers in the private sector, by men's and women's shares, 1982—9*

	Men		Women		Men + women
Year	Number	%	Number	%	(number)
1982	4,354	97.4	114	2.6	4,468
1983	4,835	97.3	132	2.7	4,967
1984	5,111	96.8	168	3.2	5,279
1985	5,127	97.2	148	2.8	5,275
1986	5,353	96.5	197	3.5	5,550
1987	5,486	96.3	211	3.7	5,697
1988	5,962	96.0	247	4.0	6,209
1989	6,127	95.5	291	4.5	6,418

* The group of senior managers is defined as position categories incorporating the word 'director'.

Source: Danmark Statistics (1983—90) *Salary and Income Statistics*.

The Equal Opportunities Act

This Act deals with the competence and composition of the Equal Opportunities Council. The Council consists of 8 or 9 members, including representatives from the Danish Employers' Confederation and the Danish Confederation of Trades Unions, and was established administratively by the Prime Minister in 1975.

The major roles of the Equal Opportunities Council are to promote the equal status of men and women in society, in the labour market, in education and in family life (Equal Opportunities Council, 1990) and to arbitrate in disputes regarding equal pay and disputes eligible under the Equal Treatment Act.

Table 6 Senior managers within local government, by total numbers and women's share of total, 1983−7*

Year	Total	Total women	Women's share of total (%)
1983	265	2	0.8
1984	263	4	1.5
1985	259	6	2.3
1986	301	7	2.3
1987	605	15	2.5[†]

* The group of senior managers consists of hospital administrator, chief principal of schools, municipal director, social director, and inland revenue director. From 1987 onwards, the position category 'other managers' was removed. The category 'municipal director, social director, and inland revenue directors' is included in the group of top managers.
[†] Notice that women's share of senior manager positions is still very small, even when a larger group of senior managers is considered.

Source: Statistic Information (1985:16, 1986:20, 1988:18, 1989:3, 1989:20) *Labour Market*.

The Equal Treatment Act

This is a very broad-ranging Act. In principle, it concerns any matter that has to do with equal opportunities. The Act includes various protective provisions, including maternity leave rules. Cases regarding sexual harassment are also treated according to the provisions of the Equal Treatment Act.

In the private sector, an employer him- or herself may, in principle, decide whom to employ. The Equal Treatment Act, however, contains a provision restricting the employer's free choice. The Act stipulates that employers are under an obligation to treat women and men equally in connection with recruitment, transfer and promotion.

According to the Equal Treatment Act, an employee cannot be dismissed on the grounds of pregnancy or because she utilizes her entitlement to leave of absence. In such a case the employer may be ordered to pay compensation corresponding to up to 78 weeks' pay or to reinstate the employee. These cases require reversed burden of proof and it is up to the employer to prove that the dismissal was not due to circumstances such as pregnancy.

The Equal Pay Act

This Act stipulates that there must be no disparate treatment with respect to salary on the grounds of sex. A few cases regarding this issue have been heard before the Danish courts, including the so-called Danfoss case. Certain guidelines regarding equal pay cases exist, but the rules cannot be described in brief because the number of judgements passed by the courts in these cases is limited.

Maternity leave

Parents are entitled to leave of up to 28 weeks as follows.

The mother

Pregnancy leave from 4 weeks before the expected delivery. Maternity leave for 14 weeks from confinement. The mother is entitled to parental leave in the last 10 weeks from the 15th to and including the 24th week of confinement. The parental leave may be shared by the mother and the father.

The father

Two weeks from the day of birth or the day on which the child comes home from hospital (these 2 weeks may be taken within the same period as the mother's 14-week maternity leave subject to agreement with the employer).

As a general rule the mother is entitled to maternity benefit amounting to DKK 2,506 per week. Female white-collar employees ('salaried employees') are entitled to receive half a salary during a period typically running from 4 weeks before the expected delivery to 3 months after it. If the half salary is lower than the maternity benefit, the salary will be supplemented up to the amount of the maternity benefit.

As a general rule the father is entitled to paternity benefit. Some employers, however, pay a full salary during the paternity leave.

Maternity benefit is paid by the government, while the salary is paid by the employer.

Childcare

Women in the Danish labour market have the highest participation rate of women in the workforce within the European Community (EC). In Denmark 44% of the 0−2-year-old children are minded in crèches and 62% of the 3−6-year-olds are minded in nursery schools. The capacity of Danish childcare institutions is very large compared with other EC member states.

PENSIONS

Statutory rules regarding pensions are the same for men and women, although pensionable age was different for men and women until a few years ago, typically 60 or 62 years for women and 65 years for men. The application of the actuarial principle, whereby the amounts of the premium and the pension are calculated in proportion to the expected lifetime of the insured, means that pension payments for men and women differ. Premiums for women would increase if they were to receive the same pensions as men because women generally live longer than men. A proposal for an EC Directive on these matters is being prepared.

Women who work part time tend to receive smaller pensions than men because pension contributions are charged as a percentage of the employee's pay.

THE GOVERNMENT'S ACTION PROGRAMME

The Danish parliament generally takes an active interest in equal opportunity matters. In 1987 the government adopted its so-called equal opportunity action programme, which called upon the public authorities to promote equal opportunities.

In 1991 the Equal Opportunities Council prepared a 3-year status report on equal opportunity efforts in various government departments, including local government. The report examined the number of women in managerial positions in 1987 and again in 1990. This gave an overview of equal opportunity developments towards the end of the 1980s. The equal opportunity situation has improved but the situation still leaves something to be desired.

THE PUBLIC SECTOR'S POLICIES TOWARDS WOMEN

This section describes how the public sector has been strengthening women's job opportunities by staff policy and by improving access for women to managerial positions.

Government action programmes for equal opportunities

In 1987 Danish ministries and boards under the Danish Parliament were directed to work according to the government's action programme for equal opportunities. Of the various areas covered by the programme, the public sector paid particular attention to staff policy, concentrating on the three areas of organization, improvement of office workers' qualifications, and increase in women's share of positions at management level. In many ministries and boards initiatives have been taken and constructive plans made in these three areas, but reports from the ministries show that there are still many unsolved problems, especially in the field of women and management.

In the first of the three selected areas, organization of work, the aim has been to improve the co-ordination of work and family life, through the introduction, for example, of flexible hours and career planning. It is hoped that it will become easier for both men and women to reduce their work time while they have small children without reducing their chances of promotion.

In the second area the aim is to improve the qualifications of office workers, 90% of whom are women. Increased staff training is becoming increasingly essential as many routine jobs are superseded by new technology, but only a few organizations have made specific plans.

In the third area, where the aim has been to improve women's share of managerial positions, there is at least a positive trend with a small increase in women's share from 9% in 1989 to 11% in 1990. Of the vacant positions in ministries and boards since 1987, 25% have been filled by women although only 21% of applicants have been women. To improve the situation further it will be necessary to concentrate on recruiting procedures and on enabling those women aspiring to management to obtain better qualifications.

During the last two years the public sector has actively worked on appointing more women to managerial positions, and the result has been that women's average share of the managerial positions within government institutions has increased from 8.7% in 1987 to 11.2% in 1990 (Equal Opportunities Council, 1990, p. 20).

Several ministries have introduced staff appraisals and increased activity on job development, which has helped strengthen the equal status of men and women.

In about half of all ministries and boards equality committees have been set up, and often it is in these committees that the work on equal status has achieved the best results (Equal Opportunities Council, 1990, pp. 29–32).

Women's representation on councils, boards, and committees

In 1985 the Committee Act was passed in Denmark, according to which authorities and organizations must propose both a man and a woman when members are appointed. This Act has led to an increase of women on public councils, boards and committees. In those councils which were appointed after 1985 the percentage of women is 37%. In 1990 the Act of Equal Representation on Boards within the State was passed. The minister decides which of the appointed persons are to be elected.

Women decision-makers in counties, local councils and Parliament

The government's action programmes include the Danish counties and local authorities. Denmark consists of 14 counties and, of these, five have equal status committees today. They work mainly with staff policy, but in general the work with equal opportunities problems in the counties' political life is almost nil. In the county councils the percentage of women is 29%. Denmark has 273 local authorities and, of these, 20 are working actively with equal opportunities, primarily on staff policy. The representation of women in local politics is 26% and Denmark has 20 female mayors (Equal Opportunities Council, 1990, pp. 34–7).

At the general election in 1990, 59 women were elected to Parliament. The percentage of women in Parliament is 33%. Four of the 19 ministries are women (Equal Opportunities Council, 1990, p. 38).

'Do I want to be a manager?': a project by three Danish companies

Three Danish companies (The Danish Broadcasting Corporation (DR), SAS Airlines (SAS), and the Danish State Railways (DSB)) have during the years 1988–90 arranged courses with the title 'Do I want to be a manager?'

The purpose of these courses was to give women the chance to discover whether or not they wanted to become managers. The aim was to encourage more women into managerial positions. The target group for the course was women aged between 30 and 40 who wanted to test themselves, develop in new ways and find out whether they really wanted to be leaders, and, if so, whether they had the necessary abilities. They were not yet managers but were in jobs that involved both responsibility and independence.

Each course had 24 participants, 8 from each company, and was a mixture of theory, practice, discussions and problem solving in collaboration with other participants. After the course the women had the opportunity to participate in networks which would give them the chance to exchange experiences and receive new inputs. About a year after the course there was a follow-up meeting.

The primary aims of the course for the individual women were:

- knowledge of and training in managing;
- self-insight and personal planning;
- insight into the differences/similarities between women and men;
- insight into company culture.

(Report from DR, SAS, DSB, 1991, p. 3)

A total of 150 women have participated from the three companies and 65% of the women think that managing is worthwhile. They want to become leaders, and over a period of 1–2 years 20% of the women have succeeded in becoming managers, some have applied for managerial positions, and others have become 'visible' as candidates. This shows that it is a myth that women do not want to become leaders.

The three companies involved have all concluded that it is beneficial to make special efforts to promote more women to managerial positions (DR, SAS, DSB, 1991).

THE PRIVATE SECTOR'S POLICIES TOWARDS WOMEN

Several companies in Denmark are working on recruiting more women to managerial positions, for instance by introducing specific action programmes and objectives. One of their reasons for this is that more companies have realized how important it is to develop female leadership potential. Another is that the number of young people in Denmark is declining, and therefore the recruitment of managers may become a problem in the future.

The number of women in the labour market almost equals that of men: quantitatively there is balance but not qualitatively. The women have competences which need to be utilized and developed, first of all to facilitate the companies' long-term recruiting, but also in terms of efficiency and economy. Several Danish companies have an equal opportunities policy to alleviate a situation where only a comparatively small proportion of the female employees are managers at middle and senior levels. The women's potential has not been realized in the same way as the men's, but an equal opportunities policy will make it easier to ensure that both sexes obtain equal opportunities in the companies.

Several companies in Denmark have applied to the Ministry of Labour for exemption from the Equal Treatment Act Section 6, making it possible for them, in areas normally dominated by men, to compose job advertisements that specify that '[the company] wants a more equal representation of men and women within the different job areas. As this kind of job is normally performed by men, we do encourage women to apply' (Equal Opportunities Council, 1990).

Many Danish companies are working with various strategies and action programmes to encourage more women into managerial positions. One such company is Baltica whose principal business areas are personal, financial and pension insurance.

Baltica women into management

In 1988 Baltica's Group Co-operation Committee decided to implement a strategy for equal opportunities. The objective of the strategy was that Baltica should endeavour to ensure equal treatment of women and men with regard to employee policy by:

- giving all employees – regardless of sex – the same opportunities for personal and career development;
- demanding the same qualifications from men and women as a basis for personal development and promotion;
- discouraging discriminatory attitudes and behaviour;
- improving the opportunities for all employees, regardless of sex, to be considered for work/function areas which have traditionally been or still are dominated by one sex.

Baltica's equal opportunities' goal is based on the fact that only a relatively small proportion of the company's female employees are managers or group leaders, section leaders, division managers, deputy directors, or at director level. Women's development potential has thus not been exploited to the same degree as men's, but with the aid of an equal opportunities policy, it should be easier to ensure that both sexes are given equal opportunities.

Baltica's Group Co-operation Committee monitored the work on equal opportunities by the following methods:

- integrating the equal opportunities' issue into Baltica's employee survey which is carried out in alternate years;
- informing staff of the equal opportunities' objective during four courses/seminars:
  - Concern introductory course for new employees;
  - Baltica's basic management courses;
  - The seminar 'Women into management' (see p. 72);
  - One-day seminars for young people.
- recording the amount of male and female participation on courses as well as recording the number of male and female applicants for management/specialist positions.

A survey of this registration of men and women is shown in Figure 3. In December 1991 the total number of employees in Baltica was 4,514, of whom 52% (2,342) were men and 48% (2,172) were women. Baltica had 527 managers (410 men and 117 women), of whom 27% of

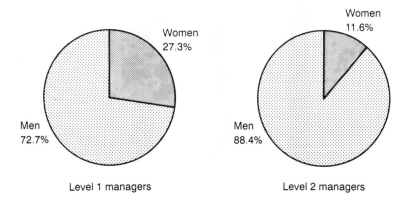

Level 1 managers   Level 2 managers

Source: Baltica Holding Personale (1991) *Equal Opportunities Report,*
            Balticakoncernen, p. 10

Figure 3   Distribution of male and female managers at Baltica at level 1
            (management responsibility for non-leaders) and level 2
            (management responsibility for leaders).

the women were in lower/middle management positions (management responsibility for non-leaders, e.g. group leaders) and 12% had management responsibility for leaders (Baltica Holding Personale, 1991).

Applicants for new jobs
Compared with the recorded number of jobs advertised in 1989, 1990 and 1991, the number of female applicants for management positions was very small, and there is a clear imbalance in the pattern of applications (see Figure 4).

Applicants for specialists' positions
The same gender imbalance is to be seen in the pattern of applications for these jobs, although there has been a gradual increase in the number of female applicants for specialists' positions in recent years (see Figure 5) (Baltica Holding Personale, 1991, p. 21).

Women's and men's participation on training courses
In 1991, on courses which contain some management element rather than courses specifically aimed at managers, 64% of the participants were men and 36% women. This shows a decrease in the number of female participants in management courses compared with 1990 and 1989 (see Figure 6) (Baltica Holding Personale, 1991, p. 26).

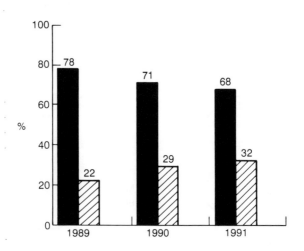

Source: Baltica Holding Personale (1991) Equal Opportunities Report, Balticakoncernen, p. 18–19

Figure 4   Male (■) and female (▨) distribution of applicants for management positions at Baltica: 1989 − 364 applications (11 positions); 1990 − 605 applications (22 positions); 1991 − 565 applications (22 positions).

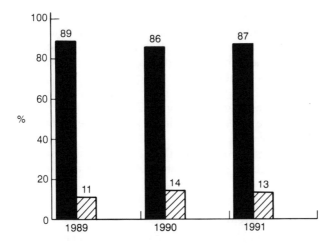

Source: Baltica Holding Personale (1991) *Equal Opportunities Report*,
            Balticakoncernen, p. 20

Figure 5   Male (■) and female (▨) distribution of applicants for specialists'
              positions at Baltica: 1989 − 859 applications (24 positions); 1990 −
              859 applications (47 positions); 1991 − 951 applications.

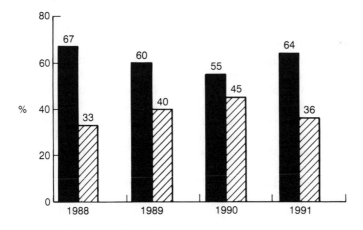

Source: Baltica Holding Personale (1991) *Equal Opportunities Report*,
            Balticakoncernen, p. 25

Figure 6   Male (■) and female (▨) participation in management courses at
              Baltica: 1988 − 170 participants; 1989 − 178 participants; 1990 − 121
              participants; 1991 − 173 participants.

'Women into management'

'Women into management' is a seminar held once a year in the Baltica group. Its purpose is to provide a setting in which women can become more conscious of their own strengths and career opportunities. The aim of the seminar is to help clarify the questions, 'Where am I now?' and 'Where am I going?' Some women are afraid of taking the next step in their career, asking themselves 'Can I manage? Have I got the know-how? Can I be a leader/specialist and at the same time have a family? *What do I want?'*

The seminar covers a number of themes, each including a presentation of theory, exercises, group work/networking and discussions, as follows:

- male and female qualities;
- androgynous leadership;
- the internal/external barriers that women have/meet in their careers;
- a female manager (guest speaker);
- assertiveness;
- images of women;
- knowledge of the organization;
- personal development;
- male/female role development (socialization process);
- participation in networking during and after the seminar.

Network groups (with company-wide membership) are set up at the beginning of the seminar and meet daily for the exchange of experiences, knowledge and information. The idea behind the network groups is that women will maintain contact with each other in the long term using the groups, formally and informally, just like men do through their clubs and associations or lodges.

The overall aim of the seminar is to enable more women to apply for management jobs at a higher level. Consequent on the findings of a pilot group in 1989, Baltica has decided to concentrate on group leaders (team leaders and supervisors) and specialists/administrators, and also on women aged 25–45 who are permanent staff. The idea of the seminar is to instigate a process without taking control. It is still up to the individual woman to take the initiative with regard to her future career.

Baltica has now held the 'Women into management' seminar twice and six of the 20 participants from the first seminar have taken on new jobs as leaders or in specialist positions. Although it is still too early to comment on the seminar's effectiveness, it is clear that since the Group Co-operation Committee decided to implement a strategy for equal opportunities, the problem has at least come into clearer focus.

A general summary of surveys by Danish companies can be seen in the Appendix.

DO WOMEN WANT TO BE MANAGERS?

Do Women Want to be Managers? is the title of a study undertaken by Højgaard (1990) for the Equal Opportunities Council to establish why women's share of managerial positions, in both the private and public sectors, is still so small.

A total of 41 women from four different companies were interviewed using a series of questions which reflected the fact that women in those companies confronted career barriers arising out of the company culture. All the women interviewed were considered to have managerial potential and were asked whether they had any idea why they had not yet reached a managerial position.

The purpose of the interviews was to ascertain whether it was true that:

- women do not apply for managerial positions;
- children and family are an obstacle;
- the demand for men and women is different;
- women are not given as much in-service training as men;
- women are afraid of conflicts;
- female leaders are better/worse than male leaders.

(Højgaard, 1990, p. 7)

The purpose of the investigation was to examine the barriers women experience when they apply for managerial positions, and the complex of male dominance and female subordination. Is the sex hierarchy at work disintegrating or are new ways of maintaining the old patterns developing? What barriers are there today, and what are the possibilities, for women who want to become leaders? (Højgaard, 1990, p. 10).

Some results from the investigation

Who has the prestige tasks?
The investigation shows that in the four companies the impression was that women and men performed almost the same tasks but in fact it was usually men who had the prestige tasks and women who had the routine work. In general, women will perform these routine tasks even though it is widely known that it is the prestige work which leads to promotion, and men, by taking on these prestige tasks, therefore have a considerable advantage on the career ladder.

The chances of promotion
In general the women were uncertain about how to progress in their careers and what the qualifications for promotion to a managerial position were. They were also unsure about what a manager's job entailed and what functions and tasks a manager performed. Several of

the women had the impression that a managerial job was a job involving control functions, conflict solving and long working days. At the same time they saw no opportunity for innovation or creativity in a managerial job (Højgaard, 1990, pp. 89, 90, 148).

Working life and family life
The investigation shows that the companies involved have a positive attitude to women managers' wish to have a family life. The women describe how in many families a power struggle takes place about who is to have a career and the division of domestic work. In most cases the woman is the loser in these struggles.

The women do not see having children as a barrier to a career and believe that a career and children can be compatible. It is men who are perceived as the problem. Several women mentioned that many men are opposed to women pursuing a career and that women often give in to this male opposition.

Women and leadership
Højgaard has divided the women into three different groups: those who are determined to become leaders, those who definitely do not want to, and those who are undecided. It is the last group, in particular, who are the cause of the myth that women do not want to become leaders. There is still a fairly widespread belief that it is not quite acceptable for a woman to aim at being a leader. Many of the women refuse to seek higher positions within their companies and believe that their career progression is due to coincidences, offers and requests rather than conscious planning. A number of these women, when asked whether they wanted to become leaders, would say no, but when specifically invited to apply for a management job, would consider doing so (Højgaard, 1990, pp. 207–14).

Why do managements not choose women?
If the women are qualified and want to manage, why then do the managements of the companies not choose women? The women themselves have no simple answer, but many of them believe that the reason is that men choose men:

- either because of tradition;
- or because the qualifications required for the managerial positions are just the qualifications that the men possess;
- or because the men do not 'see' the women and overlook their qualifications.

(Højgaard, 1990, pp. 194–219)

The reason why there are so few female leaders is due to several factors: male dominance, female resistance and indecision, and finally managements' lack of will to appoint women. The managements of these companies must learn to notice women and recognize their potential, and to see the positive aspect of the differences between men and women with regard to qualifications, characteristics, and points of view (Højgaard, 1990, pp. 194–219).

Do women want to be leaders?

Højgaard concludes from her investigation that the statements of her women interviewees give no clear picture of the reasons why more women do not reach the highest levels of management. *Do Women Want to be Managers?* focused on the workplace environment and it can be inferred from this that it is the ethos of the organization which is of prime importance in determining a woman's chances of promotion. Højgaard emphasizes that a company's culture must engender and reinforce women's self-confidence, which is a precondition for managerial success, if women are to realize their potential (Højgaard, 1990, p. 214).

CONCLUSIONS AND RECOMMENDATION FOR THE FUTURE

European Women in Business and Management is the title of this book and the conclusions to be reached will depend on what kind of business and what level of business is considered.

In Denmark the representation of women in business in general is almost equal to the representation of men and current trends indicate that this pattern will not alter drastically in future. Women have entered the working arena and intend to remain there.

However, a look at women's representation within management gives a totally different picture. In the private sector in Denmark in 1989, of 6,418 directors, 4.5% (291) were women. For middle management the figures were 26,385 managers, 10.65% (2,797) of whom were women. The percentage of women in management is very small, and this picture, or an even worse one, is repeated all over Europe.

There have been many surveys into why women are so poorly represented in management and when these studies are investigated, there seems to be no evidence to prove that women are less suited to management positions. The figures seem to indicate a waste of leadership potential, a waste Denmark cannot afford today and certainly not in the future, when it is anticipated that there will be a shortage of qualified leaders and managers. This means that we must start now to use these untapped resources and instigate education of our future potential leaders. Four recommendations, in particular, must be stressed:

Visibility

One reason for the lack of female leaders is that many women are just not visible in their companies. If women want careers, they must learn to be visible, but how are they to do this? Must they use the same methods as men or do they have to use specific ways to become visible?

Role models

The women today who possess top positions in Danish business life, are 'the pioneers'. They are the few who have broken through the 'glass ceiling'. This means that there are not many women with whom future female managers can identify. Role models are important and one way in which companies can work to provide them is by establishing mentorships, where each 'pioneer' is nurturing two or three future female managers in Danish business life.

Networks

There are many established networks, clubs, and experience groups both inside and outside the companies. Women do not usually participate in these networks; sometimes they are not even allowed to. However, it is extremely important, that women should participate in networks, clubs and experience groups, as these give them the opportunity to gain much formal and informal information, which is a part of the career culture, and this will increase the possibilities for women to interfere with that culture. If women are not allowed to participate in existing networks, clubs or experience groups, they must form their own. In Denmark we have several networks for women, both national (for example, Erhvervskvinder Business Women and Zonta, a women's network group) and international (for example, European Women's Management Development Network).

Female managers at different management levels

When we work on obtaining more female managers in companies, we often seem to forget that there are various management levels in the companies and that these different levels mean various needs for training and qualifications, both personal and professional. It is important to be aware that we cannot generalize and say that all women must work on achieving the same qualifications; we have to bear in mind the levels at which they belong and at which they are aiming.

In this chapter we have described the experience of women in business and management in Denmark including various developmental and educational activities for women. To us there is no doubt that these activities for women will yield results in the long run. It is, however, important that they are adapted to women's physical and personal qualifications and positions.

The most essential point for us, however, is that *women do want to become managers*!

APPENDIX

A general summary of surveys by Danish companies

A number of Danish companies have carried out surveys to find out why they have so few female managers. The general conclusions listed below are taken from surveys by three Danish companies: Bikuben (1989, 1990), The Danish Post Office Service (1990/91) and Baltica (Baltica Holding Personale, 1991).

- Very few women apply for management positions in Danish companies.
- The reason why so few women apply for management positions is that women still do not form part of the companies' career and management culture.
- The companies' leadership profiles are often created by men and are often maintained by the fact that men tend to hire men.
- Career and management cultures are on the whole self-elective with male candidates and therefore do not look for potential female candidates.
- The career path in most companies runs through prestigious work areas and assignments (cross-concern projects and negotiations). Women are often employed in non-prestigious areas such as administrative assignments and rarely take part in research and development project work.
- Women are more likely to consider that having less time to spend with the family is the greatest sacrifice connected with a managerial position, but women who have become managers and directors do not consider having children a hindrance.
- In general women do not have the same career opportunities as men.
- Women lack confidence in their own leadership abilities − but so do many men.
- In many companies there is an informal recruitment of managers, where unofficial values and criteria for success are a decisive factor.
- The real barriers are the traditional leadership role and the *'jante law'* culture ('no one should think they are better than the rest'), which are prevalent in Danish companies.
- The formal career and promotion structure does not recognize women who are interested in becoming leaders, and women do not carry through their ambitions, either at home or at work.
- The structures and attitudes prevalent in most families represent a considerable obstacle for women as far as their career is concerned.
- The choice of education and lack of subsequent opportunities to make a career at a later date represent a real barrier for women.

- Women lack self-confidence, which means that they are afraid of criticism. Thus they suppress their own ideas and attitudes out of fear of encountering opposition.
- In general women have a greater need for security than men. This is one of the reasons why women take on routine work assignments rather than seeking challenges in new work assignments and methods.
- Most women know they are competent but often hold themselves back, which prevents them from making any impact or gaining respect in companies.

but

- A large group of women are interested in having responsibility as leaders or in increasing the responsibility they already have.

REFERENCES

Baltica Holding Personale (1991) *Equal Opportunities Report*, Baltica-koncernen, Copenhagen.

Bikuben (1989) *Ta' roret — Barrierer for kvindernes karrieremuligheder i Bikuben*, Copenhagen.

Bikuben (1990) *Ta' roret*, Copenhagen.

Børsens Nyhedsmagasin (1991) Forlaget Management *The Golden Magazine*, Tillæg til dagbladet Børsen, November.

The Danish Employers' Confederation (1991) *Equal Opportunities — Introduction to a Debate*, Copenhagen.

The Danish Post Office Service (1990/1991) *Career, Sex and Culture*, Copenhagen.

Danmarks Statistik (1900) *The Register-Based Labour Force Statistics (RAS)*, Copenhagen.

Danmark Statistics (1983–90) *Salary and Income Statistics*.

DR, SAS, DSB (1991) *Er ledelse noget for mig*, A report about the course: 'Do I want to be a manager', 1988–90, Copenhagen.

Equal Opportunities Council (1990) *Equal Opportunities Council Annual Report*, Copenhagen.

Højgaard, L. (1990) *Do Women Want to be Managers*, The Equal Opportunities Council, Copenhagen.

OECD (1990) *Employment Outlook*.

Statistic Information (1985:16, 1986:20, 1988:18, 1989:3, 1989:20) *Labour Market*, Copenhagen.

Statistic Information (1991) *Labour Market*.

Vestergaard, V. (1991) Director 1991 in *The Golden Magazine*, Børsen, Copenhagen.

5.

THE NETHERLANDS

Kea Tijdens

INTRODUCTION

The population of the Netherlands tripled from 5 million in 1900 to 15 million in 1990.[1] The labour force increased even more, from 1.9 million to 6.4 million, of which 2.4 million are women. Women's participation rate has been increasing steadily for more than two decades. This trend is due to women's rising educational level, decreasing family sizes, changes in public opinion, growing demand for labour in women's jobs, and an increasing demand for part-time labour. In 1990 approximately 47% of the female population aged 15−64 were in work, compared with 32% in 1973.

Between 1975 and 1990 registered unemployment increased as a result of recession in the early 1980s. This rate decreased subsequently, but in this 15-year period unemployment swung from 5% to more than 15%, and back to 5%. At the worst period of recession unemployment among women was 4 percentage points higher than among men.

According to Kessel *et al.* (1986), the history of women's labour can be divided into several periods. Between 1870 and 1930 there was a major migration from the countryside to the towns. Men, boys and girls went to work in newly built factories, while women worked in their own homes and those of others. In the 1930s the government tried to combat the Depression by prohibiting married women from undertaking paid work. Therefore, the years from 1930 to 1947 are known as the period of women's forbidden labour. After the Second World War, manufacturing and building boomed and increased the demand for men's labour, and women married early, creating the baby boom. The general consensus was that women ought to be full-time housewives. The period from 1947 to 1960 is called that of women's caring labour. In the 1960s the very rapid growth of the service sector generated an increasing demand for female labour, because many women were employed in this sector. The government removed the legal barriers to married women's paid work, and the contraceptive pill made planned motherhood possible. The period 1960 to 1975 was a time of high demand for female labour. Women met these demands, resulting in a continually increasing participation rate from the late 1960s onwards. But it was not until the mid-1970s that the Dutch government followed international guidelines on equality policy, thus the years after 1975 are known as the period of women's achievement.

Compared with other European countries, the Netherlands has just about the lowest percentage of women in paid labour and the highest percentage of women in part-time work. The low participation rate can be attributed mainly to the high percentage of women leaving the labour market, either for marriage or, increasingly, for the birth of a first child. A relatively small percentage of these leavers re-enter the labour market. But women's labour-market behaviour is changing in all age groups. Young women, like young men, tend to participate less because they continue education. Women in their twenties and thirties tend to continue paid work, and women in their forties tend to re-enter the labour market, most of them in part-time jobs. Participation rates of women in their fifties are stable, as early retirement is balanced by re-entry.

Not surprisingly, part-time labour is closely related to civil status. In 1985 the percentage of married women working fewer than 15 hours per week was 82% of the total number of women in this group, whereas the percentage for men was 37%. On the other hand, labour force statistics show that only 36% of women working at least 35 hours a week are married, compared with 71% of men.

The Dutch labour force is highly segregated by sex (Tijdens, 1989): men are employed primarily in agriculture, manufacturing, construction and transport, whereas women are employed in sales, services, health-care and education. Men and women also have different occupations: men are engineers, bricklayers, bookkeepers, managers and clerks; women are nurses, shop assistants, secretaries, typists and clerks, or they perform domestic services. In the 1970s and 1980s occupational segregation remained constant for a number of reasons. Firstly, the number of women workers grew much faster than the number of male workers; the latter number is actually decreasing. Secondly, employment in women's occupations increased and employment in men's occupations decreased. Thirdly, women's entry into men's occupations is still hampered by exclusion structures. Segregation is an ongoing process, in spite of government policies to stimulate girls to choose traditionally male jobs.

The positions held by men and women are at different levels; on average women are one level below men. Thus, segregation also has a hierarchical character. Not surprisingly, career development and options differ for men and women. Men have a greater chance of moving up to a higher job level than women. According to statistics collected by the Wages Service, women hardly have a chance of moving up from the lowest level (LTD, 1987).

As in all countries, women earn less than men, even if they are the same age and have the same education and the same tenure. In the Netherlands women's average gross hourly wages are about 70% of men's. These wage differentials have remained almost constant since 1970. Two-thirds of this difference is explained by variables like age, job level and part-time labour and one-third is explained by gender.

Whether or not they have a paid job, women do most of the household work. In the late 1980s 65% of the Dutch adult population believed men and women should share housekeeping equally, but reality is very different. It is increasingly usual for women to have two jobs — paid work and responsibility for running a home. According to a major time-budget survey carried out by the Central Bureau of Statistics in 1987, on working days women spend an average of 15% of every 24 hours on housekeeping, whereas men spend only 4% (Stoop, 1991). The large majority of the female labour force takes care of the house-keeping, they cook the meals and they care for the children. Women in managerial jobs try to relieve the burden of their dual roles in several ways; according to their own answers, they clean less often, they pay for a home help, they buy home appliances, and do their shopping by car (Berends, 1988).

WOMEN AT THE TOP

As in other countries, the percentage of women in managerial occu-pations in the Netherlands is low. In 1990 almost 13% of managers were women, whereas 38% of the total labour force were women. Fewer than 3% of all working women have a managerial position. This figure is low compared with a managerial 12% of the male labour force. The labour force statistics provide detailed information about managerial jobs. Managerial jobs are not classified as a single cat-egory in these statistics, but are distinguished according to individual sectors. The Central Bureau of Statistics uses the International Standard Classification of Occupations (ISCO), as shown in Table 1, which was designed by the United Nations. According to this classification, the three-digit level occupation code defines 13 job titles as mana-gerial jobs.

In the managerial jobs working hours per week are long compared with normal working hours, for men and, particularly, for women. Table 2 shows that 94% of male managers work more than 35 hours per week, compared with 84% in the general labour force. For women the figures are 70% and 39% respectively.

The large majority of female managers are aged between 25 and 44.

Table 1 Numbers of male and female workers in managerial positions in 1990

Managerial jobs	Men (000)	Women (000)	All (000)	Percentage women (%)*
Managing directors	62	—	66	—
Self-employed managing directors	35	11	45	24
Managers – general	29	—	31	—
Managers – production	26	—	27	—
Higher managerial positions	81	18	99	18
Managerial clerical positions	30	13	44	30
Managerial positions in transport	27	—	28	—
Managers – wholesale business†	28	—	31	—
Managers – retail trade†	14	5	24	26
Managers – catering industry	7	8	15	53
Managers – housekeeping	8	7	15	47
Managers – agriculture	5	—	5	—
Managers – manufacturing industry	119	7	127	6
Total	471	69	557	12
Labour force	3,951	2,405	6,356	38

* Groups with fewer than 5,000 workers are represented by a dash (—). Therefore total figures can be more than the sum of the figures of men and women.
† Including 'self-employed'.

Source: Labour force statistics, 1990, Central Bureau of Statistics.

Only one-fifth are over 45. There are hardly any young women or men in managerial jobs (see Table 2).

Managerial job titles can be found in all sectors, but also at almost all job levels. The latter might be explained by the fact that managerial qualifications are not based on an educational category but on the fact that experience is supposed to be more important. If positions are broken down to a scale of 8 levels (8 being the highest level), 11% of female managers are working at level 3, 56% at level 4 and 24% at level 5, whereas 39% of the male managers are working at level 5, 32% at level 6 and 11% at level 7. Thus, on average, women managers are working one job level below male counterparts, as is the case in the labour force as a whole, according to the results of a large survey in 768 firms in private industry in 1984 and 1985 (LTD, 1987).

As mentioned previously, women earn less than men. In this respect the management field does not deviate from other occupations. In fact, the opposite is true. The few available statistics show that average earnings of female managers are 40% below those of their male colleagues. This wage gap is much larger than in the labour force as a whole, where women's earnings are 30% below men's. In general, one of the main variables causing wage differentials is tenure, but years of service differ less than in the labour force as a whole, as is shown in

Table 2   Breakdown of male and female workers in the 13 managerial
categories and in the labour force by working hours and age in 1990

	13 managerial categories		Labour force	
	Men (%)	Women (%)	Men (%)	Women (%)
Working hours per week				
<20	2	15	8	33
20−34	4	15	8	28
35−44	82	70	73	36
>45	12	—	11	3
All*	100	100	100	100
Age groups (years)				
15−24	—	—	17	25
25−44	59	80	57	55
45−64	41	20	26	19
All†	100	100	100	100

* Excluding 'working time unknown'.
† Excluding 'age unknown'.

Source: Labour force statistics, 1990, Central Bureau of Statistics.

Table 3   Average wages and average years of service in private industry in
1987 (sample of firms employing at least 20 people in private
industry, excluding agriculture, mining and public utilities)

	Average net hourly wages (DFL)		
	All	Men	Women
Managerial jobs	40.50	43.00	25.00
All jobs	20.50	23.00	15.50

	Average years of service		
	All	Men	Women
Managerial jobs	13.9	14.3	11.0
All jobs	9.0	10.5	6.0

Source: LTD (1988) *Labour Conditions of Men and
Women*, Wages Service, Ministry of Social
Affairs and Employment.

Table 3. Job level segregation is probably one of the main reasons for
this wage gap.

The question of why so few women reach the top of the organizational
hierarchy was raised in the 1970s. During the mid-1980s a number of
Dutch and translated books on this topic appeared, including both
interviews with women at the top and advice on how to reach the top.

In line with the expanding market for these books, OPZIJ, a Dutch feminist monthly, conducted a survey about leadership relations at work in 1988 (Berends, 1988). The sample was drawn from the Dutch labour force, its readers, and women in managerial positions. The results indicate that career aspirations of men and women do not differ. One-fifth of both the male and female labour force are planning a career, whereas the majority of the labour force believed they would still be in the same job 5 year later. Male and female employees rate their female superiors higher than their male superiors, in particular on 'masculine' subjects: they are better at work organization, they have more authority over their subordinates, and they dare to take drastic measures. According to opinions in the labour-force sample, female and male managers deal with people equally, they reach the same professional standards, and they are equally daring in taking day-to-day decisions. One difference was that, in contrast to women bosses, male superiors were said to be always busy with their work (Berends, 1988).

Whether male and female managers differ in their leadership styles has been debated recently. It was found that female university managers stimulated their subordinates, and preferred a co-operative leadership style, whereas male managers preferred control, aggression, and analytical and strategic thinking (Brouns and Schokker, 1990, p. 223). A study on managerial behaviour showed that male and female managers demonstrate significant differences in three of the 21 aspects to be distinguished (Management Ontwikkelings Groep, 1989). These three aspects were, firstly, that male managers rely more on tried solutions than do female managers; secondly, that male managers also show more individualistic behaviour than do women managers; and thirdly, that women managers stick to the rules more than male managers do. No differences were found in the way male and female managers cope with people, or in their creativity. Both groups were equally effective in their leadership styles. It is quite clear that the results of all surveys show that women managers demonstrate no difference in their leadership style; in some respects they even perform better than their male colleagues.

ENTREPRENEURIAL WOMEN

The number of female entrepreneurs in the Netherlands is increasing. Between 1975 and 1985 their number rose from 15,000 to 55,000, the latter being 18% of all registered entrepreneurs (Koopman and Walvis, 1986). In the labour force statistics, entrepreneurs are not counted as such, but are included in the self-employed group, which is far larger. The former group consists of enterprises registered at the Chamber of Commerce, whereas the latter group also includes farmers and the self-employed without personnel, who are rarely registered. In 1990, about

184,000 self-employed women were counted − 30% of all self-employed people. In addition, in 1990 the labour force statistics also counted 115,000 women assisting members of their family, being 83% of all workers in this group. Although they may not be counted as self-employed or entrepreneurs as such, many of them function in daily life as if they were.

Table 4 shows that 420,000 self-employed men and 184,000 self-employed women were counted. There are comparatively fewer self-employed women than self-employed men: 7.7% versus 10.6%. Self-employed women and men show different patterns: half of the self-employed women can be found in the public sector, with industry in second place. Self-employed men show a different pattern: 30% work in agriculture, followed by industry. In agriculture, nearly 14% of the female labour force is self-employed, whereas the figure for men is almost 60%.

Within the occupational group of managers, nearly a third of women are self-employed. Maybe this confirms the oft-heard statement that it is better for women themselves to be self-employed in case they meet problems in their career development. Among self-employed women, the largest group are 'professionals', with 53,000 women, immediately followed by service workers with 52,000 self-employed women (see Table 5).

Focusing again on entrepreneurs, several generations of female entrepreneurs can be distinguished since the Second World War.

Table 4 Number of self-employed women and men and their percentage of the sector's employment in 1990

Branch	Self-employed women (000)	Self-employed women (%)	Self-employed men (000)	Self-employed men (%)
Agriculture	11	13.6	124	59.9
Mining	—*	—	—	—
Manufacturing	10	0.4	25	2.6
Public utilities	—	—	—	—
Building	—	—	33	8.6
Trade	41	7.9	109	16.0
Transport	—	—	11	3.6
Banking	26	10.2	53	13.4
Public sector	91	7.7	61	6.4
All†	184	7.7	420	10.6

* Groups with fewer than 5,000 workers are represented by a dash (−). Therefore total figures can be more than the sum of the figures of men and women.
† Including 'sector unknown'.

Source: Labour force statistics, 1990, Central Bureau of Statistics.

Table 5   Numbers of self-employed women and men and their percentage of
occupational groups in 1990

Occupational group	Self-employed women		Self-employed men	
	(000)	(%)	(000)	(%)
Professionals	53	8.3	80	9.2
Managers	11	29.7	35	14.8
Clerks	8	1.2	—*	—
Shop and marketing sales workers	33	11.1	81	20.5
Service workers	52	9.5	27	11.7
Agricultural and fishery workers	12	16.0	125	52.3
Craft workers, operators, assemblers	15	10.6	69	4.9
All†	184	7.7	420	10.6

* Groups with fewer than 5,000 workers are represented by a dash (−).
Therefore total figures can be more than the sum of the figures of men and
women.
† Including 'sector unknown'.

Source: Labour force statistics, 1990, Central Bureau of Statistics.

Whereas the women who became entrepreneurs in the 1950s and 1960s
tended to take over a firm from a husband or parent who had died, the
women who became entrepreneurs in the 1970s and 1980s established
their own firms much more frequently, as has been shown in
an anthropological study on generations of female entrepreneurs
(Aalten, 1991).

A quantitative survey among enterprises established after 1978 and
still operating in 1985 shows that during the whole period almost 18%
of new firms were established by women (Ministry of Social Affairs
and Employment, 1985). This percentage differs greatly by sector.
Women entrepreneurs can be found mainly in the service sector, as
well as in the personal and sociocultural services, the food industry,
textile and leather industry, and in retail trades and repair services.
Around 86% of the firms are one-woman businesses. At their start,
women's firms are smaller on average than male and mixed firms (1.5
versus 2.7 employees). This was still the case in 1985 (2.2 versus 4.1).

The survey also provided some statistics about female entrepreneurs.
On average, the woman is 34 when she starts her business, and she
has a general education. Eighty-three per cent are married and 79%
have children. More than half of the female entrepreneurs are
re-entering the labour market, but this is the case more often in the
countryside than in urban areas. Not surprisingly, female entrepreneurs
work on a part-time basis more often, both when starting up, and
according to the 1985 survey.

How do women entrepreneurs run their businesses? According to
the survey, only 34% of the female entrepreneurs realized a growth in

volume between 1978 and 1984, compared to 50% of all entrepreneurs. Of the married female entrepreneurs 82% considered their firm's profits as additional income, whereas more than half the single female entrepreneurs considered their profits as their main income. On average, those women who said their firm's income was additional, earned half of the income made by those women who said it was their main income. On average, the latter group earned DFl 30,000 (approximately £12,000) per year (Ministry of Social Affairs and Employment, 1985).

POLICIES ON WOMEN'S PAID LABOUR

The women's movement in the late 1960s and early 1970s made it very clear that the government should respond to changes in society. An Equal Rights Commission was set up in 1974 as an advisory body, and since 1978 the government has made funds available to stimulate equal rights policy throughout society. In 1986 the Equal Rights Policy Plan passed through Parliament, followed by an Equal Rights Policy Action Programme in 1987. In this programme special attention was paid to positive action at work, to women as entrepreneurs, to women in men's jobs and to the economic independence of girls who reached 18 after 1990. The Ministry of Social Affairs and Employment introduced a grants scheme for companies wishing to carry out positive action programmes which will run until 1993. Although no final conclusions can be drawn as yet on the effects of these grants, quite a number of organizations have put together positive action programmes, which are discussed at several hierarchical levels in the firm, have appointed positive action consultants, and have organized training courses for their personnel (van Amstel and yan den Berg, 1991).

A review of Dutch legislation on women shows that the focus has been on equal rights, but that legislation took a long time. For example, it was not until 1957 that the law dating back to 1935 which prohibited married women from employment in the civil service was removed. The government did not ratify the Equal Pay Act until 1975. It took another 5 years for the Equal Opportunities Act to be passed. According to these laws, women, or groups of women, who feel they have been treated unfairly at work, or paid unequally, can submit complaints to the Equal Opportunities Commission. Equal rights legislation does not guarantee equal positions on the labour market; that has now become clear. According to the 1989–90 report of the Equal Opportunities Commission, many problems women encounter, for example demands for equal pay in segregated jobs, need solutions other than legislation.

Not surprisingly, the increasing supply of female labour, particularly of women with small children, has led to an increasing demand for childcare facilities. The state used to finance playgrounds for 2–4-year-olds, but only for a few hours a day; these facilities were not intended for working women. A few full-time facilities were subsidized: in 1985 the care of only 1% (i.e. 10,000) of all children between 0 and 5 years was covered by daycare centres. This was extremely low compared with other EC countries (OECD, 1990, Ch. 5). Supply did not meet demand in any way. For example, it is estimated that 29,000 women who had their first child in 1988 were looking for childcare facilities (Tijdens, 1991). According to decisions taken by government, budgets for childcare services will be increased gradually from 1990 onwards. These funds can also be used for childcare initiatives taken at workplace level, either by employers or by trades unions. Regulated daycare is expected to increase rapidly in the coming years, but it is still an open question whether supply will be adequate.

Maternity leave used to be 14 weeks in the Netherlands but has recently changed to 16 weeks; it is still one of the shortest leaves in Europe (OECD, 1990, Ch. 5). Parental leave is regulated by legislation and, additionally, in collective agreements. According to recent government decisions, it is possible for women and men to reduce working hours to a minimum of 20 for a maximum of 6 months when they have children the under the age of 4. There is a great need for parental leave, but because it is unpaid it is not yet certain how many women and men will make use of it.

According to a research project carried out in 878 private firms with a collective bargaining agreement, 13% of them used preferential treatment as recruitment policy to attract more women (LTD, 1991). Large firms, employing more than 100 people, were much more likely to do this than small and medium-sized firms (22% versus 6% and 12% respectively). These policies on women focus mainly on recruitment and hardly at all on promotion and turnover, in spite of results of personnel data analysis proving such policies would be more fruitful (Siegers, Timmerman and Wittink, 1987).

Half of 161 large private-industry collective agreements, covering 2.3 million workers, included sections on women's emancipation in 1989. The main items were childcare and parental leave, but only the latter could be characterized as agreements, whereas the former were declarations of intent to carry out research. In nearly all 52 collective agreements in the health and welfare sector, special attention is paid to women. A substantial number of these include agreements on childcare facilities (DCA, 1990).

PROBLEMS OF WOMEN IN BUSINESS AND MANAGEMENT

Public opinion on women in managerial and entrepreneurial positions is changing. In 1970 30% of the Dutch population agreed that it would be unnatural for women to manage male subordinates. In 1987 only 12% agreed (SCP, 1988). But female leadership is still not fully accepted in Dutch society. In contrast to men, women as a group are perceived as non-hierarchical. When asked 'Who has the most difficult job?', male and female workers say that the male superior with male subordinates has the easiest job. The male superior with female subordinates ranks second, and the female superior with female subordinates as third. The female superior with male subordinates has the most difficult job (Berends, 1988). In line with expectations, in the same survey female superiors report they have to deal with male subordinates who are unable to co-operate with their female superior. The survey indicates that 83% of the labour force has a male and 17% has a female superior.

It is quite clear that leadership at work is not a gender-neutral point. But it is not only a point between superiors and subordinates. Employers have no gender-neutral preferences either. The results of a large survey in 768 firms in private industry in 1984 and 1985 (LTD, 1987) indicate that employers do not prefer gender-neutral filling of managerial positions. In one out of four lower managerial positions, employers say they prefer a man, and also they prefer a male in one out of 20 higher managerial positions. In four out of 10 cases where they prefer a man, they argue that this is consistent with men's and women's roles in society. Even if employers say that they do not have a preference, they tend to recruit men for managerial positions, particularly for positions on higher levels. Managerial jobs are strongly sex typed and recruitment procedures are in line with this. The results of the survey by the feminist monthly OPZIJ mentioned previously indicate that a large group of managerial women obtained their jobs because of the withdrawal of the man nominated initially (Berends, 1988). The implication is that female managers have to overcome more aversion and traditional prejudices than their male counterparts, not only at the time of recruitment, but also during their careers.

A more detailed study, including a questionnaire completed by 875 teachers and principals, concerning women's position in managerial jobs in schools, was conducted by Ruijs (1990). The percentage of women in school management is low, compared with the percentage of women teachers. Some years ago, following integration of different school types, the percentage of female principals decreased, due to the fact that women used to be principals at girls' schools and smaller schools. These schools had a weaker position at the time of integration. Almost half the female heads believe that they encounter problems because they are women. They are evaluated more critically, they encounter greater distrust, and they have to show more persuasiveness. The research indicates a slight difference in ambition to become principal in favour of male teachers. The respondents said that female principals performed better, because of tact, patience, professional standards good communication skills and the abilities to represent others and create a distinctive atmosphere. Male principals performed better on ambition, authority, practical attitude and self-esteem.

Another major problem, for female entrepreneurs in particular, is that they have to deal with banks who believe that female entrepreneurs' companies will be less profitable than those of male entrepreneurs. As a consequence, banks are less inclined to provide credit facilities for female entrepreneurs, although, on average, the loans women apply for are much lower than men's loans, according to the results of a large investigation (Koper and Vermunt, 1985). Recently, two large Dutch banks, RABO and NMB, have officially launched positive policies for female entrepreneurs. They have made video courses for the staff to draw their attention to the specific problems of female entrepreneurs.

CONCLUSIONS AND RECOMMENDATIONS

In the Netherlands women's participation rate in paid work is low but increasing. A decreasing number of women leave the labour market at the time of marriage or a child's birth. An increasing number of women re-enter the labour market, mainly in part-time jobs. The majority of the female labour force works part-time. As in other countries, fewer women seem to be employed at higher job levels.

Women's share in the ranks of managerial occupations is low: only 13% of managers are women. Fewer than 3% of all working women have a managerial occupation. The highest percentage of female managers can be found in the catering industry, whereas hardly any female managers are found in male-dominated sectors like manufacturing, transport, wholesale business and agriculture. The gendered wage gap in managerial occupations is 40%, 10 percentage points higher than in the labour force as a whole. Hierarchical job-level segregation is one of the main variables.

No clear definition is given of female entrepreneurs and self-employed in the available official statistics. Nevertheless, the number of female entrepreneurs and self-employed seems to have increased substantially. In 1990 nearly 8% of the female labour force were self-employed, mainly in the public sector and industry, and in professional and service occupations. Whereas the women who became entrepreneurs in the 1950s and 1960s were likely to have taken over a firm from a husband or parent who had died, the women who became entrepreneurs in the 1970s and 1980s established their own firms much more frequently. The large majority of the married entrepreneurs see their firm's profits as an additional income, but more than half of the single women consider it as main income.

Legislation on equal pay and equal opportunities has been implemented slowly in the Netherlands. Childcare facilities have not met demand for many years. In 1990 the government decided to increase budgets, and daycare is expected to increase rapidly in the years to come. Maternity leave is one of the shortest in Europe and parental leave is unpaid. The women's movement seems to be more influential at industrial level than at governmental level, because an increasing number of collective agreements have additional regulations on leave, childcare and positive action for recruitment. There is a national Equal Rights Policy Action Programme, but this only provides subsidies for firms to appoint consultants.

Positive action plans must be realized on a broader scale than is currently the case. They should also include measures on career development and turnover. Employers have to be convinced that women must have equal career opportunities and that special measures are required to prevent turnover. Better childcare and parental leave facilities might help in this case. In fact, entrepreneurial women should have the same facilities for childcare and parental leave; government policy should focus on this.

Women in managerial jobs and in business encounter problems that are related to the fact that they are women, for example distrust about their professional abilities and persuasiveness in terms of leadership, because female leadership contradicts fixed role patterns. However, the performance of female superiors and school principals is good, according to the evaluations of their subordinates and colleagues and there is thus no ground whatsoever for low self-esteem. Policies, therefore, should focus on influencing opinions about female leadership. These policies should be aimed at male and female employees, but also at employers and at clients, as well as at the general public.

REFERENCES

Aalten, A. (1991) *Zakenvrouwen, Over de Grenzen van Vrouwelijkheid in Nederland sinds 1945 (Female Entrepreneurs, beyond the Borders of Femininity in the Netherlands since 1945)*, Sara/Van Gennep, Amsterdam.

Berends, H. (1988) *Vrouw en Werk. 'Vrouwelijk Leiderschap' en 'de Combinatie van Rollen Waarin de Werkende Vrouw Terecht kan Komen'. Een Onderzoek van het Maandblad OPZIJ (Women and Work. Female Leadership and the Combination of Working Women's Roles. A Survey of the OPZIJ Monthly*, Weekbladpers, Amsterdam.

Brouns, M. and Schokker, A. (1990) *Arbeidsvraagstukken en Sekse (Women at Work)*, STEO, The Hague.

DCA (1990) *DCA-Bevindingen 1989 (Findings 1989)*, Dienst Collectieve Arbeidsvoorwaarden, Ministry of Social Affairs and Employment, The Hague.

Kessel, E. van, Kuperus, M. and Pott-Buter, H. (1986) *Hoezo, gelijk belast? (What is meant by an equal burden?)*, De Populier/Amazone, Amsterdam.

Koopman, G. and Walvis, C. (1986) *Vrouwen Zelfstandig: Perspectieven op Vrouwelijk Ondernemerschap (Self-employed Women: Perspectives)*, Equal Rights Council, The Hague.

Koper, G. and Vermunt, R. (1985) *Vrouwen en Bedrijfskredietverlening. Een Vergelijkend Onderzoek naar de Belemmeringen die Mannen en Vrouwen Ondervinden bij Bedrijfskredietverlening (Women and Credit. A Comparable Research on Men's and Women's Hindrance on Loans)*, Department of Social and Organizational Psychology, University of Leiden.

LTD (1987) *Gelijke Behandeling van Mannen en Vrouwen Tijdens Dienstverband 1984, 1985 (Equal Treatment of Men and Women at Work, 1984, 1985)*,

Wages Service, Ministry of Social Affairs and Employment, The Hague.

LTD (1988) *De Positie van Mannen en Vrouwen in het Arbeidsproces (Labour Conditions of Men and Women)*, Wages Service, Ministry of Social Affairs and Employment, The Hague.

LTD (1991) *Arbeidsmarktbeleid in een Aantal CAO-Sectoren (Labour Market Policies in a Number of Branches)*, Ministry of Social Affairs and Employment, The Hague.

Management Ontwikkelings Groep (1989) *Vergelijkend Onderzoek Vrouwelijke en Mannelijke Managers (Comparative Research on Male and Female Managers)*, The Hague.

Ministry of Social Affairs and Employment (1985) *Door Vrouwen Opgerichte Bedrijven (Firms Established by Women)*, The Hague.

OECD (1990) *Employment Outlook*, OECD, Paris.

Ruijs, A. (1990) *Vrouwen en Schoolmanagement (Women and School Management)*, Swets & Zeitlinger, Amsterdam/Lisse.

SCP (1988) *Sociaal en Cultureel Rapport 1988 (Social and Cultural Report 1988)*, Social and Cultural Planbureau, Staatsuitgeverij, The Hague.

Siegers, J. J., Timmerman, C. and Wittink, R. (1987) *Analyse van Personeelsbestanden ten Behoeve van Positieve Aktie (Analysis of Personnel Data for the Benefit of Positive Action)*, Ministry of Social Affairs and Employment, The Hague.

Stoop, I. A. L. (1991) Alles heeft zijn uur; tijdsbesteding per dag van de week en uur van de dag (Everything in time, time budgets per day of the week and hour of the day), *Statistisch Magazine*, no. 2, pp. 54–69, CBS, The Hague.

Tijdens, K. (1989) *Automatisering en Vrouwenarbeid. Een Studie over Beroepssegregatie op de Arbeidsmarkt, in de Administratieve Beroepen en in het Bankwezen (New Technology and Women's Work. A Study Concerning Occupational Segregation on the Labour Market, in Clerical Work and Banking)*, Ph.D. dissertation, Van Arkel, Utrecht.

Tijdens, K. (1991) Arbeidsparticipatie en bedrijfskinderopvang (Labour force participation and firm's day care centres), in E. Singer and K. Tijdens (eds.) *Uit en Thuis (At Home and Out)*, Van Arkel, Utrecht, pp. 97–110.

van Amstel, R. J. and van den Berg, T. (1991) *Evaluatie Stimuleringsregeling Positieve Actie voor Vrouwen, Interrimrapportage 1990 (Evaluation of the Policy on Positive Action for Women, Report 1990)*, Ministry of Social Affairs and Employment, The Hague.

ENDNOTES

[1] The data in this chapter are based on labour force statistics from the Central Bureau of Statistics (CBS) in The Hague, and on wages statistics from the Wages Service (LTD) from the Ministry of Social Affairs in The Hague.

6.

GERMANY

Camilla Krebsbach-Gnath and Ariane Berthoin Antal

INTRODUCTION

Until 3 October 1990, the date of German reunification, there were 61.3 million people living in the Federal Republic of Germany,[1] 29.3 million men (48%) and 31.8 million women (52%) (Volkszählung, 1987). Since that date there has been an increase in population of 16.4 million people, 8.5 million women and 7.9 million men, citizens of the former German Democratic Republic (Winkler, 1990, p. 16). What are the implications for women in business of this major merger of two labour forces, coming from two different economic and social systems? It is still too early to tell, because the formal process of reunification does not yet allow for a unified look at the situation of, development of and outlook for women in German business. Political and economic backgrounds, developed on both sides over the last 40 years, are still too different. However, by comparing data on women in East and West German business, one can lay the groundwork for a better insight into the impact, effectiveness and reliability of factors promoting or hindering their equal opportunity in business.

WOMEN IN EMPLOYMENT IN WEST AND EAST

In 1987 10.1 million women aged 15–65 years were working in West Germany, that is 38.7% of all working people. Of these, 5.9 million (55%) were married, and approximately 2.3 million (22%) had children younger than 15 years. Although the labour force participation rate[2] of women has not changed significantly, as it has in other industrialized countries since the 1960s (1960 49%; 1987 54%), there has been a dramatic change in special age groups as Table 1 shows.

Despite economic and employment difficulties since the middle of

Table 1 Labour force participation rate of women in West Germany

Age (years)	Total		Married	
	1987	1961	1987	1961
25–30	67.2	52.8	57.2	40.4
30–35	62.2	44.1	54.7	36.0
35–40	62.5	45.1	56.7	37.2
40–45	63.2	45.2	58.0	37.7
45–50	58.8	41.5	54.1	34.6

Source: BMJFFG, 1989; p. 32.

the 1970s, the absolute number of working women has increased in West Germany. This is mainly due to the increase of part-time work which has doubled since 1972 (BMJFFG, 1989, p. 32). In 1989 23% of all working women had part-time work (BMJFFG, 1990, p. 3).

The picture is somewhat different in East Germany. Here the labour force participation rate of women has dramatically increased from 1955 (52%) to 1989 (78.1%). When female apprentices and students are included, the rate rises to as high as 91.2% in 1989. The increase was visible in all age groups (Winkler, 1990, pp. 63, 64). The working woman, or rather the working mother, in East Germany is the rule and the role model.

Even as more and more women have entered working life in East and West Germany, sex segregation of occupations appears to remain a fact of life in both systems.

In 1987 67% of all working women in West Germany were concentrated in 10 occupational groups. Most of them occupied traditional administrative and secretarial jobs, followed by sales personnel and jobs in health care.

Furthermore, women are still concentrated at the lower levels of company hierarchies, and they are overrepresented in routine work, where the introduction of new technology has and will still have a severe impact in replacing people. Women are underrepresented in technical occupations and in management jobs, where they hold about 6% of all positions. At the level of managing board members in public companies (*Aktiengesellschaften*) women accounted for only 0.7% of the positions in 1988 (Hochstätter, 1989, p. 47), and 0.3% of supervisory board members. In comparison, companies owned by women tend to have more women in management positions: according to a study conducted by the Association of (West German) Women Business Owners in 1989, 10% of the upper management positions were held by women (Hübner, 1989, p. 19).

In 1987 more than half of the 10 million working women in West Germany were white-collar workers (57.9%), about one-third had blue-collar jobs, and 5% were working as civil servants. Around 6% were self-employed or entrepreneurs. The number of self-employed women is increasing in the labour market. While in 1975 1 company out of every 10 was founded by a woman, it is today 1 out of 3. In 1989 1 company out of every 6 was led by a woman (BMJFFG, 1989, p. 34).

Although there has been some improvement, there is still a tremendous income gap between men and women. In 1988 the income of female blue-collar workers was on average still 30% lower than that of their male colleagues (40% in 1960). Female white-collar workers earned on average DM 2,989 per month (404 DM in 1960), while their male colleagues earned DM 4,654 (723 DM in 1960). In 1987 approximately 66% of all working men had a monthly net income of DM 1,800 and more, in comparison with 23% of women. The income gap also exists in upper hierarchical levels. Not only are women in management scarce, they do not receive the same pay as their male counterparts: their salaries are roughly 20% lower than those of male managers (Wirtschaftswoche, 1985, p. 70). The income gap is probably attributable primarily to structural differences, namely the fact that women work fewer hours than men and in jobs and sectors which are lower paid. The issue of 'comparable worth' is now being raised in West Germany, largely as a result of pressure from the European Community (EC) (BMJFFG, 1989, p. 37).

Sex inequality also makes itself felt in the unemployment figures. Since 1970 the unemployment rate of women has been disproportionately higher than that of men in West Germany. In 1990 48.6% of all unemployed were women and 8.4% of all working women were unemployed, while the comparable rate for men was 6.3% (BMJFFG, 1991).

The labour market in East Germany also shows significant signs of sex segregation, although along somewhat different lines than in the West. Exact comparisons between East and West are not possible, because the East German definition of the 'working class', which was valid until 1989, had an impact on the way statistical data were compiled and categorized. Nevertheless, the *Frauenreport 90* (Winkler, 1990), the first solid study on the situation of women in East Germany to be published after the opening of the East clearly shows that:

- Women are concentrated in specific economic sectors such as PTT (in 1989 69% of all employed in this sector were women), trade (71.9%) and the 'non-producing sector'[3] (72.6%). The light, textile, food producing and electronic industries are the main female-dominated sectors in industry. This pattern has not changed significantly over the past 20 years (Winkler, 1990, p. 66).
- Women are concentrated in routine jobs, they lack the power of decision-making and form the lower levels of company hierarchies. However, since the 1950s the percentage of women in management positions has increased although mostly in those areas where women have traditionally worked and are still employed: in education,

healthcare and trade almost two-thirds of managerial functions are held by women; in light industry or in services 40–50% of all managers are female. In transport and local government the percentage is still approximately 25%, and in heavy industry, construction, and science women in management are still a minority. But these initially impressive figures have to be interpreted with care: 'women are mostly employed in lower and middle management positions, in top positions they are still the exception' (Winkler, 1990, p. 95; our translation).

- Part-time work is not unusual in East Germany: in 1989 27.1% of all working women were part-time workers. The percentage has almost doubled since 1960 (14.9%), although the 'peak' was in the mid-1970s, when in 1975 32.6% of all women employed were working 25–35 hours per week.
- Working hours, working in low level jobs and in female domains are all factors which have led to a significant income gap between women and men, as Table 2 shows.
- Unemployment was officially unknown in East Germany before 1990. Since reunification, it has risen very significantly, and has affected more women than men. As of 1 January 1992 61.6% of the 1.3 million unemployed in the East were women.[4]

Comparing the situation of women in East and West, one gets the impression that, although there are differences, the basic patterns are very similar. Is the East compared to the West just 'more of the same'? Or have the different situations led to different attitudes?

EDUCATION AND VOCATIONAL TRAINING

Education and vocational training are important prerequisites for quali-

Table 2 Percentage of East German women on different pay scales, 1988 (full-time jobs only)

Pay scale (DM/month)	Percentage of women
400–500	63.1
500–600	73.9
600–700	77.7
700–800	72.4
800–900	60.7
900–1,000	45.3
1,000–1,100	36.9
1,100–1,200	32.5
1,200–1,500	28.2
1,500–1,700	17.0
Over 1,700	15.7

Source: Winkler (1990) *Frauenreport 90*.

fied employment, and in these areas the situation of women has changed dramatically over the past two decades. Today almost half of the East German university students are women (48.6% in 1989; 25.2% in 1960). In West Germany the percentage rose from 30.2% in 1972 to 38% in 1987. But at university — and, as will be shown later, also in vocational training — the basis is laid for the sex-segregated labour market.

In 1987 11.8% of all engineering students at West German universities were women (4% in 1983). In law, economics and social sciences (38.6% on 1987) as well as in mathematics and natural sciences (31.4%) the percentage is significantly higher, yet there is no equal representation. Women are concentrated in arts, languages, cultural science and sports (60.6% in 1987), and in 1987 71.8% of all students wanting to become teachers were female (BMJFFG, 1989, p. 24). It is significant that the most popular degree for both men and women is economics, and that women now account for almost 40% of law students: both courses of study lead into management in Germany, where there is no MBA degree.

The increase in the number of women graduates and their expansion into areas more suited to management careers in the public and private sectors might lead to a scenario where the younger generations of women will achieve higher ranks than their mothers. However, one has to take into account that higher education is no guarantee of employment, let alone access to management positions. In fact, female university graduates in West Germany are suffering from higher unemployment rates than male graduates: although women represent 25% of the working population holding a university degree, they account for 45% of the unemployed with a degree (BMJFFG, 1990, p. 38).

A similar pattern is visible in East German universities. Women are concentrated in educational and teaching professions (73% in 1989; 62.2% in 1971) and in literature and languages (62.2% in 1989; 63.4% in 1971). In economics their percentage has increased from 38.4% in 1971 to 66.7% in 1989, yet in medicine it decreased from 70.7% in 1971 to 55.2% in 1989. In mathematics and natural sciences, however, women are no longer underrepresented (46% in 1989) and in technical sciences (comparable to the West German engineering) their percentage increased from 15.8% in 1971 to 25.3% in 1989 (Winkler, 1990, p. 43).

The system of vocational training is much more extensive in both West and East Germany than in most other countries, accounting for 60% of school-leavers. Since 1970 the percentage of working women who have completed vocational training has risen in West Germany from 38% to 65% in 1985 (compared with 65% to 77% for men during the same period). Women without vocational training are mostly to be found in the age groups of 50 years and older and in rural areas. In East Germany 86% of working women have completed occupational training (Radtke, 1989, p. 12).

However, a closer look indicates that the problem of sex-specific segmentation has its roots also in vocational training: here women are also concentrated in selected areas. Although 355 occupations qualified for apprenticeships, women choose (or in a socialist planning economy were rather chosen for) only in a range of 28 (Meyer, 1991, p. 1,329). In 1987 95.2% of all hairstylist apprentices were female (75.2% in West Germany) and 95% of all East German apprentices training as sales personnel in retail were women (around 85% in West Germany). Office and administrative jobs are also female domains (Winkler, 1990, p. 44; BMJFFG, 1989, p. 18). In training for technical occupations, women are still a minority.

INFRASTRUCTURE AND LAWS FACILITATING THE BALANCE BETWEEN WORK AND FAMILY

The constitutions of both the Federal Republic of Germany and of the former German Democratic Republic include articles specifically recognizing the equality of men and women. But as the selection of data provided above shows, there is still a big gap between intention and reality. There are two particularly significant differences between the two societies in this respect that are relevant for the integration of women into business and their career development. Firstly, the constitutional 'right to work' in East Germany was actually a 'requirement to work': the manpower needs of the economy were so high that the state could not afford to have women not working. Secondly, as East German sociologists now point out, 'the equality of women was treated as achieved in the official GDR propaganda, the women's question was seen as resolved' (Meier, 1990a, p. 10; our translation). The subject of the existing inequality between men and women could not be raised, as critical voices in general were not tolerated and 'the placement of taboos on problems on the one hand and the dissemination of success stories on the other, blocked the development of critical consciousness, of a women's consciousness in the GDR' (Nickel, 1990, p. 8; our translation). So the women's movement, that in the West was vocal and effective in pushing the issue of inequality to the fore and getting it integrated into political parties' and labour unions' agendas, had no equivalent in the East.

A number of laws in the Code of Civil Law in West Germany (*Bürgerliches Gesetzbuch*) impose equality into working life, but there is no specific anti-discrimination law. A proposal for such a law was officially discussed at a hearing of the German *Bundestag* in 1982 and again in the late 1980s, but no political majority could be obtained to pass it. The compliance with and the improvement of existing laws was and still is officially regarded as sufficient to achieve equal opportunity in working life.

As early as 1952, the West German Parliament (*Bundestag*) passed the Maternity Protection Law (*Mutterschutzgesetz*), which regulates maternity leave and the protection against dismissal for pregnant women. This law has been revised and improved over the subsequent decades. Today fully paid maternity leave is possible for 6 weeks before and 8 weeks after the birth of a child. Since 1 January 1992 mothers or fathers have the right to stay at home after that period of time for 36 months to care for the baby. The government pays them compensation (*Erziehungsgeld*) for 24 months, the level of which is calculated according to income and not exceeding DM 600 per month. Non-working mothers are also entitled to this benefit. During this period of time the employee cannot be given notice. To date 97% of those eligible have taken the parental leave, but in only 1.5% of the cases has it been the father who has taken the leave, and 70% of fathers had been unemployed before doing so.

Since 1969 civil servants in West Germany have had the right to take up to 10 years of unpaid leave of absence if they have children under 16 years at home. Since 1974 working parents can take a paid leave of 5 days each year when their child younger than 8 years is sick.

Until 1990 the legal provisions for working mothers in East Germany were even better and included:

- fully paid maternity leave of 26 weeks;
- paid leave (with up to 90% of monthly net income) for 1 year after the birth of the first or second child and 18 months after the birth of the third child;
- paid leave to care for sick children of up to 6 weeks per year;
- an entitlement of 1 paid day off per month ('household day') for working women who were married or had children under the age of 18 or were single and older than 40, and for single fathers with children up to 18 years.

The quantity of childcare provisions was excellent in East Germany: 94% of all children aged 3−6 years were in nursery school (79% in West Germany). Of all children aged 6−10, 82% had daycare (*Kinderhort*) after school, whereas in West Germany only 4% of children aged 6−10 years needing after-school care receive it. As West German primary schools − unlike schools in most other European countries − are only open for 4−5 hours in the morning, and hours can vary from day to day, parents obviously have difficulties if both work full time and they do not want their small children to stay at home alone.

In particular, the latter figures explain why more East German women were working compared with the West: the infrastructure allowed for a better combination of work and family. Of course, one has to take into account that East Germany urgently needed a high female partici-pation rate in the labour force, and the government provided the infrastructure that enabled women to participate fully.

As the figures on women in employment in clearly show, quantities, i.e. the high female participation rate in East Germany, do not necessarily change the qualitative structure of the female workforce. In East Germany, too, women are still working in 'female domains', on lower hierarchical levels, rarely in top management positions. More needs to be done to equalize opportunities for working men and women. There is still the need for private and public sector activities and a change of attitudes to change the qualitative opportunities of working women.

PUBLIC AND PRIVATE SECTOR ACTIVITIES

Examples of particular public and private sector activities which are changing the qualitative structure of opportunities for women in business are not known from East Germany. In West Germany, however, a variety of projects and recommendations have been launched since the end of the 1970s and beginning of the 1980s (for further information see BMJFFG, 1989). For instance:

- a programme funded by the federal government to open up male-dominated jobs (*gewerblich technische Berufe*) to women (1978–1985);
- a project on vocational training for women to improve their job opportunities when new technologies are introduced (1987);
- several projects on the reintegration of women into working life after having stayed at home to bring up their children (since 1986);
- special computer courses for women (since 1987);
- development of a set of guidelines of equal opportunity measures for use in the public and private sectors (1984).

The results of these projects showed (not surprisingly for some observers!) that women do have the capabilities to work in so-called untraditional jobs, that they can meet the challenges of new technologies, and that employers can do a lot to remove the barriers preventing equal opportunities in all areas and levels of work.

Yet – as the general mood in Germany is against regulating on such issues – guidelines and project results and recommendations are submitted purely for voluntary application. And as long as employers do not acknowledge the need to strengthen their efforts to change the situation, progress will be very slow.

There are signs of pressure for accelerating change, however. Political pressure in favour of women has increased over the last decade. Labour unions as well as the political parties have all made equality in living and working conditions one of their top issues. And the power of a 'public issue' has surely helped bring about the following changes.

- Some major companies have established the policy of parental leave (unpaid leave of up to 7 years) with the guarantee of a job when returning to the company to work. Some of them have added provisions for the parent to keep in touch with colleagues and changes at the workplace, through seminars and vacation work. It is no surprise that the majority of applicants are women and therefore provisions such as these agreements could prove a mixed blessing, if (a) men do not take the leave, thereby making the recruitment of women an even greater 'risk' for a department, and (b) management then feels that it has 'done enough' to help women balance children and work and does not try to introduce other measures or organizational changes.[5]

- In 1986 the federal government passed the 'Guidelines on the occupational promotion of women in the federal administration' (*Richtlinie zur beruflichen Förderung von Frauen in der Bundesverwaltung*). These guidelines, which have also been adopted by public administrations in several states and large cities, cover measures to increase the recruitment, promotion and further training of women, and measures designed to balance work and family responsibilities (e.g. part-time work). The need for strong measures in public administration is obvious, since women are no better represented in the management ranks here than in the private sector in Germany.

One of the key elements in the policy provisions at this time is the requirement that all government agencies identify a person or group as 'equal opportunities officer' to monitor developments that affect women in the organizations. Unfortunately, these officers have not always been given the necessary support and competencies. However, where they have been taken seriously, the manifold barriers to equalizing women's opportunities have become clearer and concrete solutions are being worked out in practice (Bulmann *et al.*, 1990).

A first report on the results was issued in 1990 (Deutscher Bundestag, 1990) and showed that:

- more women are participating in occupational training courses;
- more men and women are choosing family-oriented working hours (flexitime, part-time, etc.);
- the situation of women in top positions has not really changed;
- the consciousness on the issue has increased as well as the readiness to work for change.

Although, as the report on the results points out, there is still a lot to be done, the public sector has pioneered change by implementing these guidelines.

CHANGE OF ATTITUDES

Although the legal framework and the level of skills among women have improved over the past decades, and in spite of the fact that more is known about the mechanisms of equal opportunity as a result of research and pilot projects, change towards real equality in working life is rather slow. The mind-sets, the 'software' in the form of attitudes and the behaviour of men and women as employers and employees and as partners in private life, are not keeping pace with the rate of change in laws and needs of the labour force. It is therefore worth looking briefly at such questions as: What are the attitudes of German women towards work? What are the attitudes of employers? And, do men and women share their private work?

Surveys show that, as was the case in the 1950s, women today work mainly 'to earn money', but the aspect of 'satisfaction' is today more significant than the aspect of 'necessity'. Working *and* having a family is for the majority of young women the most favourable option for life, the either/or decision has lost its importance in West Germany (Schmidtchen, 1984). In 1959 only 57% of men were in favour of their wives working; by 1979 the percentage had already increased to 73%. In East Germany women feel that work is a central part of their identity: it provides for their economic independence, self-determination and independent life planning (Winkler, 1990, p. 80).

So, women want to work and men no longer object. But the family is still the female domain, although men have increased their small share in household work (Table 3).

In-depth interviews, however, show that these figures reflect more the 'verbal attitude' of men, less their actual behaviour. The 'dual burden' (*Doppelbelastung*) is still a fact for the majority of women (Table 4). Although relatively more East German men participate in household work, the pattern is the same as in West Germany. A real sharing does not exist (Winkler, 1990, p. 127 ff.).

Table 3   Male participation in housework in West Germany (%)

	1975	1983
Never	51	30
Once in a while	38	48
Often	8	16

Source: Hartenstein *et al*. (1988).

Table 4   Men's and women's stress ratings of daily housework

Stress level	Women (%)	Men (%)
Very strong	5	1
Rather strong	13	5
Moderate	60	29
Low	17	47
Not worth mentioning	4	19

Source: Winkler (1990) *Frauenreport 90*, p. 129.

Employers do recognize that the labour market is sex segregated, but they attribute this primarily to 'tradition'. In a representative survey on hiring practices of employers and job opportunities for women, two-thirds of all company respondents stated that women/men work in female/male jobs because 'women/men have always worked in these jobs' (Sozialforschungsstelle Dortmund, 1988). More than half of all companies surveyed believe that only men/women were qualified for these particular male/female jobs.

Since the majority of companies do not believe that they are discriminating against women and 'women's lack of stress stability, qualification or self-assertiveness' is not seen as a reason for their not climbing up the corporate ladder, it seems only logical that three-quarters of all companies must believe that 'women's responsibilities for the family are the main barriers holding them back from top and/or managing positions' (Sozialforschungsstelle Dortmund, 1988). Asked what they as a company could do to improve equal opportunities for women, most companies see little that they can do themselves. Instead, they point to the responsibilities of the educational institutions and to role modelling in family life. The majority of top managers reject corporate affirmative action plans.

OUTLOOK

Given the facts and figures of today and the experiences and achievements of working women in East and West Germany over the last decades, what will their future look like in a united Germany at the turn of the century? There are now some facts supporting a scenario that could be characterized as 'forward to the past'. In other words, it is quite possible that the situation for women in business might worsen and inequality of opportunities intensify again.

The labour force in East Germany is suffering an extraordinarily high level of unemployment with 1.3 million out of work at the beginning of 1992 and it is probably not surprising that the female unemployment rate is higher than that of men. Women accounted for half of the labour force, but at the beginning of 1992 they accounted for 61.6% of the registered unemployed in East Germany (and it is estimated that the number of unregistered women is higher still). It has been reported in several German newspapers that some East German women are actually welcoming the opportunity to take a break from employment, but this seems to us to be only anecdotal evidence with limited relevance. Considering how central paid work, as a part of their identity, has been for East German women, it is unlikely that many are choosing to leave the labour market willingly. The fact that more and more company-owned and public kindergartens have been closed is certainly contributing to forcing women out of the labour market.

There are various forecasts of how long it will take to revive the economy in former East Germany, but the majority of them expect that by the end of the century a significant turnaround will have been achieved. But what will happen during the transition period? Historically, such economic conditions have squeezed women out of the labour market. The well-established mechanisms, whereby men tend to hire, keep and promote other men, reinforce themselves during such times.

But there are also facts supporting a different scenario, possibly the opposite trend, that of strengthening efforts to equalize opportunities further. There is reason to hope that women just will not accept the sweeping away of their achievements. Energy for resistance will most likely be found with the women in East Germany. They may well start fighting for those things they had come to see as their birthrights: the right to work and the right to childcare. Furthermore, the current threat to the survival of these more extensive rights for women in the former GDR has strengthened the demands of West German women in these directions. If East German women can link forces with women in West Germany, who have already learned to fight for their rights the hard way, the combined energy could help to turn around the negative trends and make the achievements of today irreversible.

As the former Minister for Family, Women, and Youth in West Germany and current President of the *Bundestag*, Rita Süssmuth, says,

> A glance at history documents that women have never received their rights voluntarily, they have always had to fight to claim them....This is still true, and for this reason women should and must continue to fight for the necessary changes in our societal structures, because when we stop fighting, we cannot move anything anymore.
>
> (Süssmuth, 1989; p. 92, our translation)

There are other facts that support the scenario of a trend for progressive change. The active networking of women, belonging to different political parties, labour unions, professional associations and other interest groups, has intensified over the last few years and this might add fuel to the energy working for change. All political parties have targeted women voters, particularly those aged under 40, and have made equal opportunity an issue. All analysis shows that they will strengthen their efforts for these voters. Furthermore, Article 31 of the Unification Treaty stipulates that government should further develop equal rights and anti-discrimination legislation, as well as legislation that enables women and men to combine employment and family life.

But standards formulated at the political level, necessary as they are, cannot change reality if they are not translated into practical requirements. Organizations, and especially managers, must be required to set reasonable targets for the quantitative and qualitative employment of women — just as they do for other management tasks — and then be held accountable for achieving those goals. These requirements can achieve significant behavioural changes, particularly if the costs of not meeting the standards are high enough. The topic of equal opportunity will remain on the agenda in Germany as a goal to fight for — not only for a minority.

REFERENCES

Bulmann, E. *et al.* (1990) *Frauenförderung in der Kommunalen Verwaltung*, Gesprächskreis Frauenpolitik, Forschungsinstitut Friedrich Ebert Stiftung.

Bundesministerium für Jugend, Familie, Frauen und Gesundheit (BMJFFG) (1989) *Frauen in der Bundesrepulik Deutschland*, BMJFFG Bonn.

Bundesministerium für Jugend, Familie, Frauen und Gesundheit (BMJFFG) (1990) *Daten zur Frauenerwerbstätigkeit*. Unpublished paper, BMJFFG, Bonn, August.

Bundesministerium für Jugend, Familie, Frauen und Gesundheit (BMJFFG) (1991) *Daten zur Frauenarbeitslosigkeit*. Manuscript, BMJFFG, Bonn.

Deutscher Bundestag (1990) Bericht der Bundesregierung zur Umsetzung der *Richtlinie zur beruflichen Förderung von Frauen in der Bundesverwaltung*, Bundestagsdrucksache 11/8129, Bonn.

Hartenstein, W. U. A. (1988) *Geschlechtsrollen im Wandel: Partnerschaft und Aufgaben in der Familie*, Schriftenreihe des BMJFFG, Band 235.

Hochstätter, D. with Schünke, M. (1989) Cherchez la femme, *Wirtschaftswoche* no. 9, 24 February, pp. 46–61.

Hübner, E. (1989) Untitled statement published in *Forum: Frauen in Führungspositionen*, Proceedings of the seminar organized by the Social Democratic Party in Northrhine-Westphalia, Düsseldorf, 27 November, pp. 18–19.

Meier, U. (1990a) Women at work: The German Democratic Republic, *EWMD News*, no. 25, Autumn, pp. 5–6.

Meier, U. (1990b) Nachdem die Panzerschränke geöffnet sind..., *DJI Bulletin, Deutsches Jugendinstitut München*, no. 15, June, pp. 7–12.

Meyer, D. (1991) Einheitsverliererinnen, Zur Situation ostdeutscher Frauen, in *Blätter für Deutsche und Internationale Politik*, no. 11, Bonn, pp. 1326–33.

Nickel, H. M. (1990) Zur Sozialen Lage von Frauen in der DDR, in S. Gensior, F. Maier and G. Winter (eds.) *Soziale lage und Arbeit von Frauen in der DDR*, Working paper 1990–6 Arbeitskreis Sozialwissenschaftliche Arbeitsmarktforschung (SAMF), Paderborn.

Radtke, H. (1989) *Der Einsatz von Frauen in verantwortlichen Funktionen von Wissenschaft und Technik — Möglichkeiten und Grenzen*. Unpublished paper, Akademie der Wissenschaften der DDR, Institut für Soziologie und Sozialpolitik, 15 May.

Schmidtchen G. (1984) *Die Situation der Frau*, Berlin.

Sozialforschungsstelle Dortmund (1988) *Einstellungsverhalten von Arbeitgebern und Beschäftigungschancen von Frauen*, Dortmund.

Süssmuth, R. (1989) *Kämpfen und Bewegen: Frauenreden*, Herder Verlag Freiburg, Basel, Vienna.

Winkler, G. (ed.) (1990) *Frauenreport 90*, Report to the Beauftragte des Ministerrates für de Gleichstellung von Frauen und Männern, Dr Maria Beyer, Verlag die Wirtschaft, Berlin.

Wirtschaftswoche, *Frauen im Management: selten, tüchtig und unterbezahlt*, no. 18, 26 April.

ENDNOTES

[1] We use the terms 'East' and 'West' Germany here although the political terms applicable until 1990 were 'German Democratic Republic' and 'Federal Republic of Germany', respectively, and since reunification the former territory of East Germany is referred to as 'the new federal states'.

[2] Defined as the ratio of the female labour force to the total population of women aged 15–65.

[3] The term 'non-producing sector', although often used, is nowhere exactly defined in the official statistics of the former GDR. It includes, however, education, healthcare and parts of the federal government, the political parties and the security systems.

[4] Unpublished data obtained from the *Bundesministerium für Arbeit und Soziales*, Bonn.

[5] It may be a positive sign for change that when IBM Germany started with a remote office work organization for qualified employees at the beginning of 1992, the company found that demand on the part of both men and women for such work facilities was immediately greater than the number of fully equipped work stations foreseen for the programme.

7.

FRANCE

Jacqueline Laufer

INTRODUCTION

The status of women in the workplace in France has changed considerably over the last 20 years. This development is undoubtedly one of the most profound factors for change in French society as a whole, going hand-in-hand with the growth of the service sector, the transformation of family structures and the appearance of new modes of consumption.

Greater numbers of women are taking up a career and wishing to combine domestic and professional roles. They are also anxious, at least the younger ones among them, to have not only a job, which they look upon as a source of personal development and economic independence, but also a qualification and a career.

Although there are more and more women middle and senior managers, as well as teachers, doctors and lawyers, and although a few of them become government ministers or airline pilots, a great number of women remain in unskilled, low-paid or temporary jobs. The picture of women's status in the workplace can therefore only be one of contrasts and the stakes for women are very different according to their professional status, age, educational level and family situation.

The laws and measures which aim to implement greater equality of opportunity undoubtedly show that society as a whole recognizes women's right to play a full part in the world of work. Even if equal opportunity schemes drawn up by companies have only affected a limited number of women as such, they show that corporate preoccupation with better use of their human resources does now include women and should enable them to gain easier access to training, qualification and a career.

In a context where growing numbers of women with children are now working, the issue of combining professional and domestic roles seems to be a challenge shared by families, the state and companies. The domestic situation of working women appears to be a determining factor in women's capacity for commitment to their work. Beyond the crucial problem of childcare lies the issue of measures to be implemented to facilitate this combination of roles, particularly within companies.

THE EVOLUTION OF THE STATUS OF WOMEN IN EMPLOYMENT

Rapid and continuous growth of women's professional activity

For the last 30 years women's professional activity has grown unceasingly. Since 1962 the working population has increased by 4.2 million and four-fifths of this increase is due to women entering the job market. The number of working women has increased from 6.5 million in 1962 to 10.5 million in 1990 and today women make up 43.5% of the working population. In 1968 36.2% of women were in employment. This has now increased to 45.6% (INSEE, 1991).

There are many reasons for this evolution: the growth of salaried employment − 75.5% of working women are salary earners, 59% in the private sector and 41% in the public sector − changes in family structures, evolving lifestyles and consumer habits.

From an economic point of view, the growth of the service sector and administrative employment has undoubtedly furthered the progress of women's professional activity. At present, three-quarters of working women are employed in the service sector, an area where half of the employees are women, whereas only 27% of industrial sector jobs are held by women (Lacroix, 1990).

The rise in the level of women's employment is demonstrated by a very noticeable increase in the number of working mothers with one or two children. In 1979 64% of mothers with one child and 46% of mothers with two children were employed, whereas now 77.6% and 71.4% respectively are in the same situation. Thus, the traditional model of alternating domestic and professional roles characterized by cessation of salaried activity during the years devoted to the birth and upbringing of children, has been succeeded by a model of combined roles characterized by uninterrupted professional activity. This development means a relative similarity can be seen in work-related behaviour between men and women among the younger generation. Young women give up work for shorter periods of time, breaks in activity are more frequently work related, and those caused by unemployment have increased, relatively speaking. However, women's professional activity remains strongly influenced by the number of children they have: only 40% of women with three children are in employment (Desplanques and Saboulin, 1990).

The precariousness of women's employment

Despite this evolution, women's position in relation to the job market remains a specific one. Apart from the differences in levels of activity due to the number of children, women are more vulnerable to unemployment and occupy an important position in the development of new types of job status, particularly in the service sector.

With regard to unemployment, 12.2% of women compared with 7% of men were unemployed in 1991, and among young women the proportion is 24% as against 16% for men. Although women account for 44% of the working population, they represent 57% of the long-term unemployed. Since 1989 adult women constitute the only category among which unemployment continues to rise. Gender inequalities in unemployment grow more acute as the level of qualification decreases. In March 1989 38% of young women without formal qualifications were unemployed compared with 27% of young men. Women's greater vulnerability to unemployment is due both to the recent changes in those sectors of activity in which women are more numerous, for example the recent restructuring of the textile and clothing industries, and to the fact that women belong to the most fragile socioprofessional categories workwise, due mainly to their lower qualifications. Finally, the career guidance given to young women fails to prepare them for the professions most sought after by companies (INSEE, 1991).

New types of employment such as fixed-term contracts, temporary and part-time work have developed in response to the need for companies to be more flexible in managing their workforce. If women have succeeded in remaining on the job market despite the unemployment crisis, it is precisely because they have occupied a central position in the transformation of the dominant model of full-time salaried employment. They are present in greater numbers in new types of employment like part-time work and fixed-term contracts. The only exception is in the area of temporary work, which represents almost 3 million jobs in France today compared to 2 million in 1982, where women make up only one-third of personnel (Jacquier, 1990).

Part-time jobs, which make up 12% of salaried positions compared with 9% in 1982, and 80% of which are held by women, are particularly widespread in sectors such as the hotel industry, catering, cleaning and retail activities. This phenomenon also affects the public sector which accounts for one-third of part-time jobs. These are generally unskilled jobs and the proportion of women in part-time employment decreases as their educational level improves, but grows larger as their family responsibilities increase. In 1989 42.3% of working mothers with three children were in part-time employment (Belloc, 1987).

The unequal access of women to different professions

The unequal numbers of men and women in different professions and trades bear witness to the fact that women's mass entry into the job market has not been accompanied by a proportionate diversification of their occupations and points to the lasting nature of the sexual division of jobs, qualifications and roles (Huet, 1983).

Thus, only 20 professions account for 5% of working women while in 167 professions the percentage of women remains below 10%. There are only 20 professions where the percentage of men is less than 10%. Among the professions occupied by a majority of women are the following: childminder (100%), secretary (98%), nurse (92%), unskilled worker in the clothing industry (92%), clerical worker (78%), primary school teacher (77%), and shop assistant (78%).

This unequal distribution of the sexes is also found within professional categories. Thus women represent 20% of factory workers but account for only 12.9% of skilled workers and for 39.2% of unskilled industrial worker. However, they constitute 75% of employees and, among working women of 35 years of age, one in two belongs to this category.

Women have made most progress in middle management,[1] particularly in administrative positions where their numbers have increased

Table 1 Female staff by socioprofessional category

Socioprofessional category	Percentage of female population employed		Share of women in category's employment	
	1982	1989	1982	1989
Farmers	6.8	5.1	38.3	37.0
Manual workers	2.8	2.2	26.7	24.3
Retailers .	4.4	3.9	47.6	47.0
Heads of firms (≥ 10 persons)	0.2	0.2	15.6	16.4
Professionals	0.8	0.9	31.9	30.9
Civil service officials	0.6	0.6	22.9	23.5
Professors and scientific professions	1.7	2.4	42.7	17.7
Professionals in communication, media and entertainment	0.5	0.8	43.9	48.6
Administrative and commercial managers	1.1	1.7	19.1	25.0
Engineers and technical managers	0.3	0.5	6.4	9.8
Primary school teachers	5.8	5.5	64.1	62.4
Social work and health professionals	5.1	5.8	75.1	75.5
Middle-range civil servants	2.0	2.1	52.0	50.6
Administrative and commercial middle management	4.2	5.5	39.8	44.0
Technical staff	0.8	0.9	10.0	10.4
Foremen and supervisors	0.4	0.4	5.3	6.6
Civil service clerks	14.5	15.5	77.0	78.0
Police and military	0.2	0.3	4.3	6.5
Administrative clerks	17.8	17.2	77.6	81.4
Retail clerks	5.8	6.2	79.3	78.4
Skilled workers in industries	2.4	2.1	2.9	13.2
Workers in industries	3.2	6.3	39.2	38.0
Agricultural workers	0.9	0.5	23.4	19.7

Source: INSEE Employment Survey, 1989.

by 20% between 1975 and 1989. They account for more than 60% of accountants, executive secretaries and qualified professionals in insurance.

As regards administrative and commercial managers (19% in 1982 compared with 25% in 1989), they have made most progress in administrative positions. However, they are also progressing in new careers such as marketing, advertising, public relations, auditing, human resources and computing.

The sales and marketing functions in sectors where the products were traditionally considered to be technical and therefore 'masculine', such as computers and, to a lesser extent, cars, now employ a growing number of women middle and senior managers.

The proportion of women managers varies according to the sector of activity. Women have made more rapid progress in industry, increasing from 9% in 1980 to 14% in 1986, than in the service sector where they were already more numerous − from 29% in 1980 to 31.5% in 1986. In industry the presence of women among managerial staff is proportional to the feminization of the sector. Thus, in the textile and clothing industries 22% of executives are women, while in the petroleum and aeronautical industries, two sectors where women are underrepresented, only 5% of executives are women (Alexandre, 1990).

Women's progress in gaining access to the engineering profession should be emphasized, even if they account for only 9.8% of engineers and technical managers compared to 6.4% in 1982 (Marry, 1989). Women engineers, who make up 19% of engineering students, no longer dedicate themselves almost exclusively to research and teaching. The majority of women engineers have third-level qualifications, which is the case for only 38% of salary earners in this category, since many men have become engineers through internal promotion. They are also younger than their male colleagues, 29 years old on average compared with 39, and 65% of women engineers are under 35. They are still largely absent from traditionally male sectors such as the motor industry, mechanics and the building trade, but are asserting themselves in newer sectors more accessible to women such as chemistry, and computer industries and electronics. In addition, new technologies have facilitated their access to new activities such as production and quality control.

However, this ability to break into the world of technology and production techniques remains limited for women, except in the case of industrial workers. Only 6% of women are supervisors and foremen and too few women occupy new technology-linked jobs promised to be important developments in the future. While women are fairly numerous among research laboratory technicians (30%) and computer programmers (23%), they are very few in production functions in areas such as electronic construction, electronics and automation, where they account for only 2−4% of the technicians (CFDT, 1990a).

In conclusion, even though women have benefitted from the general improvement in the level of education among the workforce and from the decline in unskilled tasks performed by factory workers and employees, they remain overrepresented in these categories. A whole range of occupations remains the preserve of women. Childcare, cleaning, low-skilled administrative positions, social and health work, primary school teaching, all remain largely female professions. Finally, although women have made progress in management, this progress has been limited to middle management and they have not reached chief executive or senior executive positions.

With regard to the category of heads of companies, women account for 33% of directors, but as company size increases, the number of women decreases: only 6% of heads of companies employing 10 or more salary earners are women.

It should, however, be noted that growing numbers of women are setting up their own businesses. In 1986, they accounted for 26% of entrepreneurs setting up industrial enterprises. Of these female entrepreneurs 43% set up textile and clothing businesses but others were in sectors such as building, commerce, car repairs or furniture, where few women are represented (Ministère du Travail et de l'Emploi, 1991).

Since women tend to work in low-skilled jobs and are more numerous in areas where salaries are lowest, such as textiles, clothing and the retail trade, and as they occupy positions with fewer responsibilities, they receive on average 25% less pay than men; women managers receive 30% less. In addition, large wage discrepancies remain even when the level of qualification is the same for men and women: 20–30% for executives, 15% for middle managers, 21% for skilled workers, 20% for unskilled workers and 12% for supervisory staff.

Several factors come into play here: in the case of factory workers or employees, the differences in basic salary, the number of working hours, the amount of overtime worked, length of service and the amount of allowances or bonuses. In the case of managerial staff, women's lesser salary-negotiating capacities, the fact that they frequently occupy administrative positions which are less visible in terms of performance, a lesser ability to make the most of their qualifications and diplomas due to family roles, and slower career development are the main contributory factors (Rotbart, 1990).

As far as pension schemes are concerned French schemes in the private sector include a basic allowance from social security contributions and eventual additional allowances from various types of retirement funds. Due to the smaller amount of the 'reversed' pensions women are entitled to after the death of their husbands or after career breaks, women receive on average half the mean monthly income of men. However, for those women who have completed a full career their income is on average 36% smaller than men's; this reflects the difference in average salary of men and women throughout working life.

The educational status of women

The difference in positions held by men and women reflects the traditional division in male and female roles. Generally speaking, women are at the lower end of the scale in each profession. Men devise, invent and issue orders. Women carry out orders and assist men.

These differences also reflect the way in which education and training contribute to the continuation or to the development of this division of labour between the sexes. Even though the general educational level of girls is higher than that of boys − for the last 20 years more girls than boys have taken the *Baccalauréat* − the differences in career orientation for boys and girls remain.

While 42% of girls compared with 32% of boys pursue their studies to *Baccalauréat* level, 70% of girls go on to take a literary, administrative or medicosocial-type *Baccalauréat* and only 22% a scientific or technical one. This reflects the lack of diversification in career guidance for girls (Baudelot and Establet, 1990).

The same phenomenon continues in short-term third-level education. In IUTs (*Instituts Universitaire de Technologie*) − where girls make up 37% of students − they choose tertiary subjects − information and communication, legal or social work careers. Biology and chemistry, 50% of students studying the subject are girls, are the only scientific area in which girls are well represented, whereas only 8.5% study mechanical engineering.

In the universities, where girls constitute 53.6% of the student body, they form the majority of students in arts subjects (70%), pharmacy (64%) and law (55.7%), but only 46.5% study medicine and 34.5% science subjects.

At the *Grandes Ecoles* girls account for 19.3% of total students, an increase of 7.5% since 1987. Although they constitute the great majority of students in liberal arts schools, in interpreting (80%), *Beaux-Arts* (60%), and the *Ecole du Louvre* (80%) (fine arts), they have also made considerable progress in business schools, where they now constitute 35−50% of the student body according to the standard of the school. They are, however, still underrepresented in engineering schools since on average only 19% of students are women. Chemistry and food technology are the areas which attract most women and technical and industrial subjects the ones which attract the least.

However, this phenomenon of differentiation between male and female education is most acute in the area of vocational training, and with serious consequences for young women's careers. Secretaries can hope to find employment in service sector areas with an 80% female presence but the 95% women holders of CAP (first-level vocational diploma) hairdressing diplomas will not be so fortunate given the rate of unemployment in this occupation. On the other hand, boys, who account for 95% of technical CAP diplomas (electronics, mechanics, building), will find skilled employment in industry (INSEE, 1991).

Company policies and the status of women

Although the status of women in employment is rooted in a whole series of cultural factors such as the division of labour and social roles along sexual lines, family structures and stereotypes about 'men's' and 'womens' occupations, company employment policies as such also affect women's status.

Because women's qualifications are often ill-suited to companies' most pressing needs for qualified personnel, and because of long-standing stereotypes about womens' skills and roles, they are often given positions which do not match their qualifications or ones in which they merely carry out orders or assist men. These types of job are supposed to correspond to their abilities and motivations but make it difficult for women to achieve any worthwhile career development once they are in them (Laufer, 1986).

Women are often perceived to be less interested in qualifications and careers (Laufer, 1982; Battagliola, 1984) and are less able to take advantage of company training schemes and, more importantly, of training courses leading to new skills (Divisia and Cagan, 1990).

The emphasis now placed on the development of human resources as a factor for improved business performance, the determination of companies to evaluate more accurately the types of skills they require to fulfil their economic objectives, and the introduction of new technologies in the industrial and administrative sectors, are key elements which could provide valuable opportunities for women factory workers and secretaries.

However, as far as new technologies are concerned, certain studies underline the fact that far from representing an opportunity for women to obtain more highly skilled posts in new professional environments, they could even constitute a new threat of exclusion. Given that technology has always been a male preserve and a source of power, the introduction of new technologies could help to strengthen the division of men's and women's respective roles and skills. Thus, in certain industrial sectors, the introduction of new technologies has led either to deskilling and mass entry of women as in the case of keyboard operators in the printing industry or to limited access for women to certain skilled jobs in the textile or automobile industries. The development of new technical skills would then work to men's advantage (Hirata and Rogerat, 1988).

In the banking and insurance sectors, which have been transformed by computers and office automation (40% of personnel use VDUs), two-thirds of women working on VDUs are in clerical positions while only 22% are technicians whereas the largest group of male employees are the technicians.

As far as France's 900,000 secretaries are concerned, new technologies may provide an opportunity to reduce time spent on typing and to acquire new skills but a great deal remains to be done to ensure that secretaries, whose profession is rapidly changing to that of genuine personal assistants with some functional expertise, can gain proper recognition of these new skills and enjoy real careers (Mandon, 1987).

Although women's presence is taken for granted in secretarial and administrative functions, it continues to provoke reactions or at least questions as soon as women begin to make their presence felt in areas, jobs or careers where men are still in the majority: the male foreman supervising a young women who recently completed training wonders about her ability to be a 'real skilled worker' (Laufer, 1990); workers in the book trade refuse to consider women keyboard operators as their professional equals (Maruani and Nicole, 1989); computer salesmen and product managers worry about 'too many' women entering their profession, thus reducing its prestige (Laufer, 1982); managers are surprised by the fact that their secretaries actually have professional ambitions. Finally, there is much evidence that on the whole both men and women subordinates generally prefer to work for a male boss (Serdjenian, 1988).

Thus, the greater continuity of women's professional activity and their growing presence in areas which were formerly the sole preserve of men have not put an end to covert discrimination against women in corporate personnel policies or to opposition by men − and women − to women acquiring positions which demand greater technical skills and/or greater responsibility and leadership.

Women in the public service

With more than 1 million women in the public service − 51.2% of personnel − the state is the biggest employer of women in France. Although numbers vary according to the sector of activity − 5% in the police and 73.7% in the health sector − and despite the fact that principles of equality in recruitment and career progression are enshrined in the public service charter, the situation differs little from that of the private sector. Generally speaking, the higher up one goes in the ranks, the fewer women one finds. They make up 10% of grade A civil servants, the highest category, 30% of grade B, and 75% of grades C and D. (Grade A corresponds to senior executives, grade B to middle managers and grades C and D to clerical positions.) The situation varies according to the ministry since in the Ministry of Education women account for 50% of grade A civil servants, compared with 10% in the Ministry of Industry, and for 75% of grade B, as the great majority of primary school teachers belong to this grade.

EQUAL EMPLOYMENT OPPORTUNITIES FOR MEN AND WOMEN: LEGAL MEASURES AND POSITIVE ACTIONS

The legal framework of equal opportunity

The increasing numbers of women on the job market and the acknowledgement of the many obstacles blocking the way to real equality for men and women have resulted in France, as in other European countries, in several laws being passed, notably those relating to equal pay (1972) and to professional equality for men and women, which was passed in July 1983. In this egalitarian logic, the only 'specific' measures deal with maternity leave on the one hand and, on the other, with affirmative actions designed to ensure greater equality of opportunity[2] (Laufer, 1984).

Given the inefficiency of the principles of equal pay and non-discrimination, the main purpose of the 1983 law was to provide businesses with tools to evaluate the work situation of women and to promote equal opportunity, through comparative employment status reports and positive action schemes.

Each year companies must draw up a report on the comparative status of women and men in relation to recruitment, training, promotion, qualifications, working conditions and pay. This report must be discussed with the elected work council. An assessment of this first measure shows that most companies have not taken full advantage of this opportunity to examine their employment policies relating to women, even though several companies have exceeded the target set by the law by carrying out general sociological studies on the status of their women employees or by setting up working groups comprising members of different personnel categories (Laufer, 1987).

The second tool concerns the positive action schemes which companies are encouraged to negotiate with trades unions to improve the status of women in areas such as recruitment, training, promotion or working conditions. Financial aid can be granted by the state if the proposed measures are judged to be 'exemplary'. In addition, since 1987, firms can sign contracts concerning the training and promotion of individual women. These contracts are designed to promote a greater number of women in positions or skills traditionally occupied by men or in jobs linked to new technologies where women are underrepresented. This initiative is directed at small and medium-sized businesses in particular and leads to government financial support for the training schemes.

Measures to promote equality of opportunity in the workplace

About 35 firms,[3] including Moulinex, Amora, Superba, Cogema, Belin, IBM and Roussel Uclaf, have implemented positive action schemes, the majority of them through negotiating with the trades unions a *plan d'égalité* as defined in the 1983 law. This relatively low figure would indicate that most companies do not feel it necessary to include equality of opportunity among their objectives or at the very least do not wish to assert a specific policy concerning this matter. As for the public sector, it has not played the leading role in this area which might have been expected of it (Ruault, 1989). Only four public sector companies, which often have a high technological profile, have negotiated positive action schemes. As for the trades unions, they have done little up to now to promote a matter they felt largely unfamiliar with (Doniol-Shaw *et al.*, 1989). With very few exceptions, company management has initiated action schemes and guided their content.

The measures covered by these schemes include all the areas relating to the status of women in employment: recruitment, career development training, compatibility of domestic and professional roles, and awareness raising among employees and management of the issue of equal opportunity.

Recruitment and greater access to positions available within the company
In this area, action schemes have striven to readjust recruitment policies in favour of women executives, engineers and technicians to jobs where they were underrepresented and to provide more information concerning vacant positions within the company so as to encourage more women to apply for them.

Career development
Action schemes have helped to promote women to male-dominated managerial positions and to define new career paths enabling women working in administrative functions to enter marketing and sales functions, and to promote the more widespread use of individual career and performance evaluations. They have also led to a more systematic inclusion of women in career development programmes and to the setting up of working groups to identify and evaluate the changing content of secretarial functions and the consequences for future secretarial skills.

Training
Training is crucial to equal opportunity schemes. Efforts here have been directed towards factory workers and employees. Faced with technological changes and a growing demand for higher quality in their products or services, the companies have taken it upon themselves to transform or upgrade the skills of large numbers of female factory workers and clerical staff ill-prepared to confront technological changes or to take on positions requiring initiative and greater responsibility. Thus in several companies the schemes have involved between 100 and 200 carefully selected unskilled factory workers from each company, who were able to gain a CAP (first-level vocational) diploma after

400 hours of training, allowing them to take up jobs on semi-automated assembly and packaging lines. In some other firms, all employees below secondary school level were given courses in economics, banking and communication which could grant them access to further managerial training so as to allow them to take up managerial positions in administrative and marketing areas.

Greater compatibility of domestic and professional roles
The taking into account of maternity leave for seniority bonuses and the introduction of an interview with the employee's immediate superior after her return from maternity leave to evaluate her career development, have allowed motherhood to be integrated into women's career development in a positive manner. Access to part-time work and measures which need to be taken in the areas of training and career development to ensure that this type of job does not penalize women unduly, are also mentioned in some positive action schemes.

Awareness raising among personnel of the importance of
equal opportunities
The studies carried out by certain companies among personnel, working groups and meetings of company personnel directors constituted essential tools to raise awareness of the importance of equal opportunities and have allowed suggestions thus gathered to be included in company policies. In one of the firms an internal information sheet reviews equal opportunity initiatives taken in the various companies in the group in order to encourage new ones (Laufer, 1990).

More than 250 individual affirmative action contracts have been drawn up, which shows the usefulness of individual schemes within the framework of small and medium-sized businesses. They are mainly concerned with factory workers and technicians and the training schemes needed to help them obtain more skilled positions. Until recently this measure has only marginally affected women managers.[4]

Direct government action to promote equality of opportunity

Various measures and actions have aimed to promote equal opportunity on the job market by reducing unemployment and helping women to re-enter the job market in the context of greater unemployment among women, especially younger ones. Specific actions have been taken for women within general retraining programmes devoted to the unemployed. Regional plans to reduce unemployment amongst women have been set up (Secrétariat d'Etat chargé des Droits des Femmes, 1990).

Financial assistance in setting up small businesses has figured prominently in government policies concerning job seekers. More women have taken advantage of this measure and, in 1989, they represented

24% of beneficiaries and 28% of businesses established[5] (Ministère du Travail et de l'Emploi, 1991).

Training schemes have been set up to encourage diversification of vocational and professional orientation among girls. Other schemes have aimed to encourage girls to take up careers involving new technologies. In several regions of France companies have lent their support to these programmes aimed at encouraging a greater variety of career options among women by participating in meetings and informing young girls about potential careers open to them after appropriate training.

Finally, awareness-raising actions have been organized for officials dealing with employment and training at the local and national level such as the *Délégation à la Formation Professionnelle* (National Training Authority), the *Comité de Co-ordination des Programmes Régionaux de Formation Professionnelle* (Regional Training Council) and the *Agence Nationale Pour l'Emploi* (National Employment Agency).

As far as public service is concerned, various legal dispositions state the principle of equality between civil servants and the principle of neutrality for recruitment of civil servants. However, age limits for mothers of at least one child have been pushed back for certain types of recruitment tests. Recommendations have been made that attention should be given to women civil servants' careers and access to training. Parental leave of up to 3 years can be granted to all civil servants.

COMBINING PROFESSIONAL AND FAMILY RESPONSIBILITIES

The increase in the number of working mothers of two children has altered the traditional view of the link between domestic and professional roles which emphasized the 'choice' women were obliged to make between the family and work or between a career and the family. However, women's family responsibilities still largely affect women's ability to make a full commitment to their work.

Beyond the protection of pregnant women or of women's right to work, beyond also the provision of maternity leave, the issue is to promote the changes necessary in the areas of childcare or work schedules in order to allow women to fulfil their professional ambitions and to have a family, and to improve equality of employment opportunity between men and women.[6]

Family status and professional commitments

Women's professional activity has changed greatly but is still a function of her family status in a society where domestic and family roles are not yet equally shared. Working mothers devote 48 out of every 100 hours to domestic work and 52 to professional activities while men devote 28 of every 100 hours to domestic work and 72 to professional activities. In 1985 the average father of two children whose wife worked outside the home devoted only 15 minutes more to domestic tasks than a father in the same situation in 1975 (Roy, 1989). While women's educational level affects their professional activities − 75% of university-educated women with three children are in employment compared with 45% of mothers of three without qualifications − their ability to make the most of their training is not as great as that of men or single women without children (De Singly, 1990).

Combining domestic and professional responsibilities: the legal framework

In the beginning the legal framework was concerned exclusively with maternity leave and its implications for working mothers. However, it has now expanded to include parental rights to leave for parents of both sexes.

Maternity leave

The French social security system pays 90% of the cost of the legal maternity leave. Dismissal during maternity leave is prohibited if the women has a long-term contract of employment.[7]

Parental leave

This measure, which was introduced in 1977, allows any salary earner of more than 1 year's standing, who belongs to a company employing more than 100 people,[8] to take year's unpaid leave, which can be extended to 3 years. The contract of employment is suspended but not terminated and the employee remains entitled to claim social security benefits. At the end of the period of leave the employee resumes his or her old job or a similar position with an equivalent salary. The period of leave counts for half when calculating the employee's seniority. Since January 1991 the employee is entitled to a refresher course when he or she resumes working.[9]

Part-time employment

An employee is entitled to request part-time employment. The conditions are the same as for parental leave and the employee must be guaranteed a return to full-time work.[10]

Childrearing allowance

This allowance, introduced in 1986, is an incentive to those mothers who wish to take a career break after the birth of their third child, to give up work temporarily. However, given the amount of the allowance, it tends only to be of interest to low-paid women with few qualifications.

Leave to care for sick children

Several in-company agreements and special arrangements within the public sector allow for paid leave to look after sick children — 12 days a year in the case of the public sector. The current debate hinges on whether a legal measure could extend this right to all the salaried workforce (Conseil Economique et Social, 1991).

Childcare

The childcare situation for young children in France is characterized by a principle of shared responsibility (OCDE, 1990) between parents and the public authorities. This means that, in principle, all parents who request it should have access to childcare services (crèche services, approved childminders and daycare centres) and to nursery schools when the child reaches 2½ or 3 years of age. The reality, however, is somewhat different, since over half of children under 3 are looked after outside the public childcare system[11] (Hatchuel, 1989).

The gap between the existing supply of childcare structures and parents' demands seems relatively wide. A recent study indicates that about one-fifth of parents of children[12] under 3 consider 'crèches' as the most satisfying solution when the mother has a job. However, 57% of those who prefer the crèche solution are unable to gain access to it. On the other hand, while only 30% express a preference for individual care through childminders, 41% employ them to look after their children. Furthermore, those who use crèches are satisfied with the chosen solution while half of those who employ approved childminders do not think it is a satisfactory solution. Finally, four out of 10 parents are forced to choose a solution to the problem of childcare which would not be their first preference. Many would prefer to use one of the official structures but are forced to use non-approved childminders or to turn to their families for help, especially to grandparents.

The perceived inadequacy of childcare arrangements and the problems of reconciling professional and family life in general may be a determining factor in the changes in women's attitudes to professional commitment. Thus a recent study reveals that working women without qualifications would definitely prefer to give up work temporarily in return for financial assistance greater than that provided by the *allocation parentale d'education* (childrearing allowance) and which would be paid over a 3-year period. As for women managers, they seem also more and more aware of the tension between professional commitments and care of young children: in 1984–6 only 10% agreed that women with young children should never work, while in 1989 this percentage had risen to 14%.[13]

Firms' policies and reconciliation of domestic and professional responsibilities

In the context of an increase in women's professional activity, various aspects of the role of companies in helping to reconcile family and domestic responsibilities are appearing in an area hitherto the preserve of the family and State.[14]

Company day nurseries

These were set up at the turn of the century by paternalistic employers in response to the needs of large numbers of factory workers and clerical staff and to face the demands of trades unions. However, company day nurseries now reflect companies' determination to respond to the expectations of relatively well-paid employees who have come up against the inadequacy of official childcare structures. These day nurseries which are found mainly in large service-sector companies are usually 'mini-crèches' jointly managed with the *comité d'entreprise* (staff council). They can also be located in areas where large numbers of company employees live[15] (Leprince and Penet, 1989).

Leave to care for sick children and sick children insurance schemes

Although some companies allow parents of sick children to take a certain number of paid days off, other companies have chosen to take out insurance policies for their employees which provide for child-minders to look after sick children at their home. This type of scheme is mainly used by women managers in the companies concerned but growing numbers of young male managers are now making use of them.

Flexible working hours

These can be very varied and range from flexible working hours during the day or the week, to part-time work or time off during school holidays for those who do not wish to work at all during these periods.

Administrative and service-sector professions are more adaptable to these innovations than industrial ones and numerous companies have introduced 'flexitime' schemes which combine personalized work schedules with fixed periods of attendance for all personnel.

Outwork

Although it would be difficult to carry out a systematic evaluation of experiments in the area of outwork, or working from home, they do not appear to have met with much success among those women concerned. Thus, in two different insurance companies, all volunteers asked to return to their former working arrangements after several weeks, because they felt a lack of social integration away from their work team.

The question of part-time work

While in other European countries the development of women's professional activity has been based on widespread use of part-time work, in France it is a more recent phenomenon which grew out of the economic crisis of the mid-1970s and the need for greater flexibility of firms' human resources policies.

Although part-time work is growing rapidly and is confined almost exclusively to women (83% of part-time workers are women), only one working women in four is working part time compared to 43% of working women in Sweden (Anxo and Daune-Richard, 1991).

The debate about part-time work is based on an opposition between part-time working imposed by businesses, department stores or super-markets for instance, and that chosen by employees. In as much as part-time jobs are not chosen by women but forced upon them by company demands, in the distribution sector for example, the assertion that they help to reconcile domestic and professional roles while in fact imposing serious constraints on women, distorts the nature of the debate on the real causes of the growth of part-time employment and women's true aspirations (Maruani and Nicole, 1989).

In fact, women's ambitions in relation to part-time employment are varied. Some who work part time would like to find full-time jobs but fail to do so because of the shortage of such jobs.[16] Others who wish to take advantage of a part-time job for a limited period are unable to do so due to the rigid work organization in many companies and to their reluctance to introduce more varied work schedules.[17]

WOMEN MANAGERS: PROGRESS AND OBSTACLES

The increasing numbers of women middle and senior managers in business, their higher levels of education and qualification reflected in the growing proportion of women among young executives recruited,[18] their entry into new professions such as personnel management, public relations, marketing, finance and even sales, which are more open to women managers than other more traditional and/or technical sectors, still have not managed to wipe out the differences between male and female executives.

Even though women executives have become more numerous over the last 20 years, they still do not enjoy equal opportunities with men in terms of pay or access to decision-making posts or positions of power.

In the first place, as has already been stated, the entry of women into management differs according to sectors and professions. A recent study of 100 French companies, including some of the largest ones, indicates that half the companies studied had no more than 10% of women on their managerial staff and that only 18 had more than 25% women managers. Among these were fashion companies, department stores, travel companies, banks, communications, insurance and computer companies.

In addition, the higher in the organization the scarcer women become. The same phenomenon as found in the political and administrative spheres also applies to business. Women's access to real positions of responsibility remains the exception rather than the rule. According to a study carried out in 1987 among senior management of 5,030 major companies representing 50% of gross national product, 1,237 out of 30,000 top-level executives were women, i.e. 4.6%; 58 chairpersons out of 4,650 were women, and 77 out of 2,974 chief executive officers.[19]

A certain number of studies have tried to go beyond these statistical findings and examine the psychosociological and organizational processes underlying this reality. Such studies are, unfortunately, all too rare.

Different career strategies?

There has always been a very small minority of exceptional women in business, capable of making a career while submitting totally to the expectations and constraints of organizations culturally defined by men and, generally speaking, sacrificing all family roles to their careers.

A study was carried out in 1982 with the object of identifying the career strategies and attitudes of younger women managers (Laufer, 1982). Four different career strategies were identified among the women executives interviewed in the following sectors: department stores, banks, cosmetics, advertising and computer industries.

The first strategy corresponds to what may be called a 'traditional' model of women managers' integration into the firm's culture and role structure. This model is characterized by what could be called a 'submission to the difference' between men and women. By accepting the traditional subordinate and complementary relationship with men, along with subordinate and supporting positions, and by showing loyalty, submission and devotion, these women executives have found a way of living as women within the organization, and of integrating potentially conflicting dimensions of their roles as women and as managers, opposite men who will keep strategic decision-making and power for themselves, with the consent of these women who assist them.

The second strategy is based on the affirmation of a status based on expertise but also on the 'acknowledgment of the difference' that being a woman makes. Thus women executives are willing to limit their careers and ambitions in order to have enough time to spend with their families and will not aspire to high-level management or decision-making roles. Of course, the skills acquired by some of them may lead them to positions of leadership and responsibility, but these will come in the later part of their career and will not be based on their ability to take initiatives or set long-term objectives for themselves or their departments, but rather on their ability to carry out with precision the tasks given to them. These young women, deeply absorbed in their tasks, develop a mode of behaviour which does not encourage their hierarchy to look upon them as leaders to be called upon to exercise major responsibilities.

A third strategy leads women executives to an 'assertion of their difference' and to make the most of it by choosing sectors of activity such as advertising, luxury goods and fashion, where feminity is regarded as essential to the organization's culture and success. These women executives feel recognized, appreciated and useful for the fulfilment of the company's objectives, but this does not keep them from frequent conflict with male management. To men whose power is based on figures, charts and formal relationships, they respond by asserting the power of intuition and emotion.

Finally, a fourth strategy, more frequently found among the youngest and best-qualified women managers, consists in 'demanding both equality *and* difference', that is a desire for a career *and* a family, and by challenging the logic of the 'choice' between the two. These women, who are characterized by their desire to succeed, aspire to the same positions as men, at least at the outset, and want indeed to 'have a career'. Wishing to be dedicated executives and to gain decisionmaking posts and positions of power, they show, however, some ambivalence as to the part their careers should play in their search for identity. To have a career without giving up all the other roles linked to their status as women, to avoid taking themselves too seriously and being 'obsessed' by their career goals seem indeed their main objectives.

It thus seems that far from adopting or rejecting a 'masculine' model of behaviour, the only one considered suitable for success in management, women managers develop different career strategies in accordance with their personality, qualifications, and the sector or type of organization in which they find themselves. These strategies reflect a diversity of models for reconciling feminine and managerial roles. While the small number of women in managerial positions can explain the lack of role models for career development, the problems experienced by women in projecting themselves towards such career goals originate in the role conflict many feel between the behaviour expected from managers and the type of behaviour expected from women.

Access to management or access to power?

If competence seems to be the major asset possessed by women managers — there is not a single study or poll which does not emphasize the fact that women have to do even better than men to be accepted in similar positions (Laufer, 1985) — women are often considered as strangers to the spheres of power and authority. Although the status of *éminence grise* or roles of influence seem to suit women managers, the same does not apply to many of them when it comes to taking up formal authority or supervisory roles. A number of surveys show that among managers there is a higher proportion of female than male degree holders. It is easier to integrate women whose qualifications have been certified by external authorities than to promote them internally. However, men with few qualifications are more frequently found in technical or commercial areas which lead on more easily to managerial positions than in the administrative areas where most women are employed.

In a survey carried out in a multinational computer company, although 37% of women and 39% of men claimed not to care about the sex of their supervisor, very few men or women wished to work for a female boss. Women themselves prefer to report to a man and this tendency is even stronger among women with fewer qualifications (Serdjenian, 1988).

It seemed as though women were not really destined for roles of power and that any attempt to enter this sphere had to be regarded as direct competition with men. Women themselves, with a few exceptions, appear to be less inclined to devote themselves to this quest for power, which requires total identification with the company and complete availability. They seem more familiar with the exercise of influence rather than power whereas men consider the exercise of power the logical extension and the very purpose of their careers (Aubert, 1982). The hostile attitude of men threatened by competition from women when they take up positions of power may help to explain this situation, but women have internalized these images both themselves and for other women. Such processes are another illustration of the hypothesis of the 'glass ceiling' which prevents women from achieving positions of power, as an invisible barrier which does not allow women, even highly motivated and dynamic ones, to show that they have succeeded, or to create relationships with colleagues or supervisors which would constitute a support network for them. Men are far more successful in exploiting formal and informal networks. Women are often critical of women's behaviour, emphasizing the lack of solidarity among women themselves, the lack of confidence in other women, their passivity and lack of self-confidence (Laufer, 1982).

As long as the ideal manager was seen to be competitive, aggressive and domineering, women were considered and considered themselves to be inadequate when measured against these criteria. However, given that management now requires other qualities, such as an ability to listen, negotiating skills and intuition, considered to be closer to feminine qualities, women's credibility in roles hitherto the preserve of men can be increased.

The influence of corporate practices

According to the degree of personal involvement that companies demand of their executives, women managers experience their professional commitment as a source of varying degrees of conflict. This is the hypothesis of a recent study which emphasizes the way in which the corporate culture of a company influences not only the professional lives of women but also their personal lives. In firms which demand a strong professional commitment or great mobility women tend to exclude themselves from too deep an involvement even if this has a negative effect on their careers. Even if they are given equal opportunities at the beginning of their careers by companies which emphasize 'good' human resources policies, they come to have ambivalent attitudes to organizations which demand a great deal of commitment at the expense of their personal lives and which do not always fully recognize their merits (Belle, 1991).

Women executives in a large computer company declare themselves to be more unhappy with their careers than their male colleagues — 43% compared with 28% — and feel that the company imposes more obstacles for women's careers than for men's. They also feel that women must prove their superiority before gaining a position of responsibility, that they are not given the same chances for promotion as men and that the higher up one goes in the organization, the less equality there is for women. They attribute the fact that the company keeps them in less responsible and less prestigious positions, where their replacement does not present serious problems, to men's chauvinistic attitudes, to domestic responsibilities and to a lack of adequate training. The same survey indicates that men consider that these difficulties are due essentially to the family responsibilities of women and only secondarily to management attitudes (Serdjenian, 1988).

Furthermore, in many companies women are not given the opportunity to gain sufficiently varied experience which is the key to a 'spiral of credibility' that would allow them gradually to take on more important operational responsibilities (Laufer, 1985). Only a deliberate voluntary effort on the part of companies can correct a tendency for women's careers to receive less attention than those of men.

Finally, the question of women's difficulties, real or imaginary, when faced with professional and geographical mobility is often brought up. As to geographical mobility, recognizing that this is also becoming a problem for young male managers whose wives have careers does not alleviate the fact that this difficulty is held against women when the company is searching for the future members of its top-level management team.

Adaptation of women to management or adaptation of management to women?

In France, as elsewhere, the status of women managers shows several contradictory tendencies as shown in numerous press articles devoted to this subject. Will women managers succeed in imposing their differences on the organization or will the organization select only those women capable of adapting to the fierce competition which is characteristic of organizational hierarchies? Will organizations become more human and more flexible under the influence of women and will this influence spread to men? Will different career tracks be developed to take account of women's specific constraints or will they have to submit to mobility, overwork, to the total availability demanded by the organization? These issues in France, as elsewhere, concern the whole fabric of organizational policies and cultures and also the negotiating power of women over their professional and family environment and their will to assert new ways of balancing personal and professional life.

REFERENCES

Alexandre, H. (1990) Les femmes cadres, *APEC*, July.
Anxo, D. and Daune-Richard, A. M. (1991) La place relative des hommes et des femmes sur le marché du travail. Une comparaison en France et en Suède, *Travail et Emploi*, no. 1.
Aubert, N. (1982) *Le Pouvoir Usurpé*, Editions R. Laffont, Paris.
Battagliola, F. (1984) Employés et employées: trajectoires professionnelles et familiales, in *Le Sexe du Travail* (ouvrage collectif), Presses Universitaires de Grenoble, Grenoble.
Baudelot, C. and Establet R. (1990) Les filles et les garçons dans la compétition scolaire, *Données Sociales*, INSEE, pp. 344–7, Paris.
Belle, F. (1991) *Etre Femme et Cadre*, Editions l'Harmattan, Paris.
Belloc, B. (1987) Le travail à temps partiel, *Données Sociales*, INSEE, pp. 112–19.
Brin, H. (1991) *La Politique Familiale Française*, Conseil Economique et Social, Paris.
CFDT (1990a) *Femmes, Clés pour l'Egalite*.
CFDT (1990b) *Sondage Actuelles-CSA*, November.
De Singly, F. (1990) *Fortune et Infortune de la Femme Mariée*, PUF, Paris.
Desplanques, G. and Saboulin, M. (1990) Les familles aujourd'hui, *Données Sociales*, INSEE, pp. 276–84.
Divisia, F. and Cagan, Y. (1990) Emploi et formation des femmes: politique et action du secrétariat d'etat chargé des droits des femmes, in *L'Europe et L'emploi Féminin*, AFPA, Paris.
Doniol-Shaw, G., Genest, V., Junter-Loiseau, A., Gouzien, J. and Lerolle, A. (1989) Les plans d'égalité professionnelle: étude bilan 1983–1988. La Documentation Française, Paris.
Halpern, M. (1990) *Stimuler l'Entrepreunariat Féminin*, ICOSI, Paris.
Hatchuel, G. (1989) Accueil de la petite enfance et activité féminine, *Rapport Credoc*, no. 61, May.
Hatchuel, G. (1991) Activité féminine et jeune enfant, *Rapport Credoc*, no. 95, February.
Hirata, H. and Rogerat, C. (1988) Technologie, qualification et division sexuelle du travail, *Revue Française de Sociologie*, no. XXIX, pp. 171–92.
Huet, M. (1983) La concentration des emplois féminins, *Economie et Statistique*, no. 154, INSEE.
INSEE (1991) *Les Femmes – Contours et Caractères*, INSEE, Paris.
Jacquier, J. (1990) La diversification des formes d'emploi en France, *Données Sociales*, INSEE, pp. 58–60.
Lacroix, I. (1990) Le marché du travail dans les années 1980, *Données Sociales*, INSEE, pp. 36–49.

Laufer, J. (1982) *La Féminité Neutralisée, Les Femmes Cadres dans l'Entreprise*, Editions Flammarion, Paris.

Laufer, J. (1984) Egalité professionnelle: principes et pratiques, *Droit Social*, no. 12, December.

Laufer, J. (1985) Les femmes cadres à EDF-GDF, in H. Meynaud *et al.* (eds.) *Les Femmes à EDF-GDF. Bilan et Devenir*, EDF-GDF, Paris.

Laufer, J. (1986) Egalité professionnelle: un atout négligé pour gérer les ressources humaines, *Revue Française de Gestion*, no. 55, January/February, pp. 41−53.

Laufer, J. (1987) L'égalité professionnelle, une entreprise légitime, in C. Alezra *et al.* (eds.) *La Mixité du Travail, une Stratégie pour l'Entreprise*, Cahier du Programme Mobilisateur−Technologie−Emploi−Travail, La Documentation Française, no. 3, June, pp. 7−14, Paris.

Laufer, J. (1990) *Emploi Féminin et Mise en Oeuvre de l'Égalité Professionnelle*, Programme Mobilisateur−Technologie−Emploi−Travail, Groupe HEC, Paris.

Leprince, F. and Penet, F. (1989) Accueillir les jeunes enfants, *Espaces et Familles*, no. 3, CNAF.

Mandon, N. (1987) Bureaucratique et évolution de l'activité professionelle, in C. Alezra *et al.* (eds.) *La Mixité du Travail, une Stratégie pour l'Entreprise*. Cahier du Programme Mobilisateur−Technologie−Emploi−Travail, no. 3, June, pp. 25−29, La Documentation Française.

Marry, C. (1989) Femmes ingénieures, une irrésistible ascension? *Information sur les Sciences Sociales*, Vol. 28, no. 2, pp. 291−344.

Maruani, M. and Nicole, C. (1989) *Au Labeur des Dames, Métiers Masculins, Emplois Féminins*, Editions Syros, Paris.

Ministère du Travail et de l'Emploi (1991) Service des etudes et de la statistique: Premières informations. L'aide aux demandeurs d'emploi créant une enterprise, no. 233, July.

Le Nouvel Economiste (1987) March. no. 583, 13/3/1987.

OECD (1990) La garde des enfants dans les pays de l'OECD, *Perspectives de l'Emploi*, pp. 133−58.

ONISEP (1987) Les femmes ingénieurs, *Avenirs*, no. 387.

Rotbart, G. (1990) Salaire et restructuration du travail: une transformation massive et rapide, *Données Sociales*, INSEE, pp. 96−102.

Roy, C. (1989) La gestion du temps des hommes et des femmes des actifs et des inactifs, in *Les Emplois du Temps des Francais*, INSEE, Paris, August (Collection Economie et Statistiques no. 223, July/August).

Ruault, M. J. (1989) *L'Egalité Professionnelle entre Hommes et Femmes dans les Entreprises Publiques à Statut Réglementaire*, Projet d'Avis, Conseil Economique et Social Paris.

Secrétariat d'Etat chargé des Droits des Femmes (1990) Conseil Supérieur de l'Egalité Professionnelle. Troisième bilan d'application de la loi sur l'égalité professionnelle du 13 Juillet 1983.

Serdjenian, E. (1988) *L'égalité des Chances ou les Enjeux de la Mixité*, Les Editions d'Organization, Paris.

ENDNOTES

[1] The statistical categories *cadres et professions intellectuelles supérieures* and *professions intermédiaires* used by the INSEE (French statistical insti-

tute) should be listed in detail if one wishes to analyse the status of women in business since *cadres et professions intellectuelles supérieures* include professors, administrative and commercial managers while the *professions intermédiaires* include primary school teachers, qualified nurses and middle managers.

[2] Several new legal measures have reinforced the 1983 law among them the 10 July 1989 law which gives the opportunity to firms employing fewer than 300 persons to benefit from government financial help to audit their situation in terms of equal opportunity and formulate action plans to promote equal opportunity. A new impetus to negotiation on equal opportunity could be given by the 2 August 1989 law which sets new obligations for firms to negotiate on equal opportunity actions and by the 1989 agreement on equal opportunity which has been signed by the main unions and by the CNPF (National Federation of Heads of Firms) which commit both parties to set up specific strategies and goals to promote equal opportunity.

[3] Very different in size (between 50 and 35,000 employees, 11 of the businesses concerned employed fewer than 1,000 people) and activity (6 food-processing companies, 4 banks, the others belong to the computer, electronics and mechanics sectors), these firms employ between 50% and 10% women and have a large concentration of female jobs in the lowest qualified categories and very few women in the upper categories or in sales or technical jobs staffed by men (Laufer, 1990).

[4] The companies who have signed individual affirmative action contracts are very varied in size (from 2 to 278 employees) and sector of activity. The purpose of these contracts is promotions, recruitment or transfers. Unskilled workers have become skilled workers, employees or technicians have become heads of administrative or sales departments. The financial assistance given through these schemes in 116 cases out of 148 has concerned training.

[5] Since 1984 this allowance has been available to all job seekers in receipt of unemployment benefit. Ranging from FF 10,000 to 43,000 according to previous professional experience, it has enabled 52,000 beneficiaries to set up their own companies since 1989 and increased the total volume of businesses set up. In spite of the fact that this category has been the object of attention in recent years, and while there are 216 firms created each year in France, 20% of them by women, few elements exist on women entrepreneurs and or heads of firms. Through the European Commission Programme, 45 projects of women entrepreneurship have been financed between 1987 and 1989 (Halpern, 1990).

[6] A recent survey carried out on a representative sample of working women shows that leave of absence to care for sick children, an increase in the number of places in day nurseries, flexible working hours, parental leave and the opportunity to work part time are all important factors for improving working women's lives (CFDT, 1990b).

[7] The legal minimum maternity leave is 16 weeks for the first and second children and 26 weeks for the third child. The length of compensation can be according to the profession and to collective agreements. Thus compensation can sometimes be close to 100% in certain cases. Part of the prenatal leave can be put back until the birth of the child but must be not less than 4 weeks.

8 In companies employing fewer than 100 people the employer can refuse to grant this type of leave to the employee.

9 Debate is continuing about the possibility of granting paid parental leave, which is the only way to encourage certain men to take it. At present, parental leave is usually taken by mothers and constitutes a potential risk for their professional development (Conseil Economique et Social, 1991).

10 This is a recent measure established in January 1991. It corresponds to the acknowledgement that the complete cessation of professional activity can have a negative impact on a woman's subsequent career development.

11 It is currently estimated that approximately 700,000 children under the age of 3 need to be looked after because of their parents' professional activities. Of these children 44% are looked after in 'organized' structures (18% in crèches) and 56% in other settings (35% with grandparents, 21% with non-approved childminders and nannies) (Hatchuel, 1989).

12 Crèches are 74% financed by the state but this system seems to work to the advantage of the best-informed, and wealthiest social categories, those with higher education and parents with relatively high incomes. The current growth of crèches is based partly on creation of contracts enabling nurseries organized by groups of parents to be set up. This assumes that the parents in question have a certain amount of free time, can pay part of the money required up front and cope with the administrative details (Hatchuel, 1989).

13 Although support for women's professional activity has grown unceasingly (29% in 1978, 43% in 1989) it seems now to have come to a standstill due to a greater debate about salaried work for women with young children. In 1989 more working women were in favour of mothers of young children giving up work temporarily (72%) than in 1987 (69.7%). Although support of working women tends to come from degree holders, young people and residents of the Paris area, one-quarter of factory workers and employees feel that women with young children should not work at all (Hatchuel, 1991).

14 *Le Conseil Supérieur de l'Egalité Professionnelle* (The French Equal Opportunity Commission) published a report entitled *Gestion des Entreprises et Prise en Compte des Responsabilités Familiales* in 1989. This report puts forward a number of suggestions for improving compatibility between salaried employment and family responsibilities within a perspective of greater equality of opportunity for men and women in employment. A recent *prix d'innovation sociale* (social innovation award), awarded for innovative efforts in this area, shows the importance of the growth of the company's role in the public debate.

15 Since 1975 almost all day nurseries that have opened have been in large service-sector establishments with a strong female presence and also in companies with a large managerial staff. Hospitals and ministries also offer numerous nursery services (Leprince and Penet, 1989).

16 The desire to work part time is particularly common among mothers of young children. In the study already quoted, one-third of mothers interviewed already had a part-time job and one-third wished to reduce their working time and were willing to take a cut in salary. Among the middle-classes, part-time work is seen as a more desirable alternative to giving up work (see Hatchuel, 1991).

[17] One of the part-time solutions most sought after by women is to have Wednesdays free because children do not attend school on that day. However, this is not without problems for companies who fear to see their offices empty on Wednesdays.

[18] In 1983 women accounted for 23.9% of young executives recruited by companies and 34.4% in 1989 (Alexandre, 1990).

[19] In 1987 the proportion of women among departmental heads was: communications 10%, leisure 8%, transport and travel 7%, distribution, textiles and clothing 6%, chemistry 4%, food processing, electronic supplies and building 4%, mechanics 3% and banking 1%. The proportion of departmental head positions held by women in companies was: external or public relations 22%, training 22%, finance 20%, personnel 14%, administration 9%, marketing 8%, advertising 79%, crediting 6%, sales 6%, computer science 3%, production 2% and technical matters 1% (*Le Nouvel Economiste*, 1987, no. 583, 13/3/1987).

8.

BELGIUM

Alison Woodward

INTRODUCTION

On most European indicators, Belgium, given its position at the cross-roads between the Germanic and the Romance cultures, tends to take a place somewhere in the middle. This may be the case for women in management as well. Belgian women are relatively well favoured in terms of labour market protection related to their role in the family, yet despite social policy designed to underwrite a professional role, those with management ambitions meet conservative cultures in the workplace which make it hard to break through the proverbial 'glass ceiling'.

Unfortunately, women in top management positions are very rare in Belgium. Furthermore, Belgian academics have devoted little energy to gathering basic statistical data on the demographics of the Belgian woman manager, let alone her location according to sector. Given the dearth of statistical information and the lack of solid empirical studies, this overview of the situation of female managers is brief. It highlights the experiences of a few companies who participated in a government-sponsored equal opportunities programme and who may encourage other companies. Furthermore, government policies have been changing to make it easier for women to combine work and family. This fact, and also the recent results of research on young businesswomen, allow an optimistic conclusion about Belgian women's business opportunities in the Europe of 1992.

BELGIAN WOMEN IN LEADERSHIP POSITIONS: HOW MANY?

In comparison to her Dutch or German neighbours, the Belgian woman has 'always' been working. In this century, up until the late 1960s, approximately a quarter of Belgian women were in employment in primarily working-class positions. In Flanders agricultural employment was important for women, while in Wallonia industrial employment was more common. Nonetheless, Belgium, like her neighbours, experienced a feminization of the labour force from the late 1960s onward, in a trend which has still not peaked. According to the latest available figures (1989) 44.7% of Belgian women aged between 14 and 64 are employed and they make up 42% of the working population (Kabinet van de Staatssecretaris voor Maatschappelijke Emancipatie, 1991a). More than 75% of women between 25 and 29 years of age are employed. In 1988 66% of women with at least one child under the age of 10 were either employed or looking for work (European Commission on Childcare Network, 1990). The amount of part-time employment is virtually the European mean with some 24% of employed females holding a part-time position (Kabinet van de Staatssecretaris voor Maatschappelijke Emancipatie, 1991a; Meulders and Plasman, 1989, p. 12). No one doubts that the Belgian woman is in the labour market to stay, at least until her legal retirement as early as age 60. Unfortunately, Belgian women also suffer from a higher rate of unemployment than Belgian men, due in part to their lack of skills. In 1991 the 13% female unemployment rate was more than double male unemployment, and above the general Europaen Community (EC) average of 11.1% (van Winckel, 1992, p. 27). One area in which neighbouring Luxembourg shines in comparison to other European countries is unemployment, which in 1989 was only 1.8%. However, women in Luxembourg are still more likely to be unemployed compared to men (2.7% versus 1.3%) (Commission of European Communities, 1992).

Women seem to be there to stay both because they now want to work and because the Belgian economy will increasingly need their capacity. A number of opinion surveys have indicated that the motivations for working have changed from purely economic ones to the more expressive motivations of wanting to use one's skills or develop one's self. These changing motivations have to do with the increasing educational level of Belgian women, who are now better able to command more interesting jobs. The Belgian birthrate is low (1.55) and, barring renewed labour market immigration, most experts agree that the only reserve labour available will be female. Still, even though all agree that women have a permanent place in employment, they are, like most women in Europe, heavily underrepresented in management.

Those women at the very top of Belgian society have never actually been counted, but are undoubtedly very few in number. The formation of the present national Cabinet includes three female ministers out of 13, and this is the highest number of ministers this century. A recent study of the banking industry indicated that only seven of the top 100 directors of banks were female (*Trends*, 1991). The situation in manufacturing and other private sector firms is little different. Top female executives in this small country can be counted on fingers and toes, and in a number of cases their position is in part owed to a family connection as, comparatively speaking, the family firm is still very important in the Belgian economy.

Nonetheless, the official 1981 Belgian statistics report that 2.4% of employed women are in the highest category of company executive director, director or member of senior or middle management, and that women comprise 17.5% of this category. In total 4.7% of the employed population is in this top category (Kabinet van de Staatssecretaris voor Maatschappelijke Emancipatie, 1991a). Sztum (1988), looking only at managers in the private manufacturing sector, found that only 5.3% of the 'cadre' or top management functions were filled by women. The few qualitative studies that have been done with small samples in specific sectors indicate that these women are on the lower rungs of the management ladder (Franck, van Put and Vermeulen, 1990; Demeester and Neefs, 1991; Meersman and Vanneste, 1992; Vandevoort et al., 1990). They are generally younger than the category as a whole. These women are the ones that cause Belgian male managers to claim that it is only a matter of time before women will be represented in the halls of management in proportion to their presence in the labour force. The claims of American feminist scholars that we would have to wait until the year 3000 before parity is reached find little support in management public opinion in Belgium. They believe that time will tell.

These young managers are products of an increasing feminization of universities in Belgium. In 1975 only 18.7% of university-level management students were female, whereas in 1988 the entering class of management students was 33% female (van Herck and Verbruggen, 1991, p. 99). The majority of students studying law are now female. Since management careers in 'cadre' functions are primarily open to those with university credentials, the influx of women into business administration and law programme is now being reflected in the lower echelons of Belgian firms.

THE FEMALE ENTREPRENEUR: A BELGIAN EXCEPTION?

An interesting exception to the Belgian position in the middle ground of Europe is the relatively high percentage of women among entrepreneurs. Furthermore, the percentage of women owners of small businesses has been growing, perhaps in part due to government programmes encouraging small business (Meulders and Plasman, 1989, p. 89). From 1975 to 1985 the number of self-employed women was on the increase. Although some 10% of working women were self-employed (which is again the European median), these self-employed women contrast with those in other countries which show a high rate of self-employment. Whereas in Spain, Portugal, Italy and Greece this the employment is primarily in agriculture, in Belgium 41% of the self-employed women are in commerce (Meulders and Plasman, 1989, p. 81). Thus far no study has been undertaken looking into the specifics of these entrepreneurs. The EC experts hypothesize that Belgian women have been starting their own businesses as an alternative to unemployment. The Belgian economy, which includes many small and medium-sized firms, and a large hotel and restaurant sector, provides many opportunities in fields which are conducive to female enterprise. Given the frequently voiced opinion that women may best be able to combine work and home life by running their own businesses, these Belgian entrepreneurs may prove interesting as examples of alternative routes for women in business.

AFFIRMATIVE ACTION: THE SOFT TOUCH

In part due to the prompting of the EC and in part due to women's agitation in the women's movement and the established political parties, the issue of equal opportunity for men and women moved on to the public agenda in the late 1980s. With the appointment of a Secretary of State for Social Emancipation and the Environment in 1985, the Belgian government officially recognized the inequality of women and made a promise for action. Through the Office of Social Emancipation, statistics about the position of women were compiled across the various policy fields (Kabinet van de Staatssecretaris voor Maatschappelijke Emancipatie, 1991a; Wyns and van Meensen, 1990), and studies were initiated indicating the still-existing discriminatory patterns of wages and promotion, despite European law to the contrary.

Among the issues that were brought to the fore was the low representation of women in decision-making positions in the private and public sectors. The government initiated programmes of what it called 'positive action' aimed at addressing this problem and promoting the career chances of women at all levels of enterprise. In contrast to affirmative action programmes in Scandinavia, the USA and the Netherlands, Belgium chose a voluntary approach aimed at a total reconceptualization of personnel policy for women. The word 'quota' was never mentioned. The aim was to prepare a tailor-made package for each participating company, ranging from better rest-room facilities to allowing managers to work part time. At the national level a royal decree was passed recommending that private enterprises actively pursue equality of opportunity for men and women (14 July, 1987). To implement this the government supported pilot affirmative action projects over a period of 3 years.

In the private sector this brought mixed success, as firms failed to jump on a voluntary affirmative action bandwagon. This may have been because the approach was directed at firms with relatively sophisticated personnel policies (Woodward, 1991). Only 40 firms joined the government-sponsored pilot programme which offered personnel to support the development of action plans in co-operation with personnel departments. These firms provided good examples, which it was hoped would, through publicity, inspire other companies (Kabinet van de Staatssecretaris voor Maatschappelijke Emancipatie, 1991b). Among the different strategies and ideas that firms initiated were measures designed to improve the career chances of women at the point of selection and in terms of training policy and evaluation, measures directed at improving the conditions of work, and those directed at changing the company culture through information and consciousness raising.

Initiatives for recruitment and selection

Firms participating in pilot programmes increased the attention paid to women at the point of recruitment, both in public relations and advertising texts illustrating women-friendly aspects of the firms and, in the case of Monsanto and Volvo, through use of special videos for university recruitment. Several firms co-operated with the unemployment office in a special effort to recruit females returning to work and groups of girls following technical education programmes.

At the point of employee selection special attention was paid to diversity when preparing interviewing teams, through, for example, directives for selection, and choosing teams with both men and women. Siemens prepared an analysis of stereotypical beliefs about women to help in increasing the awareness of selection teams.

Initiatives for mobility

In the area of promotion, participating companies took initiatives to aid women in career planning. Monsanto prepared a career guide for different career paths and functions, while Mobil Plastics encouraged internal promotions through yearly career evaluations interviews where future wishes and possibilities were clearly discussed. These two firms also made good use of 'model' women, already exercising management functions, in their advising of women employees, discussing real 'examples'.

Because women frequently feel they have fewer chances for training and further education, participating firms also evaluated their educational policies for employees. Janssen Pharmaceutica began including the positive action representative in course planning and decision teams. To introduce more opportunities for female workers in lower functions, they began training 'polyvalent' assembly and production workers. Van Hool, a transport company, gave special attention to the better utilization of external educational opportunities for women.

Initiatives to aid in combining work and family

Work time variation seemed to be a problematic issue for participating firms. While part-time work is almost the rule for manual functions, it is virtually out of the question at higher levels. The only initiative in connection with work time was IBM's concession to allow some workers to work at home. Although childcare is well provided for in Belgium, some local regions have problems, and participating firms, such as van Hool and van Ommeren, helped women by preparing regional guides to childcare. The King Boudewijn Foundation has been stimulating firms to think about providing childcare on site, and a few Brussels firms and hospitals have responded to this (Jansen, 1990).

Initiatives to change corporate culture

Women in management frequently complain that next to balancing work and family, their biggest problem is the masculine culture of the workplace. The pilot programme also worked on motivating men and women to participate in equal opportunities work and thereby become more conscious of the hidden aspects of culture in their organizations. EBES organized breakfast sessions to brainstorm about various problems with equal opportunities in the company. This helped both to identify needs and to motivate employees to think more about the issue. Several firms started equal opportunities teams. Janssen Pharmaceutica also used external experts to carry out interviews about stereotypes. This material was used to raise awareness about the issues at all levels in the organization.

Several of the pilot firms were also conscious that their image as woman-friendly firms could help their public image and their ability to recruit in a wider pool. The firms have made eager use of the publicity offered by their participation in the project, which again may feed back into company culture.

The pilot programme for private enterprises resulted not only in conferences and articles designed to spread the good examples, but also in concrete guidelines on how to approach affirmative action in the firm. Handbooks on how to carry out an analysis of the status of women within the company and how to develop a strategy to improve equality of opportunity in the firm are now available from the national public administration (Kabinet van de Staatssecretaris voor Maatschappelijke Emancipatie, 1991a). The Ministry of Employment and Labour attaches special importance to the negotiations necessary to anchor affirmative actions in the enterprise decision-making structure (Ministerie van Tewerkstelling en Arbeid, 1990a). A further result of the affirmative action pilot effort has been the establishment of affirmative action units not only within the Ministry of Employment and Labour but also at several universities offering postgraduate management training or doing labour research, for example the IPO-UFSIA Management School, the University of Antwerp, the Hoger Instituut van de Arbeid at the Catholic University of Leuven and the Vlerick School of Management at Ghent.

Given the somewhat mixed experience with the voluntary approach, the mandate to improve the opportunities for women was more stringent for the public sector, where local authorities and government bodies must submit a plan of affirmative action and measures to achieve results (Kabinet van de Staatssecretaris voor Maatschappelijke Emancipatie, 1990). The royal decree of 27 February, 1990, laying down measures for equal opportunities in the civil service, and its implementation have received attention in Europe, and are generating important data banks on the location of women in public sector management and their prospects over time (Paternottre, 1991).

In 1991 pre-election appearances, the Secretary of State indicated to concerned audiences that, on reflection, firmer measures would be needed to really improve the representation of women in the higher echelons of private enterprises. At present there is no legislation which could be termed 'positive discrimination'. Furthermore, despite the presence of anti-discrimination and equal wage legislation in line with European models, there have been virtually no court cases initiated by women complaining about discriminatory hiring or salaries.

The newly elected government has, at the time of writing, made no indication of a stronger commitment to affirmative action, although the recently formed Flemish regional administration has appointed a top official to manage 'emancipation' over a period of 5 years in the government itself. The national interprofessional accords between labour and employers have, however, included affirmative action support in their last two agreements, and the Ministry of Employment started an affirmative action unit. As M. Smet, the former state secretary of emancipation, is now Minister of Employment, it can be expected that affirmative action will stay on the agenda. As far as the commitment to advancing women in private management goes, however, personal communications for this article indicated that some researchers who had been involved in action research with participating firms felt that 'affirmative action' for Belgian business had been little more than a passing fad.

THE COMBINATION OF FAMILY AND WORK: SOCIAL PROVISIONS

A major problem for many female managers is balancing the demands of the job with the demands of the life-cycle. Public policy and/or flexible employers can help lessen the strain. The Belgian state provisions for childcare and parental leave are not as generous as those to be found in Scandinavia, but are looked upon with envy by the UK and the Netherlands. A number of changes have taken place since 1990 to enhance further the possibilities of combining career and family (de Gols et al., 1991; Crombé, 1991).

Maternity and parental leave

In total, Belgian women have a right to 15 weeks' leave in connection with childbearing. They are required to take 1 week before the planned date of birth and 8 weeks after the birth of the child, and are paid 82% of their salary in the period. The following 6 weeks are compensated at a rate of 75%. This compensation is paid through the health insurance funds and funded by the general employer contribution to the health insurance funds for the employee. A number of sectors also permit so-called breast-feeding leave, allowing mothers to extend their leave, but without economic compensation. Fathers have a right to 3 days' leave, to be taken in the 12 days immediately after the birth.

Belgium's programme of career breaks is used primarily by mothers who wish to stay at home with their children for a longer period than the legally permitted parental leave. Fathers may also use it, although male career breaks are usually taken in connection with starting a new business. The programme was instituted in 1985 and includes two variants:

(1) Full career break: this allows for a break of from 6 to 12 months, which may be repeated, up to a maximum of 60 months.
(2) Part-time career break: the employee reduces work time to half time for a period ranging from a minimum of 6 months to a maximum of 5 years.

Employees do not have a *right* to career breaks, but must reach an agreement with the employer ahead of the break. Employers are required to employ someone on the unemployment rolls as a replacement. This can lead to some roadblocks, for example, in higher more skilled functions. The employee taking a career break is protected from being fired, and receives a monthly flat payment of around Bfr 11,000 (higher if it is in connection with a second or third child). Employees may also ask for leave without pay, or part-time work, and are covered by social insurance.

In addition to the opportunities presented by the career-break scheme and leave options which allow some family flexibility, there are also provisions for taking care of sick children. The employee has a right to 10 days' leave without pay per calendar year. In some sectors, such as banking and distribution, special agreements have been reached allowing employees to recoup lost hours by overtime or a reduction in the yearly vacation (de Gols *et al.*, 1991, p. 56).

Childcare provisions and after-school care

For children under 3 years of age, parents in Belgium choose from a range of alternatives. About 20% of parents of this age group can avail themselves of publicly funded services (European Commission on Childcare Network, 1990, p. 29). However, the most frequently chosen solution is care by family members and grandparents, in slightly over 50% of the cases. In second place are family daycare solutions, which are often publicly certified, with about 20% of children, while the public nursery schools take only a small percentage of children (Crombé, 1991, p. 62).

Children between 3 years of age and the beginning of primary school at age 6 attend pre-primary school between 0830 and 1530 hours. This situation is exceptional in Europe and shared only with France. The care of more than 95% of the children in this age group is covered during these hours (European Commission on Childcare Network, 1990, p. 10). However, parents do face problems with the lunch-hours and periods after school and during vacations, which they solve with a patchwork quilt of alternatives ranging from part-time work to au pair and baby-sitting schemes depending on the careers of the parents. This is an area where initiatives from both the public and private sector would be welcomed (Jansen, 1990) and eight serious public projects have been started in Flanders for the period 1991–3 (Crombé, 1991, p. 64).

However, parents report that the real problems present themselves when children reach school age. The compulsory school day lasts 7 hours, but children are free every Wednesday afternoon as well as during school vacations. There is some feeling that solutions for children after these hours have not kept pace with the growing participation of women in the labour market. Some schools offer programmes, and various organizations organize camping and excursions during the vacation periods, but the solutions are insufficient. Some banks, and various quasi-public-sector enterprises such as the television and radio companies, universities and hospitals also provide vacation camps for children.

Although public childcare is comparatively good, employers do not see the childcare concerns of their employees as their problem. Female managers are expected to manage their children as well. Although Belgian male managers expressed support for splitting the housework, in practice most still have non-working wives and thus are not likely to have very much insight into the balancing acts that working women face (Albarello, 1990). In Belgium, those in management positions are expected to clock up 60 hours a week at the beginning of their careers, just the time when families can also be demanding. In response to surveys, it was very clear that in Belgium management is seen as something that is impossible to do on a part-time basis, at least in manufacturing and finance (Albarello, 1990; Franck, van Put and Vermeulen, 1990; Demeester and Neefs, 1991). Career breaks are generally considered to be fatal to the promotion prospects of women hoping to climb a career ladder (Demeester and Neefs, 1991).

GETTING BACK TO WORK: SPECIAL PROGRAMMES

Women have traditionally stopped work with childbearing, even without career-break possibilities. With the flexible career-break schemes, Belgium has increased its population of re-entry candidates, with the attendant problems of outdated skills and low levels of confidence. The Ministry of Employment and Labour estimates that some 165,000 women would like to re-enter the labour force (Ministerie van Tewerkstelling en Arbeid, 1990b). The average age of these women is around 38. They are relatively low skilled, with experience in typically female sectors such as healthcare, childcare, and clerical and sales work. The mean time out of the labour force is around 10 years, but most of the women who have been trying to re-enter remained housewives longer than they would have preferred because of practical problems of re-entry (van Regenmortel, de Cock and Vanderloo, 1990).

The problems of these women have only recently become a matter of policy in Belgium, when they became identified as a 'risk' group in 1988. The public sector has taken action both in the form of educational initiatives, supplementing private initiatives already available, and in terms of employment initiatives. For example, re-entry candidates are now eligible as replacements for those taking career breaks. Furthermore, the state is stimulating employment opportunities and retraining for childcare – perhaps a case of robbing Peter to pay Paul but, nonetheless, a step in solving two problems at once.

MAKING IT: BREAKING THROUGH THE 'GLASS CEILING' AND LEADING WITH A PERSONAL STYLE

The public policy for working women is relatively favourable in Belgium, even if there are still many aspects which can be improved. Nonetheless, there are very few women at the top of Belgian business. The discrepancy between businesswomen and men with similar qualifications is a reality. A recent study of 400 male and female graduates from 1971 to 1984 of one of the more prestigious business administration programmes, indicates that even younger women with appropriate credentials have significant problems in the business world. Both their salaries and the number and type of non-monetary rewards, such as a private office, were less than those of male fellow alumni (Meersman and, Vanneste, 1992). Women tended to believe their chances for promotion were fewer, which may have a self-fulfilling effect on their ability to get ahead. The female graduates also tended to be more 'anti-career' in their attitudes than their male colleagues. Yet, when the researchers controlled for ambitions and beliefs about promotion, a difference in achieved status still remained. Even if the women had had an identical career pattern behaviour, without career breaks, they had a lower achieved status than men (Meersman and Vanneste, 1992,

p. 36). These Belgian results naturally mirror results from English language research on women and business, but it is significant that such studies are finally being done, as the beliefs about the real situation of women in business will have to change.

There is a firm opinion among male business leaders that there is no discrimination against women in their firm, even if they might admit that the Belgian business world in general is ill-suited to women. Fifty-five per cent of business leaders in one survey agreed that if 'women are not making it, it is the fault of society and what women themselves want; our firm can do little about it' (Woodward, 1991, p. 119). While Belgian business leaders in interviews will sometimes state that business can use female talents or, for demographic reasons, will have to use female talents better, qualitative studies of business and financial life in Belgium indicate that the culture is far from woman friendly. The women who have made it to the top in Belgium have frequently had to fit into a specific Belgian permutation of Moss-Kanter's 1977 token-stereotype model. Biographical studies of women in finance (Demeester and Neefs, 1991) and politics (van Winckel, 1991) indicate that many women have chosen a career and left family behind. The American business theory that a woman who wants to get to the top should 'Dress like a lady, act like a man, and work like a dog' (Demeester and Neefs, 1991, p. 137) is definitely applicable in Belgium.

Perhaps, however, the widespread belief that time will work wonders for women may have some basis in fact in Belgium. Younger male business leaders tend to be more open than older ones to the idea of working side-by-side with women managers (Albarello, 1990). The older generation of Belgian leaders are generally married to non-working wives, but increasingly, as upper-middle-class women expect a career for themselves, male leaders will be seeing the problems of the woman in the business world first hand. It may also be the case that younger women managers will strive aggressively to achieve their rightful place and exercise management in their own way in the future. De Rese's study of women decision-makers indicates the presence of a new style of leadership among her population of younger lower-level managers, and a will to try to change the business world from within (de Rese, 1991).

Belgian businesswomen with their location in the heart of Europe have also begun to organize to improve their position in Europe. The headquarters of organizations such as the European Women's Lobby and other professional European business groups in Brussels allows Belgian women easy access to European information, and a location at the centre of many professional networks. Belgian women themselves have begun Focus Career Services, and a Belgian chapter of Network. Other traditional organizations such as the Association for University Women are taking on new identities with an influx of profession-ally active university trained women. Such organizations will support

Belgian women in carving out a stronger place in the professional world and help in the initiation of much needed mentoring of younger women by more established ones.

As this brief overview suggests, research is only recently beginning into the situation of Belgian women in management. The Belgian business world is not the same as the American, and the style that Belgian women will have to develop to succeed in the Europe of 1992 will have to be adapted. However, the traditional female virtues of verbal ability, talent at languages, and communication skills are also virtues that have helped Belgian business in general to find a place in a rapidly unifying Europe that is disproportionate to its size. Thus, optimistically, a unified Europe may mean that Belgium will begin making better use of its potential in women.

REFERENCES

Albarello, L. (1990) Que pensent aujourd'hui les décideurs et meneurs d'opinion belges à propos de la problématique de l'inégalité entre hommes et femmes? Presentation of survey results. Le Conseil de L'Emancipation. Proceedings for conference day, *Journée de réflexion: Femmes et Hommes: Inventons l'Egalité*, Brussels, 2 October, pp. 49–53.

Commission of European Communities (1992) *Women of Europe Supplement*, no. 36, March.

Crombé, C. (1991) De collectieve benadering. *Arbeidsblad*, no. 4, pp. 59–71.

Degimbe, N. and Simon, A. (1991) Vrouwenarbeid: activiteitsgraad en deeltijdse arbeid, *Arbeidsblad*, no. 4, pp. 12–21.

de Gols, M., de Vos, D., Eggermont, M., Lantin, B., Urbain, M-P. and Vanseveren, J. (1991) Individuele maatregelen met het oog op het harmoniseren van het beroeps – en het gezinsleven, *Arbeidsblad*, no. 4, pp. 37–58.

Demeester, W. and Neefs, E. (1991) *Het Glazen Plafond: Vrouwen in de Belgische Financiële Wereld*, Lannoo, Tielt.

de Rese, A. (1991) Besluitsvorming bij vrouwelijke managers. Unpublished master's thesis, Vlerick School of Management, State University of Ghent.

European Commission on Childcare Network (1990) Childcare in the European Community 1985–1990, *Women of Europe Supplement*, no. 31, August.

Franck, P., van Put, A. and Vermeulen, L. (1990) *Personeelsbeleid en Bedrijfscultuur – Carrièremogelijkheid voor Vrouwen in Ondernemingen*, Inbel, Brussels.

Jansen, W. (ed.) (1990) *Arbeids-tijd, Kinder-tijd. De Onderneming als Draaischijf*, Koning Boudewijnstichting, Brussels.

Jortay, F., Meulders, D. and Plasman, R. (1991) *Evaluation of the Impact of the Single Market's Completion on Women's Employment in the Banking Sector: Synthesis Report*, DULBEA (Department of Applied Economics, Université Libre de Bruxelles)/Commission of the European Communities, Directorate-General of Employment, Industrial Relations and Social Affairs, Expert Network on Women in Employment, Phase 7, Brussels.

Kabinet van de Staatssecretaris voor Maatschappelijke Emancipatie (1990) *Positieve Acties in de Overheidsdiensten: Toelichting bij het KB van 27*

Februari 1990, Kabinet van de Staatssecretaris voor Maatschappelijke Emancipatie, Brussels.

Kabinet van de Staatssecretaris voor Maatschappelijke Emancipatie (1991a) *Positieve Acties in de Privé Sector: Model Gelijke Kansenplan voor Privé-ondernemingen*, Kabinet van de Staatssecretaris voor Maatschappelijke Emancipatie, Brussels.

Kabinet van de Staatssecretaris voor Maatschappelijke Emancipatie (1991b) *Vrouwen in de Belgische Samenleving 1991*, Inbel, Brussels.

Kanter, R. M. (1977) *Men and Women of the Corporation*, Basic Books, New York.

Meersman, H. and Vanneste, I. (1992) *Statusverschillen van Mannelijke en Vrouwelijke UFSIA-TEW-Alumni*, Studiecentrum voor Economisch en Sociaal Onderzoek, University of Antwerp, Report 92/272, Antwerp.

Meulders, D. and Plasman, R. (1989) *Women in Atypical Employment: Final Report*, DULBEA (Department of Applied Economics, Université Libre de Bruxelles)/Commission of the European Communities, Directorate-General of Employment, Industrial Relations and Social Affairs, Expert Network on Women in Employment, Phase 5, Brussels.

Ministerie van Tewerkstelling en Arbeid (1990a) *Het Overleg over de Plannen voor Positieve Acties in de Ondernemingen uit de Particuliere Sector*, Ministerie van Tewerkstelling en Arbeid, Brussels.

Ministerie van Tewerkstelling en Arbeid (1990b) *Huisvrouw op Zoek naar een Baan*, Ministerie van Tewerkstelling en Arbeid, Brussels.

Paternottre, M-P. (1991) Positive action in the public sector in Belgium, *Social Europe*, no. 3/1991, p. 112.

Sztum, P. (1988) *Les Femmes Cadres*, Centre de recherche et d'information sociopolitiques, CRISP, Courrier Hebdomadaire, no. 1189.

Trends (1991) Women in banking, *Trends*, 5 September, no. 34, p. 42.

Vandevoort, L., van Put, A., Woodward, A. and Triest, M. (1990) *Functioneren Vrouwen Anders? Functieclassificatie en Personeelsbeleid in het Kader van Positieve Actie*, Centrum voor Vrouwenstudies, University of Antwerp, Antwerp.

van Herck, R. and Verbruggen, P. (1991) *Vrouwen aan de Universiteit*, Inbel, Brussels.

van Regenmortel, T., de Cock, C. and Vanderloo, R. (1990) *Herintreedsters: een Risicogroep als Geen Andere. Het Profiel en de Arbeidsmarkt Perspectieven van Herintreedsters en Langdurige Werkloze Vrouwen*, HIVA, Leuven.

van Winckel, A. (1991) *Keien in de vijver*, Kritak, Leuven.

van Winckel, E. (1992) Women's situation on the labour market in 1992, *Social Europe*, no. 3/1991, pp. 23–33.

Wyns, M. and van Meensel, R. (1990) *De Beroepensegregatie in België (1970–1988)*, Study commissioned by the Staatssecretaris voor Maatschappelijke Emancipatie, HIVA, Leuven.

Woodward, A. (1991) Onderzoeksnota: positieve actie in de particuliere en openbare sectoren, *Rapporten en Perspectieven omtrent Vrouwenstudies*, Vol. 3, pp. 115–28.

9.

GREECE

Poly Miliori

INTRODUCTION

Although there are a good deal of data available concerning women's participation in the labour force, unfortunately there are few statistical analyses of women in top management positions and in business in Greece. The claims of women with regard to employment in top management positions, as well as the situation concerning women general managers, are phenomena only of the last decade.

This chapter will be based on what few statistical data are available, on studies already published, on unpublished research topics presented at conferences, on articles in specialized magazines and on the growing number of interviews in the mass media with women in top management positions. It will also be based on interviews I conducted myself during the preparation of this chapter and on my personal experience, as a Greek woman working for 17 years as an editor-in-chief of a popular women's magazine.

Topics to be discussed include Greek women's share of the labour force, the attitude of the law and the state towards equality in work, the hesitant steps of women towards top management positions in both the public and private sectors, and the creation of businesses by women. There is a common thread which runs through and unites the issues, namely, that at the beginning of the last decade of the 20th century, Greek women have consciously abandoned, albeit with some difficulty, their old, one-dimensional role. However, this old role remains both a hindrance and a qualification for the new one.

WOMEN'S PARTICIPATION IN THE GREEK LABOUR FORCE

Unfortunately, 10 years have passed since the last census was carried out by the National Statistics Service. According to the last census in 1981, 27% of the Greek working population were women. Another survey conducted by the National Statistics Service of Greece in 1984 indicated that this percentage is increasing, with the current figure standing at around 33%.

This increase is due to the development of the tertiary sector of the economy, that is the service sector, a field traditionally much more accessible to women. It is exactly this sector that seems to offer most opportunities for the creation of businesses by women, and will give women the possibility of obtaining top management positions.

These data show that about one-third of the Greek working population are women. A breakdown of the percentage of women classified in various professions reveals the following figures:

- 37% of self-employed scientists are women;
- 11% of the architects and engineers are women;
- 26% of lawyers, authors and journalists are women;
- almost half of office staff, 47%, are women.

WOMEN'S PROFESSIONS

It is important to be aware that these statistics can be misleading and that real equal opportunities in the workplace have certainly not been achieved, not even in the 'office staff' category. In the higher levels of the organizational hierarchy, at managerial and senior executive level, men hold the senior positions. The true extent of women's participation in the category 'office-staff' is about half that indicated if the lower range of employee positions is taken into account − positions in which women dominate.

Typing is a 'woman's profession'. The positions involving predominately routine work, including those of typist and secretary, are almost exclusively occupied by women. 'Typist' and 'secretary' are even female terms in Greek.

Another exclusively 'woman's profession' is that of maid where women occupy almost 82% of jobs. However, in the wider classification of the service professions, the women's participation rate falls to 41%, again because men hold the higher positions.

On entering a department store, a supermarket or a boutique, a customer receives the impression that the trade is limited solely to women. However, an examination of the statistics presents a different picture: only 32.6% of the merchants and the employees in commercial enterprises are women and therefore the large majority of women serving the consumer suggests that the majority of those making the deals from their offices must be men. In fact, 82% of shop managers, 84% of sales policy department staff and 85% of sales supervisors are men. Women merely stand behind the sale stands − the last link in the chain.

NEW TECHNOLOGIES AND WORKING GREEK WOMEN

Even after the rapid establishment of computers in both the public and private sectors, the position of women in this section of the workforce has not changed. As with the supermarket, a customer entering a printing house and seeing the large number of women working on photocomposition will have the impression that women represent the majority of employees working with computers. This is only because the computer here is simply being fed with data entered by the user. Where analysis and programming are required, the computer users are men.

Research conducted by Stefanoglou and Lampropoulou (1987) showed that 99.5% of those engaged in data entry work were women, while only 27% of analysts and programmers were female. In large organizations, like banks, where 'informatics' have radically changed the nature and format of work over the last 10 years, the same pattern is observed: women comprise 10–30% of computer programmers in banks but the data entry departments are staffed exclusively by women. There is only one bank, the National Bank of Greece, which has male staff in its data entry department (League for Women's Rights, 1989).

CHANGING CONCEPTS OF WOMEN'S WORK AND PROFESSIONS

The concept of 'women's' and 'men's' professions, deeply rooted in Greek society, is interlinked with the limited extent of women's participation in management. The idea that 'manager' *means* a man has been deeply rooted in Greek society although it is expected to weaken in the generation now growing up. Particular attention is paid to the way schoolbooks present professions. The ascent of women to the higher positions in the mass media (press, television and radio) will also play a major role in changing attitudes.

Research conducted by ERT (national television and radio) was communicated at the first joint conference of EBU-EEC, on the subject of 'Women in audio-visual media of information', which took place in Athens in 1991 (ERT, 1991). According to their findings only 27% of the senior management staff of the company (heads of department included) are women. The president of the company is a man, and none of the five general managers of the company is a woman. Only three of the 28 heads of department are women. Unfortunately, there are no data available for private radio and television stations. The only woman director general in a private radio station in Greece has now resigned.

In the area of women's magazine there are many women in managerial positions, in fact more than men. By contrast, in the daily press the number of women managers is very small. Today the mass media have the greatest influencing power they have ever had. Therefore, the image of women, which will be promoted through the media, will become the model for the coming generations. However, these images should not be confined to advertisements: they should be a reflection of a positive image of women in the real world.

I believe that the entrance of women into management positions in the printing and electronic press will provide not only the impetus for more women to enter top management positions but will also convey positive stereotypes about working women in general.

NUMBERS AND ATTITUDES

In Greece 14% of managers are women. There are far fewer general managers than this in management positions. It is not easy for statistics to represent the attitudes of a society when a decade has passed since the last population census. We must also consider that in this last decade major changes have taken place: constitutional protection of equality, change in the civil code, change in family law, and EC Directives on equal opportunities.

Only 14% of economists and computer specialists recorded in the last census were women. The continuously increasing preference for economic studies, management and computer science shown lately by young girls indicates that more and more women are making top management positions in business their professional goal.

EQUAL OPPORTUNITY AND THE LAW IN GREECE

The Greek Constitution of 1975 included provisions for the protection of sexual equality, and gave the legislature 7 years (up to the end of 1982) to abolish all provisions opposed to the principle of equality. It was through Article 22 that the equality in salaries for the same work became a constitutional order.

The European Community (EC) law also imposes equality (Greece became a member of the EC in 1981). Article 119 of the EC Convention, as well as Directives 75/117, 76/207 and 79/9, impose additional measures in every country which abolish the distinction between men and women in the field of employment, professional education and promotion and insurance. The Greek laws 1414/84 and 1483/84, for example, are measures for adaptation to the EC guidelines.

Deficiencies and violations of laws

The jurist and feminist Iris Avdi-Kalkani (1988), in her book *Feminism and Employment in Greece Today*, asserts that many discriminatory laws still exist both directly and indirectly, and consequently the constitutional will is being violated. She notes:

The new laws introduced, as well as those amended in order to fit with the principle of equality in employment, often have no practical effect. Some of them are deliberately constricted in such a way as to be difficult to apply; others are violated on a systematic basis — particularly in the private sector — or have, little by little, no effect, because of lack of supervision and lack of awareness among the working people.

(Avdi-Kalkani, 1988, p. 36)

The following are two examples of 'conditions', included in laws, which contradict the legislators' intention:

(1)   One of the main problems for working women is the care of small children. Even children at primary school present problems, especially in big cities. Because of the lack of classrooms, classes are taught alternately in the morning and in the afternoon, so the working hours of mothers do not always coincide with the school hours of their children. The establishment of day nurseries has been addressed by the law, as well as in pre-election announcements. However, only companies with more than 300 employees have to provide nursery facilities and few firms in Greece are of such a size. As noted by Avdi-Kalkani, (1988) until 1988 no company day nursery had been established.

(2)   Another law, in 1984, which deals with facilities offered to working people of both sexes with family obligations, contains the following 'condition'. For a parent to obtain leave of absence for bringing up children, there is the requirement that he or she works in a company employing more than 100 people, that he or she does not receive any salary during the whole period of the leave, and that he or she pays all insurance contributions (the employer's ones included).

The *Evaluation of the Third Long-Term Community Programme of Activity for 1986–90 regarding Equal Opportunities for Men and Women*, a study conducted by the legal department of the Secretariat General for Equality, includes examples of laws changed in favour of equality, but it also states that:

Greek Courts, mainly through some previous decisions, have applied the principle of equal treatment of men and women in a fully satisfactory way (equality in salaries, access to employment, dismissal of pregnant women, etc.). The number of legal judgments is relatively limited, given the direct and obvious discriminations that still exist, mainly in the collective work contracts and arbitration decisions, as well as the indications of direct and indirect discriminations in the Act. Important reasons for this are the lack of adequate and accurate information, the fear of reprisal by the employer, and also the hesitation of the courts to proceed, as they have to, and apply immediately the aforementioned rules.

(Secretariat General for Equality, 1990, p. 2)

Therefore, it can be concluded that although equality has been legislated for, it has not yet become a reality. A typical example of this form of 'equality' is found in the situations vacant columns where the existing distinctions are still very much in evidence. There is often an express requirement for either male or female employees, depending on whether the profession is considered to be a 'man's' or a 'woman's' or, in the most extreme cases, women are explicitly excluded.

WOMEN DIRECTORS IN PUBLIC ADMINISTRATION

The Ministry of the Presidency of the Greek government carried out a census of public employees in 1988. In evaluating the figures, the following points must be taken into account.

(1) Promotion to the four ranks of public administration takes place on the basis of the 'years of employment' and 'the employee's qualifications'. In the first (lowest) rank, 33% of employees are women, in the second rank 44.6%, in the third rank 36.6%, and in the fourth (the highest) rank 29.6% of employees are women.

(2) The relatively small participation rate in the fourth rank is possibly related to the option offered (until recently to women), in public administration to retire and receive a pension after 15 years of employment.

(3) The management positions are not occupied according to the same promotion criteria as the four ranks of the hierarchy. The 'Service Councils' appoint the managers. A report by the Secretariat General for Equality mentions that there are no data available about the man:woman ratio for management positions. It further observes that 'as far as we know, the percentage of women is lower than that of men'. (Secretariat General for Equality, 1990, p. 4.) As regards top administrative posts, such as ministry director, only in January 1991 was the first woman selected for such a position in the Ministry of Commerce.

POSITIVE ACTION FOR WOMEN MANAGERS

Aliki Giotopoulou-Maragopoulou, President of the League for Women's Rights in Greece, as well as President of the International Alliance of Women, has suggested on many occasions that women should have their share of senior positions allocated through competitive tests or evaluation criteria. But in positions which are decided through a 'selection' procedure a prejudice against women still exists. Men form the majority of officers responsible for the selection of directors, and they hold all the usual prejudices against appointing women.

The B' Annual Symposium for Women Managers of Enterprises in the Private Sector, organized by STEDIMA S. A., in June 1990, highlighted the fact that after some selection tests designed for potential bank employees, in which both women and men were successful, only men were hired (Stedima S. A., 1990). Such situations also occur in the field of public administration, and therefore, when evaluating the reasons why women are not in management positions, it is necessary to consider both the public and private sectors.

In order to enforce the principles of equal opportunity in law, a number of government agencies were established in Greece, such as the Council for Equality, the Secretariat General for Equality, Prefectural Commissions of Equality and Equality Offices, in every ministry. Together with all other matters concerning equality at work, these state agencies also deal with positive action, in order to achieve equality at the higher levels of government and the private sector.

There are other agencies, especially for businesswomen, that have tried to introduce positive action, for example EOMMEX (Greek Organization of Small–Medium Enterprises), OAED (Association of Employment) and, of course, the Network for Women in Local Employment initiatives. The situation of woman entrepreneurs is considered more closely later in the chapter.

There are many women and many women's organizations who believe that the most certain, the most effective and the quickest way to abolish sexual inequality in the workplace is through the introduction of the quota system. The Co-ordinating Committee for Quotas has been working for 3 years to establish a quota of 35% obligatory participation of women in the decision-making centres. This committee included 16 non-governmental women's organizations and women's branches of eight political parties.

Other 'positive action' strategies concentrate on women's education, offer training and the opportunity to acquire qualifications and, of course, encourage research about 'women's participation' – a necessary step, since women are often ignorant of the rights they have acquired.

'Positive action' for women managers also includes efforts to provide information to women about jobs available, the representation of both men and women on committees responsible for the selection of personnel, and encouraging women to attend business education programmes aimed at senior management positions.

An important initiative was taken by the deputy minister of transportation, Apostolos Kratsas, who, through a circular to the general managers of the Greek Post Office and the Telecommunication Associations of Greece, asked to be informed, on a 6-monthly basis, about the measures taken by these associations for the promotion of women employees.

In Greece the first private sector experiment in positive action concerning the promotion of women to top management positions is being carried out by Barclays Bank. One programme educates women executives of the bank for 2 or 3 years to enable them to take on top management positions at a later date. Another programme provides management education for women employees so that they may be prepared for positions as department heads and supervisors. However, to date, there are no data available about the results of any of these positive action programmes.

WOMEN MANAGERS IN THE PRIVATE SECTOR

At present women occupy about 8% of the top management positions in the 900 biggest companies in Greece. The National Statistics Service provides detailed information: for example, that 14% of managers and senior management executives are women. Whether those numbers represent the 'real' management position is uncertain. How many of these women are really in positions of authority? And what is the difference between a 'management executive' and a 'manager'?

Relying on a wider knowledge of Greek reality and attitudes rather than on the statistics of specific achievements, it is possible to surmise that there are four main factors barring women from promotion in the hierarchies of private sector companies, as follows:

(1) The previous lower rate of women's participation in education. However, this obstacle is rapidly disappearing. Within a period of 30 years (1951–81), the percentage of women living in and around the capital city and taking courses in higher education increased by 370%. In 1981 41.5% of students were women.

(2) The double role of responsibility for the family and a demanding professional life. Although 'equality' in household and childrearing responsibilities has been promoted in Greece, the 'double role' is still a woman's reality. When women managers talk about their work, they always refer to the way they have to deal with household affairs as well. Even the most emancipated of them often mention that in order to have a career they chose to be deprived of a family — a sacrifice never required of a man.

(3) The prejudice shown by the cultural environment. Recent research by Bourantas (see *Pantheon* magazine, August 1990, p. 27) has provided a lot of evidence about the way in which women managers are regarded. The research was conducted in 30 organizations in the private sector and 15 in the public sector. The categories of people questioned who gave the most positive answers about women managers included women themselves, younger individuals, executives of multinational enterprises and officers in the public sector. Individuals in industrial enterprises and production departments, who are not yet used to having female colleagues, are more conservative. Similar findings come from data published in the press, provided by women, who work as production managers in industry or come into contact with male working environments. Women find it easier to execute their management duties in or have contacts with banks and public services, and more difficult to deal with male shopfloor workers or to be present on the factory floor or at ports. Certainly, older Greek men are more prejudiced against women.

(4) Internalized prejudice. But there is another kind of prejudice too: our own, the internalized prejudice of women. There is conflicting evidence about the way in which women confront the new role

which, ultimately, is theirs to obtain — that is, the role of the successful career woman. Some women state that their experience with a women manager has been positive. Others accuse successful women of being untrustworthy and therefore for failing to support their own sex. Chryssi Iglessi, a psychology lecturer at the University of Ioannina, who has recently published *Faces of Women — Masks of the Consciousness*, believes that

> there are too many internal resistances. And I have the impression — somebody should investigate this in order to arrive at a meaningful answer — that in Greece, women occupying top management positions do so thanks to their husband or father, and being successful in a male-oriented position, they have therefore symbolically occupied the father's position. They have achieved it by surrendering to male role models, values and competition, and they rather dislike women. They are women who have denied their female nature. Their behaviour towards other women rests on some deeper feeling of rejection and they tend to be close to the father, because they fully obey him. They obey his values, his needs and his orders (personal interview).

This internalized prejudice naturally restrains many women from ever thinking about a career in management, even though they possess the qualifications. Iglessi offered the author one more explanation: 'I think that there is a very important reality which, though it seems external, is internal. I believe that women are not trained adequately in order to pursue a career. They are discouraged from childhood on.'

Marketing, advertising and public relations

Enterprises in the fields of marketing, advertising and public relations and businesses with women customers, such as fashion and women's magazines, have more opportunities for women wishing to reach top management levels. Enterprises of this sort are also the main areas in which women try to start their own businesses. The Stedima S. A. B' Annual Symposium for Women Managers of Enterprises in the Private Sector, held in Athens in 1990, highlighted that

- women in managerial positions in advertising companies are already a reality;
- at least five of the 10 largest advertising companies in Greece have a woman in a top management position;
- the enterprises related to communications, such as public relations, market research and journalism, have women in positions of management;
- the new trend in management is in favour of women. The Secretariat General for Equality has noted that 'It is a less authoritarian management based on co-operation.'

'FEMALE' CHARACTERISTICS OPEN DOORS

'Communications is part of woman's nature.'
'Women have a creative, female mind, which gives birth to clever ideas.'
'Women create relations more easily, they have a milder nature.
'Women are more able to solve problems.'
'Women are more open and they are used to negotiation. They are more patient than men.'

These are phrases heard during conferences about women managers and similar sentiments can be found in press interviews. They describe the traditional 'women's' virtues. It is interesting − though not unexpected − that these virtues, attributed to women who have gone beyond the usual boundaries and have become members of the 'male world of competition', that is the career world, are also attributed to women 'imprisoned' at home, uneducated and depressed. Kavounidis in an article, based on her research from 1985 and 1989, in the magazine *Synchrona Themata* (December 1989) states that:

A large number of women, at some point in their interview, referred with pride to the excellent arguments, actions and acrobatics they made in order to boost their husband's morale and limit the domestic tensions between husband and children. Some of the women who participated in the research noted the fragile nature of interpersonal relations in their homes and observed that, thanks to their successful handling of these relations, 'explosions' had frequently been avoided. There were women who used the terms 'arbitrator', 'politician', 'my clever way of dealing with things', in order to describe their role in limiting tensions between the members of the family.

(Kavounidis, 1989, p. 71)

It seems that these 'female practices' currently open doors to women managers in some companies. Little by little, they may establish a new conception of co-operation between managers and employers, no matter whether the manager is a man or a woman.

PROFILE OF A CAREER WOMAN

Iglessi (1990) conducted research based on the life stories of 25 Greek women from 30 to 55 years of age. They were all university graduates, many of them involved in postgraduate studies, and all of them active feminists. Two of the conclusions of this research project were that women hesitate before making career progress, and that they underestimate their abilities.

An article published in the Greek magazine *Pantheon*, based on research by the MRB Company, on social and economic attitudes in Greek society, contains the following assertion: 'The values, the way of thinking and the way of life of women with career goals are radically different from the values and the way of life of women working only in routine jobs in order to earn a living', (p. 31). The latter's way of thinking is similar to that of women who are not professionally employed. According to this article, career women have many ideas and visions about their work; they wish to receive continuing education, to have responsibilities and to have variety in their work. They would not change their job for a different one that might offer them more money.

WOMEN ENTREPRENEURS

No adequate research has yet been carried out on the subject of women entrepreneurs. However, there are a lot of valuable data available thanks to the work of Caroline Turner and Vassilis Papaioannou for the Commission of the European Network for Women's Local Employment Initiatives in 1988. They found that, as mentioned previously, 'Women have also gradually increased their share of business ownership as a whole: from 4.7% in 1976, they constituted 9.4% of all employers in 1986' (Turner and Papaioannou, 1988, p. 31).

A problem with the statistics provided about women in business is that it is not obligatory to be registered in the Chamber of Commerce and Industry of Greece, or in the Union of Greek Industry Owners, or in the Inter Hellenic Union of Exporters and other syndicates. There is also some confusion about how many of those registered are men and how many are women. There are three reasons for this:

(1) The names of companies are listed, not the names of the owners. Not even the woman vice-president of the Chamber of Commerce and Industry or the only woman on the board of directors of the Union of Greek Industry Owners, know the number of women in their organizations.
(2) In many enterprises a woman is registered as the owner because the law prohibits her husband from establishing a business.
(3) Many family businesses, considered as belonging to the husband, are in fact directed by the wife, who has neither the salary nor the rights of insurance and pension that she might have if she were the owner.

Nevertheless, research conducted by the Network on Women in Local Employment Initiatives confirms that 'several Chambers of Commerce and Industry around the country estimate that some 10% of the businesses registered with them are owned by women, concentrated in "traditional" sectors, such as textiles, clothing manufacture and retailing' (Turner and Papaioannou, 1988).

What is the profile of women involved in business competition? Specialized and long-term education are useful but not essential for Greek businesswomen. The willingness to be continuously creative, however, is a must. Women who deal with trade and exports have to be able to understand the attitudes of the market and adapt easily to both the objects of their trade and to changing goals, in the same way that male merchants do. Some women become very attached to the product they are selling, perhaps because it is a product of their own creative inspiration, and then conduct business in order to promote it. This is often the case with businesswomen in the field of fashion who started their career as fashion designers.

There are many women who start their careers as employees in large organizations and then later establish their own businesses. When interviewed, these women usually comment that business activity impresses them and makes them feel fulfilled as well as offering emotions, happy and unhappy moments and continuous action (Turner and Papaioannou, 1988, p. 24).

Businesswomen in their double role

Depending on their financial status, businesswomen often face the problem of combining obligations resulting from their double role: the role of business owner and the role of mother. In society at large, the woman's or mother's role is regarded as sacrosanct. Of course, businessmen rarely feel the need to refer to the way they combine their family obligations with their unstable and exhausting working hours. Women attempt to solve the problem of the double role by, at one extreme, hiring a female maid to live in the house, or, at the other extreme, creating a small home-based enterprise, such as a hairdressing salon. Women on middle incomes use any available solution, often relying on relatives to take care of the children, or on day nurseries or a combination of the two.

The 'female world': an easier field of competition

The world of fashion, including clothing, the shoe industry, jewellery and beauty institutes, and the service sector of hotels, tourism and public relations, seem to constitute easier areas of competition for women. The traditional 'female' world therefore becomes the starting point from which women make their way towards the 'male' world of business: not only a familiar world but also an 'accessible' one.

The other side of this coin, however, consists of the numerous small shops, selling clothes, gifts, shoes, cosmetics, flowers or cakes, which are owned by women. In this case, the creation of a small enterprise − very often making a loss rather than a profit − is not a natural outlet for the abilities and ambitions of a young woman starting out in life, but the delayed effort of an older woman to find herself a role, even if it is an alternative to the one she would ideally have chosen. Middle-aged, with no educational qualifications, with no knowledge of the market and with capital often granted condescendingly by her husband, the woman begins a career and, in fact, a new life. The expression 'He may establish a boutique shop for her!' is a common one in Greece when the topic of conversation is the nervous breakdown of a middle-aged woman with no profession, whose children have grown up: the husband is called in to offer a solution to the crisis of age and marriage – with his money and his permission.

Both when the creation of a small business is a form of escapism, and when it is started with no obstacles and at the right time, the nature of the enterprise is very often related, as already mentioned, to the 'traditional' female role.

Tourism enterprises

Many women have founded hostels, small hotels and restaurants and, in this limited context, established small but successful and prosperous businesses.

'Women and Tourism' was the subject of a successful conference attended by women from France, Germany and Greece, which took place at Petra in Lesvos in the autumn of 1989, at the initiative of the Secretariat General for Equality in co-operation with the French–German Association for Youth (VAFJ). Thirty women involved in the creation of businesses related to tourism exchanged their ideas and experiences.

Household work

The creation by women of small businesses dealing with so-called 'household work' is an obvious trend. Even the Secretariat General for Equality, that has made and is still making a systematic effort to reinforce business goals for women, started its programme with 'rural–touristic co-operative unions'. If offered assistance for the creation of co-operative unions for women in rural areas, who produced 'household-art' in their own homes. The unions had as one of their objectives the wider distribution of products that until recently had been destined for a limited home consumption, thus enabling women to enter the business world. As mentioned in Turner's research, 'The majority of women's co-operative enterprises today are located in rural areas and islands with a much smaller number in urban centres. Most of these initiatives operate in tourist services and craft production, with some in light manufacturing workshops' (Turner and Papaioannou, 1988, p. 20).

Advertising and public relations

Another services sector apparently favoured by women in business is that of public relations. As already noted in the section about women managers, here again the 'female world' seems to be the starting point.

In the field of advertising, many women organize small and flexible advertising agencies which focus mainly on advertising in women's magazines.

Other sectors

There is also, of course, the diffused and not yet dominant trend among Greek businesswomen to start their careers in other fields, which are not directly related to their 'female' education, in particular in creative areas such as bookshops, art galleries and television production companies. Women working in such fields are committed to being creative and have a considerable amount of freedom and independence.

There are few women business owners in Greece and most of them are wives, widows or daughters of business-owning men. Daughters succeeding their father is a new reality — until a few years ago, only sons tended to succeed their fathers into family businesses.

CONCLUSION

In the advertising world women are well represented, either as managers or as owners of companies, and it is perhaps due to them that increasing numbers of women managers are appearing in national advertising. This fact, and the increasing prominence of women in top management positions in marketing organizations, must together be largely responsible for the shift in public opinion that is starting to take place. Slowly but surely Greek society is recognizing that women deserve and have the right to participate in the social and economical processes of the contemporary world.

One half of human potential has until now been unexploited, not only from a quantitative but also from a qualitative point of view. The gate to the last decade of the 20th century stands wide open for a new, hopeful, different and substantially richer society.

REFERENCES

Avdi-Kalkani, I. (1988) *Feminism and Employment in Greece Today*, Nei Keri, Athens.

Iglessi, C. (1991) *Faces of Women — Masks of the Consciousness — Structuring of Women's Identity in Greek Society*, Odysseas, Athens.

Kavounidis, J. (1985) The family and productive relations — artisan and worker households in Athens. Ph.D. thesis, London School of Economics, London.

Kavounidis, J. (1989) Wife's control of income in artisan and worker households, *Synchrona Themata (Contemporary Topics)*, Vol. 40, p. 71.

League for Women's Rights (1989) *Women, Employment and New Technology*, unpublished selection of papers presented at two seminars in Athens.

Ministry of the Presidency of the Government (1988) Census of Public Employees, unpublished.

National Statistical Service of Greece (1981) *Statistical Yearbook of Greece*, Athens.

Pantheon (1990) magazine *H doulia ta allazi ola* (Work changes everything) May, pp. 42–45.

Secretariat General for Equality (1990) *Evaluation of the Third Long-Term Community Programme of Activity for 1986–90 regarding Equal Opportunities for Men and Women*, unpublished.

Stedima S. A. (1990) Papers presented at the B' Annual Symposium for Women Managers of Enterprises in the Private Sector, Athens, June.

Stratigaki, M. (1989) Technological evolution and gendered professional specializations in *Synchrona Themata (Contemporary Topics)*, Vol. 40, p. 31.

Turner, C. and Papaioannou, V. (1988) Women's local employment initials, research in commission for the European Network for Women's Local Employment Initiatives, Commission of the European Communities, Brussels.

10.

ITALY

Federica Olivares

INTRODUCTION: THE CHANGING RELATIONSHIP BETWEEN WOMEN AND WORK IN POST-WAR ITALY

At the beginning of 1990 more than 34% of the employed population in Italy were women, and 60% of all women between the ages of 20 and 29 were either employed or actively seeking a job. Of all newly-created jobs, 70% are taken up by women. Women are entering the workforce in greater numbers than men, and with a higher degree of education. These percentages are the highest in post-war Italy and are predicted to increase in the next decade.

However, only 30% of Italian women work, which is a lower percentage than in other European countries and much less than in the USA. Only 3% are found in upper management positions. How do we explain this contradiction in progress? First of all, we have to understand the sociological context of Italian society.

Italy is characterized by an economic and cultural split between its highly productive, relatively urban, 'liberal' north and its agrarian, economically backward, undereducated and traditional south. This difference has an impact on all aspects of Italian life, including the entry of women into the workforce: much more progress has been made in the north than in the south. Southern women are better educated than southern men yet, owing to lack of job opportunities and cultural stereotyping by men, they are less likely to find work. Only 8% of women university graduates in the south are employed.

Another important aspect of Italian society is the historic role the Catholic Church has played in determining cultural values. Although the Church has less influence in the north than in the south, its impact cannot be ignored in either part of the country. The symbolic value of marriage and motherhood is still very strong, and may help explain why many women stop working after the birth of children.

Related to this is the problem that there are fewer part-time jobs available in Italy than in other countries in the European Community (EC), so women who may want to maintain a part-time career after motherhood have little opportunity to do so.

In trying to understand why only 3% of women are in senior management, it is important to define what is meant by *dirigenti* or 'upper management' in Italy. These are senior level managers and executives, clearly defined as such by government contract, with salaries that are similarly mandated. These *dirigenti* are not the sum total of all women managers but only the upper management section. Nor do they include self-employed female professionals and entrepreneurs, who may have achieved commensurate levels of responsibility and authority. Nevertheless, most research done on women managers in Italy has been directed at the *dirigenti* level.

The growth of women in management and business can be attributed to three transformations which occurred by or after the 1960s:

(1) The great economic and class transformations which took place between 1945 and 1960. More than one-third of the Italian workforce shifted from agricultural jobs to industrial employment, with a concomitant move from rural to urban environments.
(2) The new demographic profile of Italian women, characterized by later marriages, fewer births and longer life expectancy, which became evident in the early 1970s and was later than in other European countries.
(3) The significant rise in education among women. In the period 1960−89 the proportion of women at secondary school increased from 20% to 51%, and at university from 15% to 50%.

In the mid-1970s it was already clear that these changes, coupled with the beginning of the 'double-digit inflation decade', had definitely altered women's labour-force participation and work life-cycle. The single peak and decline in women's labour-force participation that had characterized Italy, began to give way to more stable and continuous work patterns. Re-entry after childrearing remains relatively low as Italy has the lowest percentage of part-time jobs in the EC.

At the same time, unemployment has increased in recent years and remains higher for women than for men: from 11.6% in 1973 to 18.8% in 1989 (compared to 4.2% and 8.1%, respectively, for men). Starting in 1984, affirmative action programmes were introduced in 20 of Italy's major public and private companies. Inspired by the EC Council's Directives, these have been aimed at developing women's career options and equal opportunity access.

LEGAL PROVISIONS

Although Italy's Constitution of 1948 explicitly guarantees the equality of men and women before the law, a political compromise between the

Christian Democrats and the left-wing parties also explicitly made women responsible for the family. Article 37 of the Constitution thus states: 'The working woman has the same rights and the same remuneration for equal work as a man. Working conditions should permit the fulfilment of her essential family function and ensure to the mother and her child a special adequate protection.'

Legislation to reinforce this 'protection' continued from 1950 to 1975, providing working women with benefits and job protection, but at the same time making them appear to be a more costly resource. Post-war 'protective legislation' began with the 1950 Act that gave women a period of paid maternity leave of 6 weeks before and 2 months after childbirth. This was extended in 1971 to 2 months prior to and 3 months after delivery on full pay. The prohibition of dismissal covers pregnancy and 1 year after delivery. In the 1970s interest in women's issues reached unprecedented heights, due to the Italian women's movement − one of the strongest and most enduring in Europe − and to left-wing coalition governments. These two forces resulted in the passing of several major Acts of Parliament which improved the social and working status of women. Among the most significant were:

- the Divorce Law of 1974, which made divorce legal under certain circumstances for the first time in Italy;
- the Abortion Law of 1975, which legalized state-funded abortions up to the 3rd month of pregnancy;
- the New Family Act of 1975, which − among other things − guaranteed the same rights and responsibilities to women previously granted only to men;
- the Equal Treatment of Men and Women Act (ETA) of 1977, which is Italy's legal springboard for equal opportunity in the corporate environment.

These laws were made possible by, and served as a catalyst for, widespread changes in social attitudes toward women. However, the lack of efficient legal and economic sanctions for infringements of the ETA law, ensured that real equal opportunities in the work environment remained practically ineffective until the statutory bodies responsible for implementing the ETA were established in 1984. Nevertheless, the 1977 legislation represents a turning point from protective legislation to guarantees of equality, and in this respect is a step forward in the perception of women's status in society.

Two Equal Opportunities (EO) Commissions have since been set up: the EO Commission at the Ministry of Labour in 1984, composed of trades unions, women's associations and employers' representatives; and the National Commission on Equality, created by the Prime Minister in 1985, whose members are nominated by the political parties and which plays primarily a cultural role, promoting studies on women's status and supporting EO practices.

THE EMERGENCE OF WOMEN IN MANAGEMENT

The 1987 CRORA survey *Professional and Personal Profile of Senior Women Managers in Italy*, sent to 4,000 women in senior management positions working in industrial companies, is the most comprehensive study of these women in Italy. The response rate was 12%. A section of the questionnaire pertaining to lifestyles, attitudes regarding women in management, and job mobility was also completed by a group of 117 senior male managers. All the tables that follow are taken from this survey (CRORA, 1987).

While legal provisions were insufficient to secure equality and career opportunities for women, other factors encouraged women's entry into the ranks of Italian management. The growth of the urban middle class (from 40% to 60% of the total population between 1971 and 1989), with its attendant openness to northern European cultural lifestyle standards, contributed to the wider acceptance of career-oriented women.

Women redirected their educational choices in terms of both subject choice and length of study. The proportion of women in professional and business-oriented higher education increased from 12% in 1975 to 32% in 1989. By 1989 women represented 50% of the total university student population, including 43% in economics, 46% in law, 58% in sciences and 18% in engineering and architecture. Between 1975 and 1990 the percentage of women obtaining graduate degrees from Italian management and business schools rose from 5% to 26%, one of the highest in Europe.

SOME FACTS AND FIGURES

As already noted, women today constitute 3% of senior management ranks, with relevant differences among sectors: 10% in public administration, 7.5% in the service sector (not including financial services), 2.4% in banking and 2% in industry. In the top executive ranks women are only 1.1%, but again there are variations by sector − from 2.1% in services to 0.3% in banking.

The relatively low percentage of women in banking, finance and insurance − 24% as compared to 46% as an EC average − may be explained in part by the strong political influence in the large state-owned banks.

In general, women have been less active than men in organizational politics. In many cases they are less likely to be considered for entry-level positions, or for any other managerial positions higher up the organizational ladder.

Very little research has been done on Italian women in management, so data are still scarce compared with many other countries in Europe. The majority of existing studies are qualitatively rather than quantitatively oriented. The data cited in the following pages are taken primarily from the following research:

(1)   Two major studies on female employment by the Centre for
      Research on Company Organization (CRORA) at Bocconi Uni-
      versity, Milan. 'Women's professional development in the banking
      sector' (Olivares and Salvemini, 1985) was conducted by means of
      questionnaires sent to the personnel officers of Italy's top 200
      banks and interviews with a sample of 20 senior executives. The
      second study, entitled *Professional and Personal Profile of Senior
      Women Managers in Italy*, also involved questionnaires, this time
      sent to a sample of 4,000 senior women managers, identified
      through the National Confederation of Managers. The respondents
      were 12% of the sample (CRORA, 1987).
(2)   Eurisko Research Institute's qualitative survey on the 'Changing
      life/career expectations of younger women in Italy', commissioned
      by the professional network *Donne in Carriera* for its 10th anniver-
      sary. A questionnaire was submitted by three labour psychologists
      to a sample of 20 women, aged 25–38, with university degrees,
      working in industrial and non-industrial companies, with positions
      ranging from junior assistant to senior manager.
(3)   Research by the professional network *Donne in Carriera* (Women
      in Careers), which has been collecting data on its members since
      1980. It was founded in Milan in 1990 by Federica Olivares and
      now has seven chapters throughout Italy and 500 members, mostly
      women in their early forties working both in the liberal professions
      and as managers or entrepreneurs.

PERSONAL BACKGROUND OF
SENIOR WOMEN MANAGERS IN ITALY

The following descriptive data on women in senior management are
based on a study of a large number of Italian companies conducted by
the University of Bocconi (CRORA, 1987). Note that almost half of the
senior managers are aged under 45 – the result of women's reorientation
of their academic studies *en masse* into middle management positions
during the 1980s. Proof lies in the fact that this rise is concentrated in
the period 1971–84; in 1971 the same age groups constituted 37.7% of
the total (see Figure 1).

It should also be added that in the last 15 years career paths up to
management ranks have been shortened for both men and women,
from 15–20 years to 10–15 years on average. This can be explained by
the fact that new and fast-moving businesses have become part of the
Italian economy during the same period.

The majority of Italian women managers are married: almost 10%
more than a decade ago. At the same time, they are twice as likely to
be separated or divorced as they were in 1975. Given that the average
age of these women managers is less than it was 10 years ago (see
Table 1), it seems that women no longer have to renounce marriage to
pursue a career. In addition, 53% of Italian women managers have

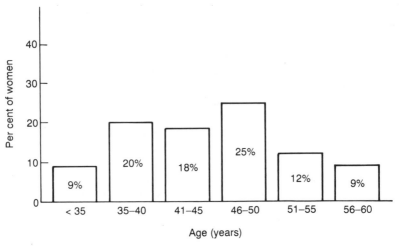

Source: CRORA (1987) *Professional and Personal Profile of Senior Women
          Managers in Italy*

Figure 1   Distribution of senior women managers by age, 1990 (mean age =
             45 years).

Table 1   Marital status of women managers (%)

Single, never married	28
Married	59
Separated or divorced	10
Widowed	3

children; the average number is 1.7. In contrast, a 10-year-old study of
a group of US women executives showed that older women regarded
their career as an either/or alternative to marriage and family.

There is high professional homogeneity between the woman manager
and her partner (see Table 2). Seventy per cent of couples earn equivalent
incomes, and only 20% are in situations where the man earns less than
the woman (see section on earnings).

Table 2   Occupations of women managers' partners (%)

Manager	32
Liberal profession	23
Employee	22
Entrepreneur	8
Retired	6.5
Other	8

Lifestyle

From the lifestyle profile presented in Tables 3 and 4, the average woman manager emerges with a considerable burden of 48 hours spent working at her job and 12 at home. Consequently, she has little time for herself. Yet it is worth noting that one male partner out of three devotes more than 10 hours a week to home and family chores. Paid help emerges as an attractive option, given the couple's dual income, and is still a viable option in Italy among this social class. Proof of the modestly supportive attitude of the woman manager's partner is the average of 8 hours per week he devotes to home and family chores.

Professional profile

Education
Senior women managers under the age of 40 have the highest percentage of university degrees of all women managers and the highest education level; 45% of them have a university degree, compared with 2% of all Italian women (see Figure 2).

Table 3 Division of domestic chores

	Woman manager (%)	Partner (%)	Other people (paid help) (%)
Housekeeping	37	10	53
Childcare	58	32	10
Family budget	59	39	2
Family errands (Banks, public services, etc.)	55	42	3

Table 4 Professional, domestic and personal allocation of time by men and women (hours per week)

Working hours			Domestic chores			Time for oneself		
Hours	Women	Men	Hours	Women	Men	Hours	Women	Men
<40	11%	20%	<10	40%	73%	<10	40%	32%
40−50	56%	47%	10−15	36%	17%	10−15	37%	38%
50−60	24%	26%	15−20	13%	7%	15−20	13%	16%
>60	9%	8%	>20	11%	3%	>20	10%	14%
Average	48 hours	47 hours		12 hours	8 hours		12 hours	13 hours

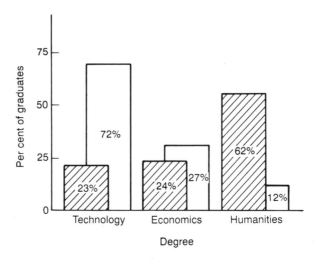

Figure 2   Percentage of degrees obtained in technology, economics and humanities by women managers (▨) and men managers (□) (40% high school diplomas, 45% university degrees and 12% postgraduate degrees).

Professional motivations

Economic autonomy and the desire to attain a highly qualified professional role seem to be the strongest motivations among Italian women managers. Nevertheless, a recent qualitative study (based on a limited sample of women 25–35 years of age) suggests that younger women find self-expression and self-fulfilment to be the strongest motivators for pursuing a managerial career (see Figure 3).

The average yearly gross earnings of women managers are 10–15% less than those of their male counterparts (see Figure 4). The reason for the relatively small differential is that in Italy most employment contracts are established by the government and the unions. A specific remuneration range is attached to each corporate job title, sector by sector, both for hourly workers and for salaried employees up to and including the management level.

Yet, despite this 'gender-neutral' process, women managers lag slightly behind. Non-management female employees fare somewhat worse, with an 18% lag, and blue-collar women earn 20% less. In addition, women managers encounter discrimination in the awarding of discretionary benefits such as low-interest mortgages and company cars, as well as the distortions resulting from job evaluations and promotion levels. Forty-one per cent of women managers are quite aware of the fact that they earn less than their male colleagues.

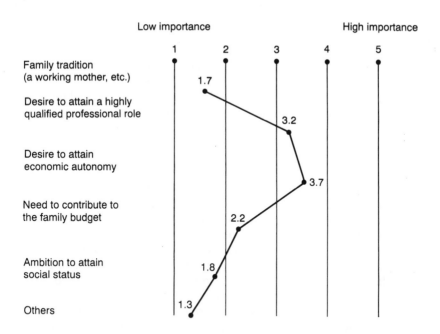

Figure 3 Women's motivations for pursuing a managerial career.

Function and role in the organization

Accounting, together with marketing and sales, are the professional fields offering the most career opportunities for women. These are followed by human resource management, that is personnel, training and recruitment, which was one of the first sectors in which women found less resistance the 1970s. Women managers in EDP are still rare,

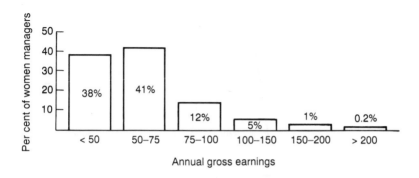

Figure 4 Women managers' average annual gross earnings.

although their numbers have increased notably in the last 5 years (see Figure 5).

THE PROBLEM AREAS FOR ITALIAN WOMEN MANAGERS

The problems facing Italian women managers are not unlike those facing their counterparts in the rest of Europe, and include sociocultural biases, men's attitudes and discrimination in organizational settings.

Sociocultural biases

As noted earlier, sociocultural biases have had a diminishing impact on women's roles in Italy in the last decade. But because of the symbolic value of marriage and motherhood in this overwhelmingly Roman Catholic country, Italy has been one of the first places in Europe to work out a 'compatibility ethic' philosophy to women's career planning. This began in the early 1980s and is simply an approach to life planning which bears in mind the goal of a balanced relationship between one's personal and professional life.

Starting in their college years, younger women are seeking 'compatibility strategies' for their management careers. These consist of:

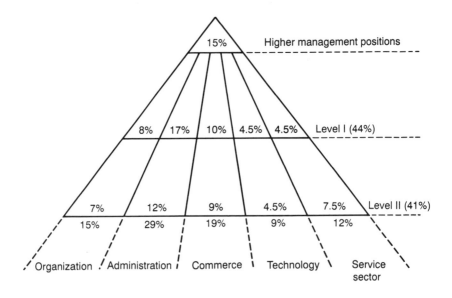

Figure 5 Functions and roles of women in management.

- marrying later than their mothers by an average of 7 years, from age 20 to 27 in the last 25 years;
- choosing partners who seem 'compatible' with their career choices;
- having fewer children and at an average age 10 years older than their mothers;
- marrying in greater numbers than the previous generation of women managers − 10% more than a decade age.

The compatibility ethic contains another key element: a demand for time for one's self and one's personal interests. Here again, younger generations of women managers clearly state their need for individual space and time twice as frequently as women managers in their fifties.

Men's attitudes

Men's stereotyped attitudes both in the home and in the work environment are additional career blocks for women managers. Although men from the north of Italy generally have more liberal attitudes than those from the south, overall stereotypes impact on women's careers in three ways:

(1) as fathers they have lower expectations for their daughters' careers than for their sons';
(2) as husbands they do not share equally in home chores;
(3) as partners they do not provide the emotional back-up that a professional woman needs.

Yet women perceive the greatest source of discrimination as stemming from male prejudice in the workplace. In male-dominated sectors, competence is often defined in masculine terms, with reference to 'macho' qualities such as competitiveness and stress endurance. To be truly competent, one simply has to *be* a man − an obviously insurmountable obstacle for the opposite sex. Personnel selection using the criterion of 'guys like us', sometimes called managerial cloning, is especially widespread in the industrial and banking sectors.

Discrimination in organizational settings

In the early 1980s researchers tried to identify discrimination in corporations through an 'organizational' approach: pinpointing the formal structures and policies that contributed to unspoken barriers for women. By the mid-1980s this approach had been enriched with a broader vision: by understanding the overall corporate culture of an organization, it was believed that certain myths, stereotypes and, consequently, discriminatory practices could be identified.

The effectiveness of this cultural analysis was borne out in the (1985) CRORA study of women in banking (Olivares and Salvemini, 1985). Almost 50% of the women staff had never been promoted. Of the other half, 35% had received only routine promotions and just 15% had benefitted from 'real' promotions based on merit in a *bona fide* career track. Not surprisingly, top bank managers, all male, expressed the view that 'banking is a man's game'.

The industrial sector tends to display discrimination both at hiring levels (hiring fewer women and for lower-level positions than men) and in promotion policies (it takes a women an average of 5 years longer to reach a managerial level). The service sector, by contrast, hires a higher percentage of women who have a better and often more specialized education, but there is still the tendency to direct women towards certain job categories. More telling is the still high degree of discrimination in promotion policies, even in fast-moving areas such as advertising or financial services. It is true that in new business sectors, such as high tech, where a male culture has not had time to take root, women are moving up faster.

TRENDS TO WATCH

Some current trends in women's career choices point to new occupational patterns for women in management:

- A marked reorientation of female professional choices: from 1981 to 1989 young women between 25 and 29 years with a diploma or university degree were five times more likely than their male colleagues to choose a non-corporate career path (a diploma in Italy is roughly equivalent to a degree from an American high school plus 2 years of junior college or technical school).

They were three times more inclined to go into business for themselves or pursue a liberal profession. This redirection (unimaginable in the early 1980s, when women were expected to pour into the management ranks) is partly a function of the gap between aspirations and reality for women in corporate management. But it is also a result of the diminished appeal of corporate life in general, which the behaviour of younger managers of both sexes increasingly illustrates.

- A new breed of women entrepreneurs are starting up small 'micro' companies. In the last decade women started up 25% of all new businesses in Italy.
- Younger educated Italian women are showing increasing indifference to the once rigidly prescribed corporate career path. They are opting in increasing numbers for different routes to professional fulfilment.
- At the same time, the 1980s have witnessed an unprecedented growth of women in Italian management, including increases in non-traditionally-female sectors and functions. There has been an increase in affirmative action and equal opportunity practices among

a great number of medium- to large-sized companies, brought about by trade union pressures *and* by growing acceptance of the need to utilize all human resources in an organization. Different value systems are also increasingly being accepted.

- The demographic squeeze foreseen for the decade of the 1990s in other Western countries is also valid in Italy. There will be 20% fewer people between the ages of 15 and 19 in the year 2000 than there were in the 1970s, while at the same time 60–80% of new entrants to the labour force will be female, with increasingly better educational backgrounds. These changes bode well for the upward managerial mobility of women.

REFERENCES

CRORA (1987) *Professional and Personal Profile of Senior Women Managers in Italy,* Centre for Research on Company Organization (CRORA), Bocconi University, Milan.

Eurisko (1990) Changing life/career expectations of younger women in Italy. Paper presented at the National Meeting of *Donne in Carriera* (Women in Careers), May. Available from *Donne in Carriera*, Via S. Maria alla Porta 1, 20123, Milan, Italy.

Olivares, F. and Salvemini, S. (1985) Women's professional development in the banking sector. Unpublished report available from Centre for Research on Company Organization (CRORA), Bocconi University, Via Sarfatti 25, Milan, Italy.

11.

PORTUGAL

Rita Campos e Cunha

INTRODUCTION

Portugal is a small country, located on the western part of the Iberian peninsula, with Spain being its only territorial border. Perhaps for this reason, Portugal has always been outward looking. The expansionist efforts of the explorers of the late fifteenth and early sixteenth centuries, as well as the number of Portuguese emigrants spread all over the world, are a reflection of this curiosity or necessity. Portuguese culture is traditionally open and tolerant of different civilizations, and the Portuguese people are characterized by their mild manners and customs.

Attitudes towards Portuguese working women, particularly those holding managerial jobs, are rapidly changing, becoming more positive and favourable. However, a rather conservative attitude can still be detected.

The political environment from the 1930s to the 1960s highly valued the domestic and family role of women in a society which was predominantly rural. Even so, female participation in the labour market grew from 13.1% in 1960 to 19% in 1970 (Nunes, 1984) and reached 46% in 1987, which is higher than the European Community (EC) average of 41% (Eurostat, 1989). The female participation rate in the labour market had, therefore, started to rise significantly, even before the entrance of Portugal into the EC in January 1986.

This high participation rate reflects (a) the need to contribute to the family budget, (b) substitution for men, mainly in rural areas, where the supply of labour was reduced by emigration and the colonial war, and (c) the creation of short-term, part-time jobs in the more developed technological industries.

According to a recent survey (Lopes, Perista and Ferreira, 1991), from 1983 onwards women have increasingly accepted short-term contracts, seasonal and temporary jobs and other forms of employment contract which are limited in duration or have a precarious quality, as opposed to full-time or part-time employment contracts.

Work as a way of satisfying social and personal development needs is becoming more and more important, particularly for those women with higher educational achievements and management ambitions. A study by Rodrigues (1990a) concludes that while many women work for economic reasons, Portuguese women entrepreneurs are often motivated by a desire for self-improvement, reflected in their high expectations of the psychological growth to be gained from their professional activity.

According to the Portuguese Association of Women Entrepreneurs (Associação Portuguesa de Mulheres Empresárias, 1992), the sectors with higher rates of female participation are agriculture, the textile and clothing industries, the services sector, education and health.

Another important development has occurred in the female employment rates by age. While in 1980 the highest employment rate was in the 20−24 age group (69.4%), it consistently declined from there on. By 1985 the rate had grown to 71.5% in the 30−34 bracket, starting gradually then to reduce, and amounting to 46.5% in the 50−54 age bracket (ILO, 1981/1985). There seems to be a trend for Portuguese women not only to increase their participation in the labour market but also to remain there, even after marriage and childbirth.

The rate of female unemployment, however, was 8.1% in 1990, that is more than double the 3.2% rate of male unemployment (Instituto Nacional de Estatística, 1990).

Portuguese working women are found mainly in the more important cities, especially Lisbon and Oporto, and in the northern, more industrialized areas of Portugal (Instituto Nacional de Estatística, 1981).

PORTUGUESE WOMEN ENTREPRENEURS

From 1960 to 1989 the percentage of entrepreneurs who are women has risen from 7.3% to 20% (Rodrigues, 1990a). This growth is more pronounced amongst entrepreneurs than amongst the general working population. It is interesting to note that during this period, in which the absolute and relative numbers of entrepreneurs declined, the number of women entrepreneurs has increased.

It should be stressed, however, that we are considering a very small percentage of the active population in the early 1980s (Instituto Nacional de Estatística, 1981). These women are concentrated in commerce (31.8% of women entrepreneurs), the textile and clothing industries (18.1%), food industries (11.6%), and services (12.9%) (Rodrigues, 1990a). While the textile industry is traditionally a female sector, in the sense that it employs a mainly female workforce, some other sectors, such as sections of the service industries and commerce, used to be male dominated. On the other hand, the majority of women entrepreneurs are between

30 and 50 years old (Rodrigues, 1990a). Whether these facts are a consequence of a profound change in social values or the result of the increasing feminization of education, is still less well understood.

By way of an example, Rodrigues (1989) has characterized the typical woman entrepreneurs in the construction, textile, clothing and food industries as being young (75% are under 40), having a university degree (40%), being a shareholder (78%) and company founder (50%), being professionally self-fulfilled (82.5%) and living in northern Portugal (52.4%). The typical company managed by the woman entrepreneur is small (82.1% have fewer than 100 employees), was founded after 1974 (66.7%), has a low technological development level (89.2%), and is usually in the domestic as opposed to the export business (60%).

A survey of 50 women entrepreneurs and managers in the top 3,500 companies revealed that women develop their professional careers in different ways. Sometimes, it is the reflection of a change process, a break with traditional or dominant social patterns; such is usually the case with company founders or career managers. In other cases, women become managers by marriage or inheritance, representing a continuous and slow diversification of women's roles and an enlargement of domestic and family duties into a public and market arena (Rodrigues, 1990b).

According to Rodrigues (1990b), the emergence of the women entrepreneurs reflects not only the diversification of women's work and the enlargement of their domains, but also a change in the social meaning of female work. Furthermore, it reflects the importance for women of new values which regard a professional activity as a way of satisfying the desire for personal development, which may be a consequence of change in the global cultural system.

Many small companies have recently been launched by women, as an alternative to employment, making use of financial incentives provided by the EC — The Local Employment Initiatives — which will be dealt with in a later section. Like all small firms, however, they face many barriers to their consolidation, and have a very low survival rate. This is due mainly to difficulties with access to information and support organizations, by a lack of management training, by difficulties in obtaining sufficient capital in the early days, and by problems with the efficient commercialization of products. Moreover, this is further reinforced by social prejudice and the perceived lack of credibility of women entrepreneurs.

WOMEN IN MANAGEMENT POSITIONS

Portuguese women in leadership and managerial positions are still underrepresented, but will inevitably increase in number as women are now a majority of university students, even in some sectors that have traditionally been considered male dominated, like law and economics. The socialization, training and expectations of young men and women will grow steadily more homogeneous and differences in the workplace will reduce. Recruitment of women for managerial positions will therefore be a natural result of the increasing feminization of universities, since access to the most talented human resources is not a luxury. For instance, in public administration, Portugal has not only the highest feminization rate, but also the highest rate of women in leadership positions, in the EC.

At the EC levels A1–A3 (equivalent to permanent and deputy secretary to assistant secretary) Portuguese women occupy 20% of the positions, followed by Denmark with 9.9%; and at the levels A4–A8 (equivalent to senior principal to administration trainee) Portuguese women hold 38.4% of these positions, Italy taking the second place with 28.8%. The averages for all EC countries and EC Commission are 5.9% and 17.3% for the A1–A3 and A4–A8 levels, respectively (European Institute of Public Administration, 1988).

GOVERNMENT LEGISLATION AND SOCIAL PROVISIONS

Since the democratic coup that took place in 1974, with the development of the women's movement, political parties, trades unions and, more recently, the EC Directives, legislation has been passed on maternity and parental leave, on employment and training policies for women, and on childcare facilities. The principles of non-discrimination and equality of rights and opportunities were sanctioned by the Portuguese Constitution in 1975.

Article 13th
(1) All citizens have the same social dignity and are equal before the law.
(2) No one can be privileged, benefitted, prejudiced, deprived of any right or excused of any duty because of ancestry, sex, race, idiom, national origin, religion, political or ideological belief, education, economic or social condition.

Article 59th
(3) It is incumbent upon the State to guarantee the right to work, granting:
  (a) ...
  (b) Equality of opportunity to choose a profession or type of work and conditions which allow access to any job, work or professional category, are not limited by sex.

(Constitution of the Portuguese Republic, 1975)

Maternity and parental leave

According to law no. 4/84 (Neto, 1984), women are entitled to 90 days maternity leave, of which 60 days must be taken after delivery and 30 days may be used totally or partially before or after delivery.

In the case of the mother's physical or mental disability, the last 30 days of the maternity leave (or last 60 days not immediately subsequent to delivery) may be used by the father. In the case of the mother's death, the father is entitled to parental leave for the same period to which the mother was entitled.

Mothers are also entitled to two work reductions per day, for a maximum of 1 hour, to allow for breast-feeding, until the child is 1 year old. Fathers have a right to 2 days leave, to be taken immediately after the birth. The full salary is paid during all these periods of leave.

Career breaks may also be used by mothers or fathers who wish to stay at home with their children over and above the legally permitted parental leave. A full career break may be requested, without any financial compensation, for a period of 6 months, which may be extended to 2 years, starting at the end of maternity or parental leave. Employees with two or more children under 12 years may also request a reduction of work time or a flexible schedule. These programmes, however, have to be negotiated with the employers and an agreement must be reached.

Mention should also be made regarding the provisions for care of sick children. Employees, both fathers and mothers, have a right to 30 days per year to attend children under 10 in the case of sickness or accident, with full pay, and if a child is in hospital one parent can take leave equal to the length of the hospital stay. In practice, these career breaks are rarely requested by individuals holding managerial positions, particularly men. Women managers who take a career break will probably have to face some barriers in their attempts to climb the corporate ladder.

Childcare

In Portugal, although some progress has been made, childcare facilities are still not satisfying the needs, either in quantitative or qualitative terms, of parents, especially those with children under 3 years.

Portugal has the lowest rate in the EC of childcare facilities for children aged between 3 and 36 months (11%), and also for children aged between 3 and 6 years (35.6%), which represents about half the EC average of 66% (Comissão da Condição Feminina, 1989). Given the high work rate of Portuguese women, it is easy to imagine the problems they face in reconciling the demands of family and work, and also to see how much needs to be done in this area, both in the public and private sectors.

Although childcare facilities are concentrated in urban areas, it is precisely here that problems are most acutely felt, since the active population is much bigger and the family structure is less traditional. In the rural areas, it is easier to find grandmothers or aunts, ready and willing to provide for the care of children when women decide to develop a professional activity.

In the bigger cities, families with greater economic resources, such as Portuguese women managers and entrepreneurs, make use of the private system of childcare facilities, which may extend later into the afternoon.

When children reach school age, the difficulties do not decrease. The compulsory state school day is 6 hours − equivalent to either a morning or an afternoon. Very few state schools or other organizations offer activities for the rest of the day or during vacations.

Private schools, which usually cater for all educational levels from kindergarten to the end of high school, can be a great help to dual-career families, by providing longer school days − up to 11 hours − as well as quality of teaching. These schools charge comparatively high prices and are, therefore, limited to families with medium or high incomes, among which we may include women managers, who must resort, particularly during vacations, to the help of grandmothers, baby-sitters and housekeeping schemes.

Nevertheless, the majority of women managers are still expected to assume responsibility for childcare, and management is considered to be incompatible with part-time or other flexible contracts. This fact, in association with the hindrance of career breaks, is likely to produce high levels of stress. This is a social problem that will have to be dealt with by society, and should lead to a profound change in the attitudes and social values associated with gender.

POSITIVE ACTION POLICIES

Positive action measures towards equal opportunities and treatment for women have been adopted by the Portuguese Institute for Employment and Professional Training (Instituto do Emprego e Formação Profissional, 1991). This organization has opted for some measures of positive discrimination, as outlined below.

- Staff training and integration. Employers are exempted from 25% or 50% contribution to training grants when they employ women in traditionally male-dominated professions.
- Bringing young people into employment. Employers are exempted from the 25% contribution to the monthly subsidy for young people when young women are employed in traditionally male-dominated professions.
- Job creation grant. For each new job created for women, in traditionally male-dominated professions, firms receive a bonus grant of 20% of 12 times the national minimum wage.
- Enterprise and self-employment allowances for women (local employment initiatives). A bonus grant of 20% of 12 times the national minimum wage for each job created will be received by women investors and managers. This allowance can be a top-up to the job creation grant.

- Enterprise support centre. Women entrepreneurs and managers will be given priority in projects in traditionally male sectors or innovative areas involving new technologies, new products, or new production or management processes, besides receiving an increase of 20% in the first cash grant for each new job, topped up by the allowance of 20% of 12 times the national minimum wage.

Besides these positive action measures, the *Instituto do Emprego e Formação Profissional* is also providing support structures, either by financing childcare facilities or by developing the conversion of training facilities. In this regard, childcare grants are given to women trainees who are responsible for children and have to leave them in care in order to be able to attend training, for the duration of the vocational training at IEFP's training centres. It has also been paying for the conversion of training centres, in order to allow women to attend them, as well as for accommodation expenses for women in training centres with only male residential facilities.

Pamphlets and other literature have been published by IEFP, some of them with the collaboration of the Commission on Women's Affairs, regarding equal opportunities, training schemes for women and career choice aid. A network of equal opportunities officers, composed of members from each of IEFP's central units and one from each regional branch, was created in 1986 with the objective of ensuring the enforcement of laws and regulations on equal employment opportunities and vocational training.

TRAINING AND EMPLOYMENT POLICIES

With the support of the European Social Fund, IEFP has been running training schemes for women, some in traditionally male occupations like carpentry, electricity and plumbing, and others in equipping women with entrepreneurial skills. These latter programmes cover such topics as negotiation, autonomy, risk and decision-taking, assertiveness, communication, interpersonal skills, internal company affairs and marketing. An assessment of these programmes shows that the main effect of the project was to instil greater self-confidence in the participants' abilities and their company projects (Instituto do Emprego e Formação Profissional, 1991). Training programmes were also created by the organization to help consolidate companies set up by women with a syllabus composed of several general management courses.

Two women's operational programmes were designed by the EC, one for long-term unemployed adult women (OP8) and another for young unemployed women (OP13), to promote equality of opportunity and treatment for women in the job market and to upgrade their participation in the professional arena and their professional status, including the widening of the range of career options available to women and the overcoming of social, economic, family and credibility problems faced by women entrepreneurs.

Two types of measures have been taken by IEFP under these operational programmes: firstly, pretraining modules, to help women draw up innovative career plans and prepare them to achieve the full benefit of technical and vocational training programmes; and, secondly, complementary training modules, designed to complement vocational training modules, in order to respond to the specific problems of women, enhancing their self-development, alongside their technical and vocational training.

The professionalization of traditionally feminine skills, in order to start a career, the development of innovative professional areas and personal development programmes are also receiving the support of IEFP.

Local employment initiatives

Another important measure in IEFP's employment policy has been to help and support women in their efforts to create companies. When starting up businesses, Portuguese women entrepreneurs frequently highlight difficulties in securing enough capital, lack of credibility by banks, clients, suppliers and local organizations, deficient management training, lack of appropriate counselling and information and difficulties in the home/work interface, as major obstacles they have to face.

Recognizing these obstacles as external impositions and not innate feminine problems, justifies some of the positive actions that have been introduced to facilitate the creation of businesses by women, either by financial grants, specific management training or development of childcare facilities (already mentioned in previous sections).

A significant number of these local employment initiatives occur in traditional activities, namely textiles, crafts and clothing. These are labour intensive, employing groups of women with a low educational level and reduced negotiation and credit attainment capacities. These initiatives are typically an employment alternative for these women.

Another group of businesses have taken more innovative initiatives, either by way of product, technology or distribution and commercialization. These companies are located closer to the urban centres, especially Lisbon, with higher common stock and fewer employees. Their female entrepreneurs usually have a higher level of education as well as a greater capacity for negotiation and better access to credit. Their main motivations are the desires to materialize an idea, for risk taking and self-fulfillment (Nunes, 1990).

Delettrez and Nunes (1990) point out that women have a tendency to create their companies in sectors where they already have experience and knowhow, which instills the confidence needed for the initiative. There is, therefore, a reinforcement of the sectorial segmentation of feminine employment; nevertheless, it should be emphasized that many of the women's initiatives, even in traditional activities, present innovative characteristics, in that:

- they respond to unsatisfied local needs, selling a rare product;
- they satisfy social needs, like childcare or community service in deprived areas;
- they explore local resources (linen growing, wool handling, etc.) while preserving the ecological and cultural inheritance;
- they have a cultural component that enhances economic activity (such as the resurgence of traditional dress/crafts).

However, these companies are still new and need to be nurtured by structures providing better management training, technical, marketing and commercial services, exchange of experiences and development of co-operative links between existing initiatives and their founders.

WOMEN MANAGERS: WHAT PROSPECTS FOR THE 1990S?

With more women now working than ever before, it is only natural that they are also increasing in the managerial ranks. The political change to democracy in 1974 brought about a complete revolution in social legislation, the laws approved being much more innovative than the laws that were in force in the more developed European countries. Nonetheless, when we are talking about equal opportunities for men and women in their managerial careers, we are talking about a major cultural and social change, which will inevitably take a long time to achieve. Women are still expected to fulfill their maternal role, which includes not only childbirth, but also the nurturing and childrearing responsibilities, while being expected to play by the same rules their male colleagues do. And while a few women put their careers first and, in order to climb the corporate ladder, choose to forego motherhood, the majority of women are still trying to pursue a serious professional career and, at the same time, remain actively involved in childrearing.

These women are 'talents' that companies should not waste, but at the same time companies should consider that these women are willing to trade off some of the perks that go with career development, for more flexibility and time to spend with their children, at least while they are young.

Companies and society in general must prepare themselves to recognize and profit from these different situations.

In the 1990s, the increase in educational levels and professional qualifications of women in Portugal, as well as the increasing diversification of backgrounds, will lead to a stronger need to recruit women for the technical and managerial ranks. In 1989/90 the percentage of women entering university courses was 54%. The majority of students studying law are now women and in business and economics around

48% are women, and more than 50% in some schools (Direcção Geral do Ensino Superior, 1991). Medicine, agronomics, industrial production engineering, mathematics and information sciences are some other areas where the female population is now the majority of all first-year students (Comissão para a Igualdade e para os Direitos das Mulheres, 1991).

In the two leading MBA programmes, however, the percentage of female students in 1991/92 was 24%. The reason for this is probably that the most common age group for entering MBA programmes is 28 to 32 years old, which coincides with the age at which most Portuguese women have very young children. There is, therefore, some room for improvement when we are dealing with the development of employees to middle and senior management positions. On the other hand, well-educated women are more likely to go back to work after the birth of their children, and to go back more quickly than the less educated ones.

Companies will have to adapt to these demographic changes through recruitment of an increasing number of women and development of their managerial talent. Management development is clearly associated with career planning and the fit between the company's strategic needs and the employee's professional interests and expectations.

Greater flexibility will have to be provided in almost all aspects of human resource management, particularly work schedules, remuneration packages and training programmes. Providing flexibility may be costly, at least in terms of the resultant lack of administrative standardization, but will surely reflect in greater productivity and job satisfaction and reduced occupational stress and staff turnover.

The increased educational level of the population, in general, is the best and surest way to produce a change in the values of a society and this change will accompany the trend that is occurring in the developed Western countries towards sexual equality.

By the turn of the century the flexibility that is now being defended as a positive action policy for women will probably be the norm for every employee, male or female, since the domestic and childcare roles will tend to be shared by both partners of the well-educated, dual-career families.

REFERENCES

Associação Portuguesa de Mulheres Empresárias (1992) Unpublished statistics, July, Lisbon.

Comissão da Condição Feminima (1989) Conclusões do Seminário: O Emprego das mulheres e as estruturas de apoio às crianças, organizado pelas Organizações Não Governamentais do Conselho Consultivo da CCF, June.

Comissão para a Igualdade e para os Direitos das Mulheres (1991) *Portugal, Situação das Mulheres*, Lisbon.

Delettrez, A. M. and Nunes, M. C. (1990) *Assessment Report on Women's Local Employment Initiatives*, European Community Commission, April.

Direcção Geral do Ensino Superior (1991) *Estatísticas do Ensino Superior*, Divisão de Estudos, November, Lisbon.

European Institute of Public Administration (1988) *Women in the Higher Public Service*, Maastricht.

Eurostat (1989) *Labour Force Survey — Results, 1987*, Office des Publications Officielles des Communautés Européennes, Luxembourg.

ILO (1981/1985) *Yearbook of Labour Statistics*

Instituto do Emprego e Formação Profissional (1991) *Employment and Training Policies for Women for Equal Opportunities*, April, Lisbon.

Instituto Nacional de Estatística (1981) *Recenseamento Geral do População*, Lisbon.

Instituto Nacional de Estatística (1990) *Inquérito ao Emprego*, 3° trimestre, Lisbon.

Lopes, M., Perista, H. and Ferreira, C. (1991) *Identificação de Domínios Prioritários de Intervenção no Âmbito da Formação/Emprego de Mulheres*, CiSEP, ISEG, Lisbon.

Neto, A. (1984) *Contrato de Trabalho, Notas Práticas* (9th edn), Actualizada, Livraria Petrony, Lisbon.

Nunes, M. do C. (1984) A mulher: entre a família e o trabalho, *Economia e Socialismo*, no. 63, October/December, pp. 71—6.

Nunes, M. do C. (1990) *Avaliação de um grupo de Mulheres que criou a sua empresa: o papel da formação e da subvenção comunitária*, CEDEFOP, Janeiro.

Rodrigues, M. de L. (1989) As Mulheres na função empresarial: problemas e hipóteses, *Organização e Trabalho*, Vol. 1, November, pp. 122—34.

Rodrigues, M. de L. (1990a) Mulheres 'patrão' e o dualismo do mercado de trabalho — Análise de dados estatísticos, *Sociologia — Problemas e Práticas*, no. 8, pp. 63—80.

Rodrigues, M. de L. (1990b) *A Emergência do Fenómeno 'Mulheres Empresárias': Sintoma e reflexo de transformações nos modos de vida?*, paper given at the symposium *Viver n(a) Cidade*, LNEC and ISCTE, 18—20 October.

12.

SPAIN

Matilde Vázquez Fernández

INTRODUCTION: WOMEN AND EMPLOYMENT IN SPAIN

In terms of law and employment, the situation of Spanish women has undergone significant transformations in the last few years, in a process similar to that which has occurred in other European countries over the past few decades. Various factors have contributed to this transformation, such as the policy of equal opportunities which the government has been operating since 1983, the setting up of the Women's Institute (a public organization with its own budget), and the Plan for Equal Opportunities for Women which was in operation from 1988 to 1990. The latter is a series of legislative reforms and other measures aimed at promoting employment and vocational training, as well as the consolidation of a system of horizontal structures through ministerial departments.

THE EVOLUTION OF THE RATE OF FEMALE EMPLOYMENT

Since 1964 the employment activity rate of the female population has increased, and this was especially noticeable in the early 1970s, concluding with a period of rapid economic growth. Between 1970 and 1974 the active female population rose from 3 to nearly 4 million, and its activity rate increased by 5 percentage points. The employment and economic crises which occurred from 1973 once again marked a stagnant period as regards women's employment. There was a large rise in unemployment, and between 1976 and 1985 there was a stage which labour market analysts have termed the 'phase of discontent' as regards job expectations. During this period the activity rate for women remained constant and this situation was maintained until 1984–5, when there was a massive influx of women on to the job market.

In annual averages, the rate of female employment rose from 20.5% in 1976 to 28.4% in 1981. It reached 33% in 1990 (see Tables 1 and 2).

Forecasts made so far about the employment rate indicate that from now until 1993 it may continue rising at the same pace, although the increase may be greater if we take into account factors such as changing attitudes and the impact of employment policies which favour women.

SOME FEATURES OF WOMEN'S INCREASED PARTICIPATION IN THE LABOUR MARKETS

Between 1984 and 1990 more than 1 million women joined the labour market, thus increasing their numbers by 27%, whereas the number of active males only increased by 5%. Moreover, there was a 23.4% increase of women who were actively employed whilst the increase for men was only 12.8%. From 1984 to 1990, 1,644,700 more people have become employed, of whom 699,800 are women and 944,900 men. This surprising increase in women's employment is a consequence of the influx of married and middle-aged women on to the labour market. This means that there has been a break with women's traditional attitude towards motherhood as these are women who previously would have left the job market early (Tables 3 and 4).

Table 1   Employment activity rates

Year	Men (%)	Women (%)
1976	78.6	19.5
1981	73.9	27.4
1985	69.9	29.6
1988	66.5	32.3
1989	66.7	32.9
1990	66.8	33.4

Source: INE (National Institute of Statistics) 1990, 3rd quarter, *Labour Force Survey*, Madrid.

Table 2   Employment and unemployment

	Women	Men
Population aged 16 years and over	15,848,300	14,603,500
Active population	5,298,200	9,750,400
Employed population	4,031,800	8,625,100
Unemployed population	1,266,400	1,125,300
Inactive population	10,550,100	4,628,500

Source: INE (National Institute of Statistics) 1990, 3rd quarter, *Labour Force Survey*, Madrid.

Table 3 Employment activity rates in groups of age and sex, 1984−90 (figures are percentages)

Age group (years)	1984			1990		
	Women	Men	Both sexes	Women	Men	Both sexes
16−19	34.3	46.0	40.4	31.8	35.2	33.5
20−24	56.4	66.6	61.8	61.5	72.2	67.0
25−29	52.3	93.4	73.0	64.8	91.9	78.6
30−34	39.1	96.6	68.0	56.4	96.8	76.2
35−39	32.0	97.1	64.3	49.6	96.7	72.6
40−44	29.6	95.3	62.4	41.0	95.8	68.3
45−49	27.4	92.8	59.0	34.7	94.1	63.2
50−54	24.6	69.3	55.8	29.2	89.4	58.5
55−59	22.6	77.0	49.7	23.0	76.5	48.4
60−64	16.0	56.1	35.1	15.2	46.4	30.1
65−69	4.8	13.9	8.8	3.9	7.3	5.5
70+	1.3	3.1	2.0	0.7	1.3	0.9
Total	27.7	69.3	47.7	33.4	66.8	49.4

Variation	Women	Men	Total
16−19	−7.4	−23.6	−17.0
20−24	9.1	8.4	8.5
25−29	23.8	−1.6	7.7
30−34	44.3	0.1	12.0
35−39	55.2	−0.4	13.0
40−44	38.5	0.5	9.5
45−49	26.6	1.4	7.3
50−54	18.8	29.0	4.8
55−59	1.7	−0.6	−2.6
60−64	−4.7	−17.4	−14.3
65−69	−19.3	−47.2	−37.4
70+	−48.9	−59.1	−55.2
Total	20.5	−3.6	3.5

Source: INE (National Institute of Statistics) 1984, 4th quarter; 1990, 3rd quarter, *Labour Force Survey*, Madrid.

In recent years, the variable factors which have influenced women joining the job market have been both family related and linked to the higher level of education reached by the female population, given that the tendency towards an increase in activity comes about as the level of education rises. Of those men who have been through higher education 83.8% are economically active as opposed to 72.1% who have only a basic level of education. With women, 80% of those who have had a higher education are active as opposed to 26% of those who have attained only elementary studies.

The bulk of the female workforce is concentrated in sectors such as the leather and footwear industry, the clothing industry, textiles (166,500 in employment), retailing and wholesaling (562,300), restaurants, cafeterias and catering (167,900), public administration (124,700), edu-

Table 4 Occupation rates in groups of age and sex, 1984−90 (figures are percentages)

Age group (years)	1984		1990		Variation	
	Women	Men	Women	Men	Women	Men
16−19	13.6	20.3	18.3	24.3	34.4	19.8
20−24	29.9	38.1	38.1	54.8	27.7	41.1
25−29	38.1	70.3	46.0	78.5	20.7	11.7
30−34	33.3	81.4	43.5	87.8	30.7	7.8
35−39	27.8	85.0	41.0	89.8	47.3	5.6
40−44	26.9	84.3	34.8	90.1	29.0	6.9
45−49	25.3	81.1	30.0	88.7	18.3	9.4
50−54	23.2	79.2	26.0	82.7	11.9	4.4
55−59	21.0	68.5	20.9	69.8	−0.3	1.9
60−64	15.5	49.2	14.5	43.0	−6.7	−12.6
65−69	4.8	13.7	0.0	7.1	−99.2	−48.3
70+	1.3	3.1	0.7	1.3	−49.2	−58.9
Total	20.8	55.2	25.4	59.1	22.3	6.9

Source: INE (National Institute of Statistics) 1984, 4th quarter; 1990, 3rd quarter, *Labour Force Survey*, Madrid (modified).

cation and research (256,200), health and veterinary services (191,600), and domestic and personal services (416,900).

An analysis of relative participation rates reveals that in 1990 women represent 45% of those employed in the textile sector, 64% in the leather and footwear industry, 42% in commerce, 38% in restaurants and catering, 47% in cleaning services, 60% in education and research, 63% in health services, 62% in social aid and community services and 83% in personal and domestic services. However, from 1984 to 1990, the number of women working in the textile industry and personal services has remained constant. On the other hand, there has been a spectacular increase in the number of women employed in the property sector.

Women's occupations and occupational status are good indicators of the quality of the jobs they obtain. The 1984 figure of 334,800 women professionals and experts has risen to 628,300 in 1990, which represents an increase of 81% as opposed to a 34% male increase. There was an increase from 5,100 women personnel managers in public administration, managing directors and company managers in 1984 to 22,100 women in this grade in 1990; this represents an increase of 245% (see Table 5). The latter is, without doubt, due to their increased presence in technical grades in the public sector.

Women employees in the public sector have also increased by 48% (see Table 6). In public administration women occupy 10% of the top grade of the professional career, but, on the other hand, their presence is scarce in top posts in private companies. It is estimated that fewer

Table 5 Active occupied population according to occupation and sex, 1984−90

	1984		1990	
	Women (000)	Men (000)	Women (000)	Men (000)
Professional, technical and similar	334.8	533.9	628.3	729.8
Members and management personnel of public administration bodies and company directors and managers	5.1	161.5	22.1	214.9
Administrative service personnel and similar	433.3	715.1	797.4	855.7
Retailing, sales and similar	431.9	644.7	612.6	783.3

Source: INE (National Institute of Statistics) 1984, 4th quarter; 1990, 3rd quarter, *Labour Force Survey*, Madrid (modified).

Table 6 Active occupied population according to occupational status and sex, 1984−90

Occupational status	1984		1990		Percentage variation	
	Women (000)	Men (000)	Women (000)	Men (000)	Women	Men
Total	2,987.2	7,371.9	4,031.8	8,625.1	34.97	17.00
Employee	33.4	325.8	65.9	421.7	97.31	29.44
Businessman without employees or self-employed	466.0	1,575.2	543.8	1,460.7	16.70	−7.27
Member of co-operative	—	—	20.6	71.0	−12.27	−10.51
Family workers	489.0	284.4	429.0	254.5	53.81	11.84
Public sector employee	532.1	1,171.8	818.4	1,311.7	47.26	27.80
Private sector employee	1,455.3	3,978.3	2,143.1	5,084.1	−4.35	−39.49
Others	11.5	35.2	11.0	21.3		

Source: INE (National Institute of Statistics) 1984, 4th quarter; 1990, 3rd quarter, *Labour Force Survey*, Madrid (modified).

than 5% of women have a highly responsible post in firms, depending on the sector, and where this does occur it is usually in service sector firms, small and medium-sized firms and newly created businesses.

In two studies carried out by the Women's Institute on Spanish businesswomen, it was found that female employers have a higher level of education than their male counterparts. This fact is confirmed in the Survey on Wage Discrimination conducted by the Women's

Institute, which reveals that the salaries earned by women who run their own businesses are higher than those of their male counterparts. Furthermore, a considerable increase in the number of women employers is forecast for the next few years (Women's Institute, 1987, 1990).

LEGISLATION

The legislative measures regarding employment which have been approved since 1988 are as follows.

- Law 8/1988, concerned with infringements and sanctions in the social arena, has clearly defined the nature of discriminatory acts in business both in terms of gaining access to work as well as working conditions. These have been qualified as very serious and carry a large fine.
- Law 3/1989 modified the Statute of Workers and the Civil Servants Act, increasing maternity/paternity leave from 14 to 16 weeks. In Spain 75% of the salary is covered by social security, and most general wage agreements state that the remaining 25% should be covered by the firm. This law allows a parent to take 1 year's leave of absence in order to look after children whilst his or her post remains open, and either the father or the mother can take advantage of the 16-week leave and the year's leave of absence. This law clearly states that cases of sexual harassment at work are covered judicially.
- The Labour Procedure Law 7/1989 includes the 'reversal of the charge of evidence', giving female workers a legal instrument with which they can report cases of discrimination. It will be up to the employer to bring forward evidence to disprove discrimination, and not the worker herself as was the case up till now.
- The Royal Decree 7/1989 has modified the General Social Security Law so that as from 1 January 1990, the spouse of a man who runs his own business, who can prove that the she receives a salary from him, should join the social security scheme as an employee.

PROFILE OF THE SPANISH WOMEN MANAGER

A recent survey was carried out by the Women's Institute asking women executives from 138 different firms, 213 questions. The firms were selected from a wide range of industries and included organizations from the food and drink sectors, the motor industry, electronics and business technology, electricity generating companies, banking, insurance, and the pharmaceutical, plastics and rubbers, chemical, refining and commercialization, and metal industries. There were replies from 49 managing directors, 5 deputies and 54 heads of departments, 62 area heads, 31 technical experts, 3 middle-grade technical experts, 4 administration heads, 9 administrative staff and 1 saleswoman. Over 50% of the sample worked for multinational companies.

According to this latest survey, a profile of the typical Spanish woman executive includes the following features. She is aged between 30 and 45 and has a university education complemented with specific courses on computer studies and personnel management, and she speaks at least one foreign language fluently. Most have acquired their jobs by means of objective tests or through professional contacts. Only 12 have done so by means of consulting agencies, which do not look favourably on women candidates for executive posts.

A large number of the women surveyed acquired the post they now occupy by means of internal promotion, some of them after many years of waiting, while they occupied administrative-type posts. Marital status seems to be an important factor in the development of a professional career and, according to our research, there are more openings for single women.

When it comes to promotion, the basic factors, and those considered most attractive by women, are the personal satisfaction which the post offers and its possibilities for promotion. Elements such as salary, prestige and length of working hours are of secondary importance. Any woman who is aiming for a responsible post must plan her career strategy. All respondents agree on this point, with most of them opting for a strategy which combines money and a career over the long and short term, respectively. Seventy-six per cent claim to have a clearly defined plan, although they are not satisfied with what they have achieved until now, since they aspire to a higher grade post or to reach the top in their present situation. The time spent at work varies between 40 and 55 hours a week. In addition, 62% also work 5 hours a week at home and 31% work between 5 and 10 hours. The volume of work and their promotion to a higher post, mean they have less free time. However, this has not stopped them living with a partner or having a family, although it has in some cases stopped them having more children; 62% of women executives are married or living with a partner and 58% have children. Children are the usual reason for a career being interrupted, for between 2 and 4 months, although this does not prevent most women from being fully reincorporated, as they do not lose contact with the firm during this time.

It is noticeable that Spanish women executives miss having the backing of a mentor throughout their professional life. This is an important consideration when it comes to being promoted to a responsible post.

A basic aspect of the survey is the women executives' assessment of their professional milieu. *Only 37% claim to receive the same treatment as their male counterparts*, and 10% consider that they are treated less well. However, 48% feel accepted and appreciated by both their male and female colleagues and subordinates. Although 50% feel that they have entered the firm on the same footing as their male colleagues, two-thirds of those surveyed claim that they have to work harder than men to prove their worth. The fact is that there are still stereotypes about women who hold responsible posts; the most frequently heard being that they are incapable of accepting responsibility or risks, that they have little interest in being promoted, and that they are excessively concerned with the running of their home.

These stereotypes are also in force when it comes to selection, as can be seen from the different assessments given to factors such as physical appearance, the interview or the CV. The candidate selected is not always the best irrespective of sex. Although 69% are convinced that Spanish women executives are capable of reaching the top posts, 54% think that large firms offer greater possibilities in this respect.

Asked to list the qualities which help to gain promotion to top posts, the women listed the following in order of priority. A woman must be enterprising, she must have a solid, up-to-date training and acute decision-making powers, she must be hard on herself and on others, self-confident, communicative and able to motivate others, she must have an overall vision of problems, be independent in her own sphere of decision-making, and be receptive to the firm's problems.

On the other hand, they highlighted *problems* which must be faced in the business world, such as the fact that women take very little part in political and economic decisions; the lack of public services which would ease women's work; men's domineering attitudes; lack of an effective policy aimed at reducing women's inequality, together with insufficient public and social recognition.

OPPORTUNITIES AND OBSTACLES IN THE PROFESSIONAL CAREERS OF WOMEN EXECUTIVES

The results of the studies conducted by the Women's Institute over the last 3 years clearly show that the obstacles faced by Spanish women executives in their professional careers are not that different to those faced by women in other countries. It is a question of cultural traditions, educational barriers and legal restrictions, although it must be said that the legislation in Spain on equal opportunities is one of the most advanced in Europe. Family pressure and even the attitudes of women themselves also play their part.

The latest study carried out by the Women's Institute has investigated the opportunities and the obstacles faced by women in the development of their careers in public administration, in comparison with women in a private company, using a qualitative methodology. Nine discussion groups were organized using participants from public administration and private companies: eight groups of women and one group of men. The women executives were from the top three grades. From public administration there was a group of managing directors, a group of deputy managers, and a group of advisers and heads of service. From private companies the first level corresponded to general directors and managing directors. The second was for deputy general directors and operating area directors, and the third level was for assistant managers and operating area heads. In total 68 women and eight men participated. The group of men was made up of directors from administration and from private and public companies and was used to contrast and compare with the women's opinions.

The analysis of the results, although based specifically on the opinion of the women executives employed in the public sector, also coincides with the opinions of the women employed by private companies.

Changes in the business world are seen as instrumental to equal opportunities. So too are changes in attitudes to childbirth; women's greater independence from their partners; advances in household technology which shorten the amount of time women spend on domestic chores; changes in the job market with over 1,200,000 women joining the workforce; a similar number of professional and technically qualified men and women on the job market; progressive cultural changes in organizations, new organizational policies and equal opportunities policies; and the fact that women are offered greater training opportunities.

However, some women take a critical view of these changes. Rather than offering them opportunities, they believe the changes enhance professional advancement at too slow a pace. They also criticize the changes for not improving the quality of life, and assert that the facilities available are too few and the benefits too little. Despite this, all the women confirm that professional fulfilment is on the horizon for an ever increasing number of women.

Gaining entry to public administration is seen as a clear opportunity factor, but the methods used to gain entry into private firms are an obstacle for women executives, since tests and interviews are biased and the usual method of selection is an analysis of a candidate's professional biography. Public administration has a set entry system which is more objective than the private sector method, because the system of competitive public examinations takes account of personal knowledge. Private companies, on the other hand, put great emphasis on a candidate's development potential and availability — two factors which public competitive exams do not take into account. (The percentage of women accepted into the higher echelons of public administration is 52%, although the percentage is slightly lower for specialized posts.)

The obstacles to women's advancement observed included discrimination, the male culture of organizations, competitiveness, male communication networks, family ties and self-imposed limitations. Discrimination is the act of treating a certain social group, in this case women, in a different way. Discrimination is related to:

- the organizational sphere: the private sector discriminates more than the public sector but there are certain spheres in public administration where it is also in evidence;
- organizational policies: there are certain companies in which women are implicitly or explicitly denied promotion to top posts;
- organizational culture: the more hierarchical the organization the more discrimination against women;
- the sector: sectors which have a strongly masculine presence discriminate more, and this is the case with private companies;
- age: whilst top executives tend to be older, there is more discrimination against women;
- hierarchical position: the lower an employee's position in the ranks, the more discrimination she will encounter;
- the fact that women are in a minority in any case, which tends to favour discrimination.

What exactly is a *male culture*? Most of the women managers in our sample point to male ways of behaviour which are different to those of women. It seems to be a question of male and female values. Masculine behaviour is thoroughly accepted in the professional world, so women are thus obliged to imitate this behaviour, especially in the private sector. But just what are these values? The following characteristics have cropped up in the course of the interviews as examples of typically male behaviour: aggressiveness, which is seen as 'elbowing one's way up the ladder'; publicizing one's actions or 'giving oneself airs' — women are seen as more modest about their work than men; and competitiveness. The women sampled in our study believe that women have not been educated to be competitive. This lack of competitiveness is an obstacle in the path of women's socialization, which leads them toward the public as opposed to the private sector.

As for exclusively male networks of communication or influence, the world of work appears to be ruled by an invisible, mutually binding network between men. It is seen that, in general, women remain on the outside of the strategic power networks, and these are precisely the groups which have an important role to play when it comes to professional promotion, especially at the top end of the scale. Many women indeed refuse to have anything to do with these communication systems and spheres of influence.

Obstacles pertaining to family ties are of a more social nature. The social role of women is linked to their role in the family, whilst for men, time spent at work is of prime importance. If being available is a prerequisite for promotion, women's family ties are a serious obstacle which stands in the way of their availability at work. It would seem, and this is a topic for debate, that the life of organizations is regulated by availability for work. Therefore, if women have to devote part of their time to the family, their domestic role and their profession may turn out to be incompatible. Despite behavioural changes with regard to marriage, it is still true that most women take time off from their professional life to devote time to their children, and it is the woman who is mainly responsible for organizing the household. Women who work in public administration have pointed out that these problems should not be expressed at work. Proposals which have been put forward for easing this situation include the reorganization of the working day, flexible timetables and greater use of team work.

Closely linked to the question of family ties is the system of timetables and availability. This is the subject which was nearest the heart of the women we interviewed, though more strongly felt by women in the public than in the private sector. Many of them rejected the system of rigid and permanent timetables at work which they associated with the male working culture. For the man, work occupies him totally; it is his absolute space and time. It is said that 'a man's workplace is his living room'.

Although many women have accepted that there is a price to be paid for their professional career, and have adapted to it, they insist that, as they stand, most work timetables are highly inefficient, as a considerable amount of time is spent just being there or waiting for something to happen.

Finally, the survey addressed itself to the limitations women impose on themselves. One hears frequently that 'women are not interested in a professional career'. Statistics confirm that, for example, there are fewer women who attend training courses or who put themselves forward as candidates for higher level posts. It is thus important to publicize training courses and to offer women incentives and encouragement to apply for senior positions.

It should also be noted that during the course of these interviews there was an excessive amount of self-criticism and a certain amount of lack of confidence and insecurity expressed by these women. For example some interviewees said that women turn down posts because they do not consider themselves capable, whereas a man would never do this. They noted that insecurity is a product of education and also a consequence of feeling constantly under observation. Being controlled and watched may produce negative effects and a sense that all one's actions must be justified.

WHAT DO MALE EXECUTIVES THINK OF FEMALE EXECUTIVES?

Male executives often claim that there must be qualified few female candidates who are willing to accept management roles, since they make do with secondary roles in public administration. Women also find it difficult to gain entry to companies in the technological sectors due to the limited training opportunities. According to men, there is not a sufficient specialized female workforce in this area. Women who have gained entry to administrative posts usually have a humanities—oriented rather than a technical background. This provokes a lack of confidence in women's effectiveness.

A second argument is that the changes which are taking place on the job market, due to the incorporation of women, are accelerating in public administration. We have already seen how more women than men are passing public competitive exams. This has a negative connotation because so many of them are gaining entry that in the end it will become a discredited sector. It is even claimed that in ministerial departments, where women are in the majority, salaries or specific perks are lower, as are the budgets which are allocated to them.

Amongst the obstacles to women's advancement listed by male executives is the fact that women have less time available due to family ties, added to the organizational pressure exerted on women, so that they continually have to prove their worth.

Finally, the question of male and female culture also arose in the male executives' group. Men also accept that there are male and female values within the organization and that these changes are preparing the way for a reunion, a drawing together of the two sets of values. They forecast that an increasing number of men will leave their companies, as work absorbs more and more of their time. If women are to be the same as men in their professional behaviour, men too will have to think about their private lives.

FEMALE BUSINESS OWNERS IN SPAIN

A study carried out by the Women's Institute in 1989 on female business initiatives analysed just what it is that motivates female employers to set up in business. It involved 105 in-depth interviews amongst women business owners with over 2 years experience, and others who were just starting on a business project.

The most commonly stated motives for women setting up in business were, in order of importance: personal and professional fulfilment, motives related to improved well-being, the desire to obtain a salary, and, finally, purely business motives. The problems faced by women are of a financial nature, problems related to the internal organization and management of the firm, and problems arising from sharing household tasks. Financial problems are accompanied by a fear of taking risks and fear that the project may not succeed. On the other hand these women have willpower, energy and dedication.

These female business owners tend to give a highly positive assessment of their objectives, knowledge and business experience obtained, and what this experience has meant to them personally and professionally. They claim that since starting their businesses they are more sure of themselves and have more determination and independence. In addition, their business experience has served to increase their organizational, commercial, negotiating and management competence. They have developed their capacity to relate to others, and have overcome whatever was lacking in their training by integrating knowledge in the broadest sense of the term.

Of the 105 businesswomen interviewed, 52.4% head the firm and the remaining 47.6% share the top post with other partners, adapting legal formulas such as those for the self-employed, limited liability companies and limited companies. The partners usually come from the circle of close relatives, husbands, friends and colleagues.

First in importance are tasks concerned with commercialization, promotion, public relations and clients, which absorb a third of an ordinary working day. This clearly ties in with the fact that women's business activities are mainly commercial. However, women employers also declare a preference for these tasks. Secondly, female employers devote their time to activities related to general management including management, organization, and co-ordination. Finally, personnel relations is the area which all find the most difficult. It is not one of the tasks they attend to immediately, and they neither prefer nor exclude it, so it could be taken that this is an awkward area.

In terms of time spent at work, 11% devote less than 40 hours a week, 40% devote between 40 and 50 hours, and the remaining 48.5% spend more than 50 hours, which represents a daily average of 12 hours, taking the working week as being 5 days. Bearing in mind that there is a tendency to overestimate the time spent at work, perhaps the actual number of hours devoted to the firm would be 10 hours a day, although periodically, at peak times, this may rise to 12, 14 or 16 hours. We must highlight the flexible nature of dedication; it is also compatible with a more flexible timetable and therefore more easily combined with the greater or lesser demands from home.

Some of the recipes for commercial successes mentioned by the interviewees included: having insight and being familiar with the market; being in a not very competitive, expanding market; having a good range of clients; offering quality and good service; and being serious, kind and attentive to clients. The personal qualities which were mentioned as being most in keeping with the business spirit were: tenacity, willpower and the ability to get down to work, trust, eagerness and ambition, seriousness and discipline as well as a professional attitude and a solid training. As regards innovation, these women are quite obviously aware of technological changes. They are concerned with their firm's image and try to project a modern, competitive, serious image, offering quality products and transmitting the idea of service and attention to the client. Theoretically at least, they work with a modern firm's conceptual field.

Relations with personnel are mainly on an integrated and personal basis. Relations with employees are good, close and, in some cases, intimate, trusting and respectful. There is a general interest in continuous training. A certain group of women employers show a clear preference for employing female employees and tend to employ fewer staff than male employers do. Female employers are more highly trained than males although there are gaps in their training as regards courses or seminars on business management, and disciplines which relate to management, organization and business administration.

The parents of female employers tend to have had a primary education while their children have usually been through secondary and higher education. Professionally, parents and husbands work with their own firms or in other firms as directors or managers. Female business owners say they have learnt from their fathers such values as tenacity, effort, competitiveness, independence, intelligence and strength, and from their mothers, fortitude, sensitivity, strictness, a spirit of sacrifice, affection and understanding.

Of the women interviewed who had their own families, 63% claimed that there was absolutely no conflict between being a woman, wife, mother and businesswoman. For them, the home is an important area, though if there are no children, or if they are grown up, the household presents fewer problems as less physical attention is required. For these women there was no question of choosing between work and family – the two of them must be juggled. Making them compatible is a question of time, attention, innovative harmonious solutions, and involving the other partner in the process; in short, a question of social organization.

CONCLUSIONS

The situation of Spanish women at work has undergone great changes in the last few years, as is shown by the fact that from 1984 to 1990 more than 1 million women joined the labour market. Most of these are middle-aged, married women, which reveals that there has been a change in the traditional attitude to work and motherhood.

The professional grades occupied by women have also changed. Thus, the number of women managers and professionals has risen by 81% between 1984 and 1990, which is due in part to their increased presence in technical grades in the public sector. The number of women business owners has also increased by 57.8%, to a total of 325,800 at present.

However, the presence of women in management posts in business is very low. In public administration the figure stands at 10% at the top level, but this figure is reduced to 5% in private companies.

According to the results of a recent survey carried out by the Women's Institute (1990), Spanish women executives are sufficiently well qualified to take on responsible posts but, despite this, two-thirds of the women interviewed claim that they have to work harder than their male colleagues in order to prove their worth, as there are still a number of stereotypes in force regarding the role of women in responsible jobs.

Prejudice and discrimination still exist when it comes to job selection, as illustrated by the different types of assessment given to female and male applicants.

Although there have been changes in the social and economic milieu, as regards attitudes to childbirth, greater independence from one's partner, fewer household chores, greater availability of training opportunities or the changing job market, there is still a whole series of obstacles which women have to overcome as their professional career advances. In the opinion of the women executives interviewed, these obstacles can be summed up as discrimination, the male culture of organizations and male communication networks, family ties, the timetable system and self-imposed limitations.

Obstacles are also present in the path of the professional career of women business owners, but they are of a different nature, basically financial, and related to organization and internal management. Women employers overcome these difficulties using effort, dedication and will-power, and claim that becoming their own boss has given them more self-confidence, and greater personal independence.

REFERENCES

INE (National Institute of Statistics) (1984) *Labour Force Survey*, 4th quarter, INE, Madrid.

INE (National Institute of Statistics) (1990) *Labour Force Survey*, 3rd quarter, INE, Madrid.

Women's Institute (1987) *The Female Business World in Spain*, Women's Institute, Madrid.

Women's Institute (1990) *Female Business Activity*, Women's Institute, Madrid.